THE NAZI SPY PASTOR

THE NAZI SPY PASTOR

CARL KREPPER AND THE WAR IN AMERICA

J. Francis Watson

 PRAEGER

AN IMPRINT OF ABC-CLIO, LLC
Santa Barbara, California • Denver, Colorado • Oxford, England

Library of Congress Cataloging-in-Publication Data

Watson, J. Francis.
  The Nazi spy pastor: Carl Krepper and the war in America/J. Francis Watson.
    pages cm
  Includes bibliographical references and index.
  ISBN 978-1-4408-2807-2 (alk. paper)—ISBN 978-1-4408-2808-9 (ebook) 1. Krepper, Carl, 1884–1972. 2. World War, 1939–1945—Secret service—Germany. 3. World War, 1939–1945—Secret service—United States. 4. Espionage, German—United States—History—20th century. 5. Sabotage—United States—History—20th century. 6. Spies—Germany—Biography. I. Title.
  D810.S8K749 2014
  940.54′8743092—dc23   2014012296

ISBN: 978-1-4408-2807-2
EISBN: 978-1-4408-2808-9

18 17 16 15 14   1 2 3 4 5

This book is also available on the World Wide Web as an eBook.
Visit www.abc-clio.com for details.

Praeger
An Imprint of ABC-CLIO, LLC

ABC-CLIO, LLC
130 Cremona Drive, P.O. Box 1911
Santa Barbara, California 93116-1911

This book is printed on acid-free paper ∞
Manufactured in the United States of America

Dedicated to my wife Elaine . . . with love and thanks for walking with me in the footsteps of Carl Krepper—and with thanks to our children, Francesca, Felicia, and Ian, for their patience, love, and support

CONTENTS

A photo essay follows p. 88

INTRODUCTION

Sailing from Lisbon, Portugal, to New York City on December 5, 1941, the SS Excalibur was at sea when Japan attacked Pearl Harbor. Five days prior to the ship's arrival in New York, Adolf Hitler declared war on the United States. When the ship arrived on December 16, 1941, the United States was at war with the Axis powers. In less than a month, the Excalibur would be recruited to the American war effort and rechristened the USS Joseph Hewes.

Among the first-class passengers who disembarked from the Excalibur in New York was a man known as the Rev. Carl Krepper.

This was not Pastor Krepper's first trip to the United States, nor was it meant to be a vacation for this German clergyman. Krepper had been sent to America on a mission that would bring him into the dark corners of the world of espionage and international intrigue. Carl Krepper was a German-born American citizen, and the man who sent him to America in December 1941 was a German intelligence officer named Lt. Walter Kappe. In 1942, Kappe would send eight saboteurs to commit acts of terrorism on American soil.

When Krepper landed in New York in December 1941, he was returning to a country he had called home for more than a quarter of a century. The shipping and immigration records for the SS Excalibur listed the bare facts of Krepper's existence: He was a naturalized American citizen, born in Altona, Germany on May 11, 1884. The place and date of his naturalization were listed as Philadelphia, Pennsylvania, at the general court, in June 1922. Krepper's address was listed as Clark Township, Rahway, New Jersey. This information was recorded on the Excalibur's "List of American Citizens." What was not listed on the Excalibur's passenger manifest was the fact that, for the past six years, Krepper had been living and working in Nazi Germany, and that he had returned to the United States on a secret mission that had been approved at multiple levels of the Nazi leadership in Germany. This mission embroiled Carl Krepper in what was potentially the most deadly terrorist plot on American soil prior to 9/11.

The telling of Carl Krepper's story was made possible by bringing together a number of different sources. This story first came to the author's attention in a sealed file maintained in the archives of the now-closed Redeemer Lutheran Church in Irvington, New Jersey. These archives are contained within the records preserved in the Lutheran Archives Center at Philadelphia. Among the archival materials that together tell the story of Carl Krepper, Lutheran pastor and Nazi agent, are German and American ecclesiastical records, contemporary newspaper accounts, and federal court records, as well as recently declassified files preserved by the Federal Bureau of Investigation.

The author is grateful to a number of individuals and agencies for allowing him access to these sources, and who have assisted in a variety of ways in the writing of this book. I wish to particularly acknowledge the assistance of the following individuals and institutions: John Peterson, Curator of the Lutheran Archives Center at Philadelphia, for assistance in researching the archives of Carl Krepper's churches in Philadelphia and Newark, New Jersey; Ulrich Stenzel of the *Landeskirchliches Archiv* of the *Evangelisch-Lutherische Kirche in Norddeutschland* (Kiel, Germany), for locating the materials from Krepper's German personnel records; the staff of the Archives of the Evangelical Lutheran Church in America (Elk Grove Village, Illinois), for their help in locating official American Lutheran correspondence related to Carl Krepper; the Records Dissemination section of the Federal Bureau of Investigation (Washington, D.C.), for providing digitized copies of its records on Carl Krepper; John Daggan, Archivist, Metropolitan New York Synod, Evangelical Lutheran Church in America, for assistance with information on President Samuel G. Trexler from the Metropolitan New York Synod Archives; my predecessor as president of the Board of the Lutheran Archives Center in Philadelphia, the Rev. George E. Handley, for help with materials on the history of Lutherans in New York City; George Hawley and Larissa Brookes of the

Charles F. Cummings New Jersey Information Center at the Newark Public Library, Newark, New Jersey, for their assistance with their clippings file from the Newark Evening News, and in locating Krepper's mug shots; Warren Grover and Dr. Tim Christ of the Newark Historical Society, who pointed me in some helpful directions, invited me to offer a presentation on Krepper at the Newark Historical Society in January 2010, and located photos of Krepper after his capture by the FBI; my brother Dr. William E. Watson, Professor of History, Immaculata University, with whom I first delved into Carl Krepper's story in 2009; Dr. Guy C. Carter, formerly of St. Peter's College, New Jersey, historical theologian, for reading the manuscript and offering helpful suggestions, and for materials related to the German Lutheran resistance to Hitler; my congregation at Christ Lutheran Church in Whiting, New Jersey, many of whom lived through, and bravely endured, the times described in this book on both sides of the Atlantic; my son, Ian Watson, with whom I explored the archives of the United Lutheran Church in America in the summer of 2012; and my wife, Elaine Petrosino Watson, MS, who walked with me in Carl Krepper's footsteps in the various communities in New Jersey in which he served as pastor.

CHAPTER ONE

Student at the School for Spies

GERMAN LUTHERANS IN AMERICA

The first German Lutherans came to the North American continent in the seventeenth century, drawn by the lure of land and financial opportunity.[1] Those German Lutherans brought with them their particular theological and liturgical traditions, which manifested themselves in congregations throughout the Dutch and British North American colonies. Germans were active in the Lutheran Church in the Dutch New Netherland colony as early as the mid-1650s.[2] From its earliest days, the Lutheran congregation in Manhattan was multinational, with as many as seven nationalities represented within its membership. By the early eighteenth century, there were so many Germans in British New York City that it was noted that there were "mostly Germans"[3] within that Lutheran community.

In the later seventeenth century, many German Lutherans emigrated to the British colony of Pennsylvania to live in Francis Daniel Pastorius' community of Germantown (first settled in 1683 through the Frankfurt Land Company, and officially organized 1691). Among these German immigrants who came to Pennsylvania was a man who became the first Lutheran pastor to be ordained in the Americas, Justus Falckner (born 1672 in Langenreinsdorf, Saxony). Justus Falckner arrived with his brother Daniel in August 1700, and he was ordained a Lutheran pastor at Gloria Dei Church, the Swedish Lutheran parish in the Wicaco section of Philadelphia, on November 25, 1703.[4] Justus Falckner served congregations in New York and New Jersey for 20 years.

German Lutheran clergy were sent to America in something of a haphazard fashion in the eighteenth century, and many who came to serve had no formal training or credentials. For a number of reasons, including lack of properly trained and ordained clergy and the sheer physical distances between Lutheran congregations, it was not unusual in the first half of the eighteenth century for Lutheran congregations to be without ordained clerical leadership for decades on end.[5]

One of the most significant developments in the organization of German Lutheranism in North America came with arrival of Henry Melchior Muhlenberg, who was sent to America from the Francke Foundation at Halle,[6] which also sent a number of Lutheran pastors to India. Muhlenberg arrived in British North America on September 21, 1742. He had official authorization from King George II's court chaplain, Frederick Michael Ziegenhagen, to serve Lutheran congregations in Philadelphia, Trappe, and New Hanover, all in Pennsylvania. Muhlenberg was a multilingual preacher who helped to organize and oversee German Lutheran congregations, particularly in Pennsylvania and New Jersey.

Muhlenberg was the prime mover behind the founding of the oldest organized Lutheran Church body in the United States, the Evangelical Lutheran Ministerium of Pennsylvania and Adjacent States, which was organized in 1748[7] (generally known as the Ministerium of Pennsylvania). When it was officially incorporated in 1854, the Ministerium's Germanic roots were evident, as the church body was incorporated as "the German Evangelical Lutheran Ministerium of Pennsylvania and Adjacent States."

Even after many Lutheran parishes began utilizing English as their primary language for worship and education, the needs of German-American congregations were addressed within the "German Conference" of the Ministerium, which was founded in 1919. The modern descendant of this organization exists as the "German Evangelical Lutheran Conference in North America."[8] This organization defines itself as a "special interest group for ministry among people of German language and/or heritage in North America."

With a growing German immigrant population in the United States during the nineteenth century, the need arose for German-speaking clergy to serve German-American Lutheran parishes throughout the country. To meet this need, 18 different mission institutes were established in Germany that, by the end of the nineteenth century, had trained a total of 1,340 leaders to serve the German-speaking Lutheran communities throughout North America.[9] Even the English-speaking American Lutherans (in particular, the parishes associated with the General Synod) ended up looking to Germany for assistance in securing German-speaking pastors to serve the growing influx of German Lutherans in the United States.[10]

As German immigration expanded throughout the world in the nineteenth century, the Lutheran churches in Germany saw the need to provide pastoral care for those immigrant communities. During the nineteenth century, foreign mission institutes in Germany trained seminarians to serve as pastors of German Lutheran congregations throughout the world.[11] From these seminaries, pastors were sent from Germany to North and South America, Australia, Romania, Egypt, and Italy.[12] Foreign mission work was also carried on by graduates of these theological institutes in places such as India and Iran. Nonetheless, the majority of men trained in these German foreign mission institutes were sent to North America.

As World War I dawned, many German-American Lutheran clergy and congregations were faced with a dilemma. Loyalty to their adopted country was tempered by a linguistic and cultural affinity with the Fatherland. Before the United States entered the "Great War," German propaganda efforts sought to utilize the press as well as German American Lutheran churches to keep America neutral. The United States went to war against the German Empire and the other members of the Central Powers (the Austro-Hungarian Empire, the Ottoman Empire, and the Kingdom of Bulgaria) on April 6, 1917. When the United States went to war with their ancestral homeland, Lutheran pastors and congregations debated the wisdom of maintaining the use of their native tongue within their congregations. The use of the German language in worship was looked on as an un-American activity by some, including members of the U.S. Senate. A number of Lutheran congregations that had previously maintained the use of their native language in liturgical worship as well as in the normal day-to-day dealings of their parish communities discarded the ancestral tongue for English. Conflicts over the continued use of the German language among American Lutherans intensified during World War I, when the Bureau of Investigation (soon to become the Federal Bureau of Investigation) investigated some German-born Lutheran clergy for attempting to subvert the American war effort.[13] Among those Lutheran pastors who were investigated at that time was a German-born and German-trained pastor named Carl Emil Ludwig Krepper, who was at that time serving as pastor of a church in Philadelphia.

CARL KREPPER'S STORY

"I was born on May 11 1884 in Altona, the son of former court assistant Ernst Krepper and his wife Pauline, née, Behrends." With these words, the Rev. Carl Krepper introduced himself to the Information Department of the Nazi Foreign Office in Berlin.[14] When Krepper wrote his letter of introduction on July 16, 1941, he was seeking sponsorship from the *Auslands-Organisation*, the Foreign Organization of the Nazi Party outside of Germany, for a trip to the United States. Krepper's one-page letter of introduction offered a brief biographical résumé of his life, as well as a statement of the intended purpose of his journey in December of 1941—to work against what he called the "plutocratic-Jewish" influence in America. This trip would end with Krepper's 10-year incarceration at the Lewisburg Federal Penitentiary for being a Nazi agent. Within five months of writing the above letter of introduction, Krepper would be on board the SS Excalibur sailing from Lisbon, Portugal, to New York City.

Carl Krepper was born in Altona, which for 200 years was administered by the Kingdom of Denmark. Altona's roots date to 1535, when it was settled as a fishing village on the right bank of the Elbe River. The town came under Danish control in 1640. In 1864, 20 years before Carl Krepper was born, Altona came back under German control as a consequence of Denmark's defeat in the Second Schleswig War (February to October 1864), after which Denmark ceded control of Altona to the Kingdom of Prussia.

Granted the status of a city in 1664 by the Danish King Frederik III, Altona existed as an independent city under both Danish and Prussian rule. In 1937, the Nazi German government reorganized the territory around Hamburg with the "Greater Hamburg Act," and in 1938, Altona became a suburb of Hamburg.

Carl E. L. Krepper was baptized in Altona on June 25, 1884. On March 4, 1900, a little over three months before his sixteenth birthday, Krepper was confirmed in nearby Blankenese.[15] The year that Krepper was born and baptized marked a turning point in nineteenth-century

Germany. At the multinational Berlin Conference (November 14, 1884, to February 26, 1885), Germany emerged as a colonial world power. While in previous centuries, Germans had migrated to many parts of the world, including America, for financial and even religious reasons, after the Berlin Conference Germans could feel proud that they had entered the world stage, as their political and military influence spread beyond the bounds of the German Empire.

Spearheaded by the King of Portugal, the Berlin Conference was organized by Otto von Bismark, the first chancellor of Germany. The conference resulted in the division of the African continent between a variety of European colonial powers, including Germany, the Austro-Hungarian Empire, Denmark, Sweden/Norway, Italy, France, Belgium, the Netherlands, Great Britain, Italy, Spain, Portugal, Russia, and Turkey. The United States of America was also represented at this conference. As a consequence of the conference, Germany took control of Namibia (German Southwest Africa) and Tanzania (German East Africa). Like the other European colonial powers, Germans spread their culture and military influence throughout their colonial outposts for decades to come. The European colonial experiment in Africa would eventually be tested and would contribute to bringing the nations of Europe into World War I. These boundaries would continue to be tested into World War II and beyond, as African self-identity and nationhood would evolve in the second half of the twentieth century.

Carl Krepper attended public schools in and around Altona. His "Mittelschule" education was received in Altona, while he attended the "Stadtschule" in Kappeln, and his "Volksschule" studies were conducted at Blankenese. As a student, he would have learned stories of Prussia's defeat of the Danes in 1864, as well as the expansion of German power and influence beyond the bounds of the Fatherland, which had started in the year of his birth. Krepper was born into a unified and expanding Germany, and he began school at a time when a German national identity and prestige was on the rise.

As he grew into manhood, Carl Krepper was very proud to be German. He grew to love the classics of German literature, and even had shelves of these books in his apartment when he was arrested as a Nazi agent in Newark, New Jersey, in December 1944.

Nonetheless, or more likely as a consequence of his pride in his German heritage, shortly before his nineteenth birthday, Krepper took a step that would eventually lead him far away from the Fatherland to labor in the *Ausland* (the foreign lands), in the United States. In 1903,

Krepper enrolled at the Ebenezer Seminary in Kropp, Schleswig-Holstein, which trained pastors to serve in German American parishes in the United States and Canada. Krepper was born two years after the founding of this seminary, at a time when Germany was entering the world stage as a colonial power. This was also a time when the Lutheran Church in Germany was responding to the spiritual needs of German expatriates by sending German-speaking and German-trained clergy to serve as pastors of Lutheran congregations all over the world.

KREPPER AND THE KROPP SEMINARY

Carl Krepper was just one of the many German-educated seminary graduates who came to the New World in the early years of the twentieth century to be ordained and live out his vocation to God. More precisely, Krepper was one of over 200 seminarians who were trained at the Ebenezer Lutheran Seminary in Kropp, Schleswig-Holstein, Germany, to serve congregations in the United States and Canada. These men were sent to the United States and Canada between 1882 and 1931 to be ordained in the New World as pastors of German-American and German-Canadian Lutheran parishes. Kropp, as it was called, was founded for the express purpose of preparing men in Germany to serve in what was called "the American mission field."

The founder and guiding light of the Kropp institution was a pastor named Johannes Joachim Heinrich Paulsen (1847–1916). Paulsen was born on June 6, 1847, in Witzhave, Schelswig-Holstein,[16] and he was ordained as a Lutheran pastor on November 20, 1870. He first held the position of "preacher" (*Prädikant*) in Kropp, and then on November 3, 1872, he became pastor in that municipality. In 1879, Paulsen established a deacon training program for 12 deacons in Kropp that became the precursor for his later theological seminary.

Recognizing the growing need to train German-speaking pastors to serve German Lutheran congregations in the United States and Canada, Paulsen founded his Ebenezer "preacher's seminary" in Kropp, which began operations on May 1, 1882.[17] Paulsen secured financial support for his institution from German-trained Lutheran clergy and German-speaking Lutheran congregations in the United States. An arrangement was made between Kropp Seminary and the Lutheran Theological Seminary in Philadelphia whereby Kropp Seminary graduates were sent to Philadelphia for a year of preparation to serve in the American context.[18] This relationship began in 1887, and at times the association between the Kropp and Philadelphia seminaries was strained. The "Kropp War,"[19] as it was called, erupted over the issue of the recognition of Kropp Seminary graduates as being fully prepared for the ordained ministry by the American church. Among the matters at issue there was a feeling among the Kropp graduates that the Philadelphia Seminary in particular and American Lutheran clergy in general considered their seminary preparation in Germany insufficient, and not as complete as the regular American graduates of the Philadelphia Seminary. Nonetheless, it became the common practice that, upon completion of their studies in Germany, Kropp Seminary graduates were sent to the Lutheran Theological Seminary at Philadelphia for a year of preparation to serve American congregations. In time, Kropp graduates entered other seminaries of the Lutheran Church in North America to prepare for their American ministries, including the Lutheran Seminary at Gettysburg, Pennsylvania, the Hamma Divinity School in Springfield, Ohio, and the Waterloo Lutheran Seminary in Waterloo, Ontario. The preparation of these Kropp graduates included instruction on American church polity as well as the different ecclesial environment they would encounter in the New World.

A major difference between the Lutheran churches in the United States and Germany was that in Germany the salaries of pastors were paid through the state, while in the United States, salaries were paid by the individual congregations that the pastors served. Because there was no Lutheran state-sponsored church system in America, the Kropp graduates had to become acclimated to a very different environment than they had experienced in Germany.

The Kropp Seminary came to be called "the Evangelical Lutheran Preacher's Seminary for Foreign Lands" (the "*Ausland*"), but because they were specifically being trained to become pastors in America, some of the seminarians at the Kropp Seminary called themselves students of "the American Theological Seminary in Kropp."[20]

The 279th seminarian who studied at Kropp was Carl Krepper, who entered the Ebenezer Seminary at Easter of 1903. He completed his studies at Kropp in the summer of 1909.[21] As Krepper did not possess a university degree prior to his seminary studies, his course of study at Kropp lasted a little over six years. He would have studied the Old and New Testaments as well as the Lutheran Confessions, the distinctively Lutheran theological documents of the sixteenth century that all Lutheran pastors were expected to study. These confessional documents included the *Augsburg Confession* (1530), the *Apology of the Augsburg Confession* (1531), the *Smalcald Articles* (1537), the *Treatise on the*

Power and Primacy of the Pope (1537), the *Large* and *Small Catechisms* of Martin Luther (1529), and the *Formula of Concord* (1577). Krepper had several classmates who entered the Kropp Seminary at the same time as he did who made names for themselves in North American Lutheranism. Among them was the Rev. Johann H. Reble, DD, who became president of the Canada Synod of the Lutheran Church, and the Rev. August Greve, pastor of Immanuel Lutheran Church in Lakewood, New Jersey, who presided at the funeral services for those who perished aboard the airship Hindenburg in 1937.

The Great Depression in the United States affected economies all over the world, and postwar Germany was no exception. Massive unemployment and a banking crisis in 1931 brought hard times to the Kropp Seminary, like many other German institutions. Together with another seminary located at Breklum, Germany, which also trained seminarians to serve in the United States, the Kropp Seminary closed its doors on July 1, 1931. The United Lutheran Church in America (ULCA), the church body in the United States that sponsored the financial grants to the Kropp Seminary, continued assistance to the seminary into 1932 to help with closing costs for the institution. In the minutes of its Eighth Biennial Convention in 1932, the ULCA summed up its appreciation for the work of the Kropp Seminary:

> These institutions have sent to America some very valuable men who are now pastors and teachers prominent in the affairs of the United Lutheran Church. Others are serving diligently and sacrificially in little-known fields. For all, the Church thanks the Kropp-Breklum institutions. The closing of these institutions will no doubt bring a feeling of regret to the many friends in this country, but it must not be interpreted as failure. To have served a purpose in God's plan, is the highest type of success.[22]

As the Kropp Seminary closed its doors, the Lutheran Church in the United States recognized the faithful service of the greater part of the Kropp graduates who served in America. While the majority of the men who were trained at the Kropp seminary were good, faithful pastors who served the communities to which they were sent with dedication, overall these graduates have been characterized as being "militant representatives of German Nationalism."[23] Their promotion of the German language has been characterized as "more romantic than realistic in the changing conditions" of the American scene.[24]

The promotion of the German language was not the sole or even the major concern of the so-called Overman Committee that investigated Kropp graduates during World War I. The Overman Committee was a subcommittee of the Senate Judiciary Committee that was established on September 19, 1918, to investigate pro-German propaganda and interests in the United States. The committee consisted of five senators: Lee Overman of North Carolina, Thomas Sterling of South Dakota, Knute Nelson of Minnesota, Josiah Wolcott of Delaware, and William King of Utah. Hearings were held by the Overman Committee starting on September 27, 1918. In June 1919, the report of the committee was released. During the course of the Senate subcommittee hearings, Captain George B. Lester of the Military Intelligence Bureau of the U.S. Army testified on the investigation of a number of Kropp Seminary graduates.[25]

Among the charges leveled by the U.S. Army at Kropp Seminary graduates during the First World War was that these German-born pastors had attempted to keep the United States out of the war by fomenting racial unrest in the Southern states. Over 1,200 Lutheran pastors were investigated for "disloyalty" to the United States. In particular, the Kropp graduates were accused of preaching "pulpit propaganda" that could ultimately subvert the United States' entrance into and participation in World War I. There was concern in the U.S. Army that German-born clergy who served Lutheran congregations near army bases had been "disloyal" to America by promoting pro-German and anti-American sentiment at a time of war between the United States and Germany. The claim was made by American politicians and army investigators that between August 1914 and April 1917, hundreds of Lutheran pastors had preached and prayed for German victory in the war, and that some of these clergy were actually paid by the German government to promote these pro-German ends. Kropp graduates were particularly singled out for participating in such anti-American activity.

A direct result of these investigations of German-born clergy for "disloyalty" was an increasing movement to change the language of Lutheran worship services from German to English in German-American parishes. There was an anti-German hysteria that spread throughout the United States after the United States' entrance into the Great War, and many German-Americans felt as if speaking their native language within their adopted country would make them seem unpatriotic. It was a sad reality that some German-American families gave up speaking German in their households during the First

World War so that their children would not be stigmatized as being unpatriotic.

In many ways, Krepper was typical of his fellow Kropp graduates. He was trained in Germany to serve German-speaking American Lutheran congregations, and all the congregations that he served in the United States were primarily German-speaking parishes. When he was investigated in 1918 by the Bureau of Investigation (renamed the Federal Bureau of Investigation in 1935) "upon a charge that he was engaging in German activities,"[26] Krepper reportedly declared that "he was proud he was a German." This, of course, was far from being a crime. In and of itself, being proud of one's German heritage did not lead any German-born pastor or anyone else to participate in subversive anti-American activities.

The German-born Pastor Krepper was described by the Bureau of Investigation as being a "shrewd alert young man, very soldiery in manner and speech." As he was serving a German-American congregation at a time of war with his homeland, Krepper was bold enough to say that he was not a naturalized American citizen, and he had no intention of becoming one. This part of Krepper's statement would likely have given pause to army investigators, who speculated on the loyalty of men who were trained in the German Fatherland specifically to serve in the United States. Neutrality on the part of men like Carl Krepper was not considered a viable option at a time of war by investigators in the U.S. Army or among members of the U.S. Senate.

Despite his declaration that he had no intention of becoming an American citizen, on September 12, 1918, a little less than two months before the armistice was declared in Europe, bringing hostilities in war-torn Europe to an end, Krepper registered for the American draft. He was listed as being neither native born nor a naturalized citizen. At the time, Krepper was serving as pastor of the "Lutheran Friedens Church," or Peace Lutheran Church, as it would later be called (from the English translation of the German "*Frieden*," meaning "peace"). Krepper was specifically called to serve Friedens Lutheran Church because he agreed to conduct all the religious services there in German.[27]

When Krepper registered for the draft he was 34 years of age, and he was listed as being tall and of medium build, with grey eyes and auburn hair.

A little over a year later, on October 3, 1919, Krepper filed his "Declaration of Intention" to become an American citizen at the District Court in Philadelphia. In that declaration he stated:

I am not an anarchist; I am not a polygamist nor a believer in the practice of polygamy; and it is my intention in good faith to become a citizen of the United States and to permanently reside therein.

After Krepper's return to Germany in 1935, he told church authorities there that after World War I, he had been a member of an executive committee of an emergency relief fund to aid Germans adversely affected by the war.[28]

Krepper became a naturalized American citizen on June 28, 1922, three years to the day after Germany signed the Treaty of Versailles, officially ending hostilities between Germany and the Allies. When Krepper formally renounced his allegiance to the German Empire in his February 13, 1922, petition for naturalization, the German Empire that he knew as a boy was no longer a reality. Listed as living with Krepper in his petition for naturalization were his wife Marie (born November 2, 1888, in Germany), and his son Ernst (born October 10, 1913, in Philadelphia). In his petition, Krepper made the standard oath: "I am attached to the principles of the Constitution of the United States." He furthermore promised that he would "renounce absolutely and forever all allegiance and fidelity to any foreign prince, potentate, state, or sovereignty," including, in particular, "the German Empire."

What had changed Carl Krepper's mind and enabled him to take the leap of renouncing his German citizenship may have been a growing awareness that the Germany he knew was largely no more. The kaiser was gone, and the international aspirations of the German Empire were over until the dawn of World War II. Another influence on Krepper's decision to become an American citizen would likely have been the first of the two witnesses for his petition of naturalization. Signing Krepper's petition as witnesses were the Lutheran minister Rev. Georg von Bosse, of 1113 West Westmoreland Street in Philadelphia, and Charles Frey, a German-American barber from the same neighborhood.

THE PASTOR AND THE BARBER'S WIFE: INFLUENCES THAT SHAPED A SPY

Pastor Georg von Bosse and Charles Frey were individuals who were significant in terms of Krepper's life story, and both men influenced Krepper in very particular and significant ways. Georg von Bosse was a Lutheran pastor and fellow Kropp Seminary graduate. Born November 3, 1862, in Helmstädt, Germany, von Bosse arrived in America aboard the ship Elbe on May 7, 1889. He had departed Germany from the port of Bremen and arrived in the port of New York. While serving as an assistant in his first call parish, St. Paul's Lutheran Church in Philadelphia, von Bosse married a parishioner, Louise Stiefel, in 1890. In March 1891, he was called to be pastor of Zion Lutheran Church in Egg Harbor City, New Jersey. He served in Egg Harbor City until December 9, 1896. After serving as pastor of a congregation in Harrisburg, Pennsylvania, and as superintendent of a German orphans' home near Buffalo, New York, von Bosse received a call in 1905 to be the pastor of the parish he had previously served as an assistant, St. Paul's Lutheran Church in Philadelphia. He remained as pastor of that congregation until his retirement in 1930.

Throughout von Bosse's career as a pastor, he strongly promoted bilingual education within German-American households. He endorsed this agenda because he believed that this would help preserve German language and culture in America.[29] Von Bosse "believed that it was possible for German Americans to live in a dual world: a German sphere of culture, religious piety, and joy in life and an American sphere that included civil and religious liberties."[30] Von Bosse has been described as "[a] leader of German Americans committed to the notion that German immigrants and their progeny should steadfastly retain their ethnic heritage."[31] As a Kropp seminary graduate, a major goal of Pastor von Bosse's ministry was to promote German culture and the German language within his parishes and within the larger American Lutheran Church. He sought to achieve this goal through a variety of routes. He was secretary of the Archive Committee of the German Society of Pennsylvania and a member of two other significant German-American societies: the *Deutscher Pionier Verein* and the German American Historical Society.

Starting in 1900 (with volume 12), von Bosse served as associate editor of *The Pennsylvania-German*, which described itself as "the only, popular, illustrated, monthly magazine of biography, genealogy, history, folklore, literature, devoted to the early German and Swiss settlers in Pennsylvania and other states and their descendants." Von Bosse's specific role in this magazine was to "elicit data respecting a. The German citizenship of our country that immigrated since the year 1800. b. the Germans in the Twentieth Century. c. German ideas and ideals in the world's history." Von Bosse's work as associate editor was seen as "widen[ing] the scope of the magazine." In these issues, von Bosse told the stories of leading German-American historical figures and he tried to point out the reality that German-Americans were involved in all aspects of American society, including the military and the agricultural spheres, from even before the American Revolution.

In 1908, von Bosse published an important book written in German, the translation of which was entitled *On the German Element in the United States* (*Das Deutsche Element in den Vereinigten Staaten*). This book was printed in Stuttgart, Germany, but it had a wide readership in the United States. While he studied at the Kropp Seminary, Krepper would likely have known of this book by an eminent Kropp alumnus. It would undoubtedly have been a standard reference book for those preparing to come to the United States to serve. Von Bosse's book had a significant impact among German Lutherans, who were given a multitude of examples of German-Americans who both maintained their German identity in the New World and participated significantly in American life. The book was advertised in all the German-American periodicals of the time, and it remains a standard reference to this day.

On the German Element in the United States told the story of German-Americans from before the Revolution up to the early twentieth century. Von Bosse placed German-Americans right in the center of the American experience, and this presentation would have influenced men like Krepper as they learned of how deeply German ideals and culture had influenced the birth and growth of what became the United States of America. Two images served as the frontispiece of the book: U.S. president Theodore Roosevelt and Kaiser Wilhelm II. The juxtaposition of the images of these two leaders spoke volumes, as it visually illustrated von Bosse's point: Germans and German culture can coexist with "English" Americans while at the same time maintaining their distinctive identity within the United States.

In his volume, von Bosse proclaimed a brief intercession that expressed a German immigrant's prayer for the well-being of both his ancestral Fatherland and his adopted country: "God protect Germany and America!" On the title page, von Bosse was identified simply as an "Evangelical Lutheran Pastor in Philadelphia." Nonetheless, by the time von Bosse wrote the book, his name was already intimately connected with the German-American community both within the United States and in Germany. As with many other Kropp Seminary graduates (including Carl Krepper), von Bosse sought to keep the United States out of World War I.

Besides being a witness to Krepper's petition for naturalization, von Bosse installed Krepper as pastor of the Friedens Lutheran Church in Philadelphia in 1911. His fellow German-American clergyman had a deep influence on Krepper as a newly ordained pastor. While Krepper immersed himself within American society, he had in von Bosse a very helpful guide. Von Bosse had become a model of how to successfully make the transition into the American way of life while simultaneously maintaining his German ethnic heritage. So it was that when Carl Krepper became an American citizen, he was following a path already blazed by pastors such as Georg von Bosse, who had maintained what was seen as a healthy balance between loyalty to German language and culture and successful involvement in American society.

Von Bosse traveled back to Germany in 1934 and in 1936, where he witnessed what he and many others at first believed was the rejuvenation of German national pride and prestige under Adolf Hitler's leadership. On his trips back to his homeland, von Bosse witnessed the effects of Hitler's rise to power in the Fatherland, and in common with other German-American pastors in the mid-1930s, von Bosse was at first very much taken with Hitler and the National Socialist movement.

When Krepper returned to Nazi Germany in 1935, Pastor von Bosse assisted him in a very concrete way by writing a letter of introduction on his behalf to German church authorities. This letter apparently detailed Krepper's support of National Socialism in Germany, as well as his work with the pro-Nazi Friends of New Germany back in America.[32] Von Bosse's letter was referenced in a March 11, 1940, report on Krepper that was addressed to the Reich's minister for church affairs in Berlin. While von Bosse's letter no longer appears to be extant, it is telling that von Bosse's name still carried weight back in Germany five years after he had retired from active parish ministry in the United States. Even more fascinating is that Dr. Hans Kerrl, Hitler's Reich minister for church affairs, thereby knew of Pastors von Bosse and Krepper.

Appointed by Hitler in 1935, Kerrl led the Reich Ministry for Church Affairs. This ministry was instituted by Hitler to coordinate the Führer's policies aimed at unifying the Nazi agenda within the German Protestant churches. This ministry replaced Hitler's previous attempts to bring the Lutheran and Reformed churches and their clergy into line with the National Socialist agenda under the leadership of Hitler's *Reichsbishop* (Reich bishop), Ludwig Müller. In 1932, pro-Nazi church leaders had created the "German Christians' Faith Movement," which sought to integrate Hitler's Nazi agenda within German Christianity. The "German Christians," as they were called, believed that Christianity and Nazism were completely compatible and wholly complimentary. While only around 3,000 out of 17,000 German clergymen affiliated with the

"German Christians," Hitler sought to bring all German Christians, both Catholic and Protestant, under the Nazi yoke. After Hitler assumed the chancellorship of Germany in 1933, pro-Nazi churchmen organized what was called the "Reich Church," which sought to force Lutheran and Reformed Christians into one ecclesial body that supported Hitler's anti-Jewish and nationalist agendas.

Reich Bishop Müller was Hitler's chosen leader for the Reich Church. Müller was elected Reich bishop in 1933, yet by 1935, the Protestant churches were not unified in support for the Reich Church. The vast majority of Lutheran and Reformed clergymen declined to become part of the "German Christian" movement. The Lutheran pastor, theologian, and martyr Dietrich Bonhoeffer was instrumental in organizing the "Pastors' Emergency League" (*Pfarrernotbund*), to which 6,000 pastors had signed on by the conclusion of 1933. Among other things, the Pastors' Emergency League supported clergy who suffered financially because of their rejection of Nazism. The German "church struggle" (*Kirchenkampf*) pitted the German Christians over against what came to be called the "Confessing Church" (*Bekennende Kirche*). The Confessing Church came forth from the Barmen Declaration of May 1934 (written primarily by Karl Barth, a Reformed theologian), which rejected the anti-Semitic position of the Reich Church and opposed Hitler's attempts to co-opt the church. The Confessing Church brought the ecclesiastical opponents of Nazism together into what they considered was the only legitimate evangelical church in Germany. Together with Pastor Bonhoeffer, the Berlin Lutheran pastor and hero of World War I, Pastor Martin Niemöller, and other well-respected pastors organized the Confessing Church, which claimed to be the true representative of the German Protestant churches. In his church in suburban Berlin, Niemöller preached sermons opposing the attempts to enforce the Nazi Aryan agenda (the "Aryan Clause") articulated within the Lutheran churches. Particularly, he fought the policy to remove converted Jews who had become Lutheran pastors from their parishes. As a result of his opposition, Pastor Niemöller was arrested by the Gestapo in 1937, and was eventually sent to the Sachsenhausen concentration camp in 1938; in 1941, he was sent to the Dachau concentration camp. In all, Niemöller spent more than seven years incarcerated by the Nazis until he and other prisoners were liberated in May 1945. For his opposition to Hitler, Pastor Bonhoeffer was executed at the Flossenbürg concentration camp on April 9, 1945. Carl Krepper knew of Pastor Niemöller's imprisonment at the Dachau concentration camp, and

when asked at his trial why Niemöller was arrested in Germany,
"Krepper replied 'Because he (Niemöller) said the German people were
bestowing upon Hitler the honors that only belong to God.'" Krepper
was clearly aware of the clerical opposition to Nazism in Germany, and
he thereby knew the theological basis for the revolt of the Confessing
Church against the German Christians. When he came to America in
1941 to act as an agent of the German government, Krepper had already
chosen on which side of the "church struggle" he stood. Krepper supported the alignment of the Third Reich and Christianity espoused by
the German Christians.

As a result of his inability to unify German Protestants in the Reich
Church, Müller resigned. Instead of putting another Reich bishop into
office, Hitler placed Hans Kerrl as head of the Reich Ministry for Church
Affairs. Dr. Kerrl would have known of Pastor Georg von Bosse's reputation as an influential German-American clergyman who had some posi-
tive things to say about the Third Reich. He would also have become
aware of Pastor Krepper through von Bosse's letter of recommendation.

When Georg von Bosse died on April 21, 1943, in Rahns, Pennsylvania,
Carl Krepper had been back in the United States for a year and a half,
and he was serving as an agent of the Nazi government.

The other witness to Krepper's naturalization petition in 1922 was a
Philadelphia barber, Charles Frey, who was likely a member of Krepper's
parish in Philadelphia. The Frey family would play a crucial role in
Pastor Krepper's life in the succeeding two decades. Krepper would
marry Frey's ex-wife Bertha on October 23, 1923, after Krepper's first
wife Marie divorced him. Thus Bertha Frey became the second Mrs.
Krepper. Bertha traveled back to Germany with Krepper a handful of
times prior to their return to the Fatherland in 1935 in order to visit
family. Even after Pastor and Mrs. Krepper moved back to Germany, the
two traveled back and forth to the United States, both together and sep-
arately, until Krepper's fateful return to the United States in 1941.

When Krepper came back to the United States in 1941 to serve as a
Nazi agent, Bertha Krepper stayed in Germany. She received Krepper's
church salary while an assistant pastor served in Krepper's stead in his
German congregation. Bertha Krepper would have supported her husband's pro-Nazi work in America prior to 1935; she also supported his
mission back to the United States in 1941. While he served his parishes
in New Jersey, Krepper became an ardent supporter of Adolf Hitler and
the burgeoning Nazi movement in the Fatherland. Bertha Krepper was a
willing participant in her husband's life, in terms of his pastoral work as

well as his support of the Friends of New Germany in New Jersey. After she journeyed with him back to live in Nazi Germany in the fall of 1935, she became a supporter and participant in his mission to the United States. Bertha passed on coded messages between her husband and Lt. Walter Kappe, the intelligence officer who sent him to the United States as a contact person with other Nazi agents and potential saboteurs.

Bertha Krepper understood and supported the relationship between her husband's vocation to God as an ordained pastor and his passion for promoting German culture and civilization as a Kropp graduate. Her sense of duty to the Fatherland was as complex as Krepper's own.

During his pastorate of the First German St. John's Lutheran Church in Newark, New Jersey, Krepper became involved with the pro-Nazi Friends of New Germany and the related German American Business League (DAWA). He supported the work of the Friends at a number of levels, and he even saw his work with these organizations as an outgrowth of his pastoral ministry. When he sought to prove his loyalty to the Nazi movement back in Germany, he proudly proclaimed that he had flown the swastika flag of the Nazi party in his church in Newark, New Jersey.

As a pastor's wife, Bertha Krepper walked down these roads along with her husband. Whatever she may have felt of her husband's involvement in the Pastorius sabotage plot, she supported him by sending him letters about her condition and the condition of Germany during the war.

When he returned to the United States as an agent of the Nazi government, Krepper lived, at least part of the time, with the Frey family in Rahway, New Jersey. Krepper listed his address on the 1941 SS Excalibur ship register and on his 1942 U.S. draft registration card as that of his stepson, Eugene Frey. When the Pastorius saboteurs were captured, it was discovered that they carried with them handkerchiefs that contained Carl Krepper's name and his stepson's address in Rahway, New Jersey.

While Krepper did not become a Nazi spy directly because of his study at the Kropp Seminary, or through his contact with either Pastor Georg von Bosse or the Philadelphia barber Charles Frey and his family, these two influences played significant roles in Krepper's life before and after he was recruited as a Nazi agent.

Krepper's particular experience at Kropp Seminary certainly placed him in a milieu that enabled him to see his work as a Nazi agent as consistent with his sense of call to the holy ministry. As incongruous as it may sound, Krepper saw no inconsistency in serving both God and the Fatherland of the Third Reich. When he was recruited for his work in the United States by the Nazi intelligence officer who brought forth Operation Pastorius, Krepper was eager to show his loyalty to Nazi ideology. Carl Krepper willingly became an apt pupil at the real school for spies after his return to Germany in 1935.

CHAPTER TWO

Carl Krepper, Pastor

COMING TO AMERICA

The recent Kropp Seminary graduate Carl Krepper arrived in New York on November 11, 1909, aboard the SS President Grant, which had sailed from Hamburg on October 31, a day of special significance to Lutherans all over the world. That day is celebrated as Reformation Day by the Lutheran Church. It marks the day that Martin Luther posted the 95 Theses on the door of the Castle Church in Wittenberg, which started the Reformation, the sixteenth-century transformation of the Western church. The fact that the ship that brought Krepper to the new world had left Germany on Reformation Day would undoubtedly have been seen as a propitious sign by Krepper. He was beginning a new phase of his life as a Lutheran pastor in America, and there would have been no better day to mark the start of this new journey than October 31.

On the original ship manifest, Krepper was listed as a 25-year-old theological student from Blankenese, Germany. The American manifest of "alien passengers for the United States" listed Krepper as a "clergyman," with his father, Ernest Krepper, in Blankenese, Germany, listed as his nearest relative. Krepper's final destination was listed as Englewood, New Jersey.

During his ministry in the United States, Carl Krepper became acquainted with a veritable who's who of German-American Lutheran clergy. In addition to Pastor Georg von Bosse, who took part in Krepper's installation as pastor in Philadelphia and who wrote an important letter of introduction to German church officials upon his return to the Fatherland, when Krepper arrived in Englewood, New Jersey, he was greeted by a pastor who also would soon be serving in another Philadelphia congregation alongside Pastors Krepper and von Bosse. The German-trained clergyman who was serving as pastor of St. John's Lutheran Church in Englewood, and who would have greeted Krepper when he arrived in America, was Pastor Fritz O. Evers. Evers served that congregation between the years 1908 and 1912. He would have provided Krepper with a welcome upon his arrival and ensured that the newly minted Kropp graduate got to the Lutheran Theological Seminary at Philadelphia for the final stage of his education in American church life.

Pastor Evers was called to serve Zion Lutheran Church in Philadelphia from 1914 to 1929, where he would have worked with both Pastors Krepper and von Bosse in the German Conference of the Ministerium of Pennsylvania. Starting in 1918, Pastor Evers chaired a Committee on Jewish Mission that was sponsored by the United Lutheran Church in America, and that was considered to be part of the "home mission" work supported by the larger church. This committee was the only such organization that existed within American Lutheranism at the time.

From 1925 to 1928, Evers chaired the committee for "Relief for German Children of the Lost Provinces of Germany and Austria," which offered assistance to children in the former territories of the German Empire that were lost to Germany after World War I. Later, as a pastor in Baltimore, Maryland, Pastor Evers would be called to testify in the 1942 wartime trial of another Kropp seminary graduate who was accused of spying for Nazi Germany, Pastor Kurt Molzahn. It is not clear how long Krepper visited with Pastor Evers in Englewood, New Jersey, after his arrival in America, but Krepper ended up soon thereafter at the Lutheran Theological Seminary at Philadelphia for his orientation in American Lutheranism. Pastor Evers went on to become the pastor of the historic Zion Lutheran Church in Baltimore. He died in 1952. Pastor Evers would play another role in Krepper's later life as a supporter of the "Pastor Krepper Defense Committee."[1] This committee sought the support of the Lutheran Church in the United States in securing a federal pardon for Krepper both during and after his incarceration. The "Pastor Krepper Defense Committee" included pastors who were active members of the "Committee on German Interests" of the United Lutheran Church in America. It should be noted that the United Lutheran Church in the United States did not support the "Krepper Defense Committee" and its goals. In time, the Committee on German Interests also tempered its public support for Krepper. The United Lutheran Church in America furthermore denied Krepper an American church pension after his release from jail. Krepper had applied for a pension from the American church even though he not been on the clerical roll of the United Lutheran Church in America since 1938.[2]

Considering his later infatuation with the Third Reich and its Aryan supremacist ideology, it is fascinating that in 1909, as he journeyed to the United States to begin his career as a pastor, Krepper shared the SS Grant with an assorted company of travelers, including Russian Jews, a Polish baker, a Hungarian housewife, and a German farmer. For his part, as was typical of German Lutheran pastors serving German congregations in the United States at the time, and similar to many other immigrant groups who came to America in the early days of the twentieth century, Krepper found comfort and support within his own ethnic community. Much of Pastor Krepper's life in the New World would be spent in the company of German-Americans.[3] Of course, in and of itself, there was nothing insidious in this. Proximity to others of one's ethnic heritage does not necessarily produce spies for foreign governments. As with immigrant communities all over the United States to the present day, there was a comfort in starting a new life in a new country with fellow expatriates. Other sinister influences would shape the pastor who would one day become an enemy agent in his adopted country.

FIRST AMERICAN PARISH: WILLIAMSTOWN, NEW JERSEY

After less than two months of preparation at the Lutheran Theological Seminary at Philadelphia, Carl Krepper underwent a theological examination conducted by the Ministerium of Pennsylvania and Adjacent States to determine his fitness for ordination. After satisfactorily passing this exam, Krepper received a call to serve as pastor of the St. John's German Evangelical Lutheran Church in Williamstown, New Jersey, on December 1, 1909. He was ordained on January 5, 1910, as a Lutheran pastor by the Ministerium of Pennsylvania.[4] St. John's Church had been organized in 1897 as a German-speaking congregation. The church building in which Pastor Krepper led worship was built in 1898, and was adjacent to the church cemetery. The church building is now located in a more prominent location in the Williamstown community. When Pastor Krepper arrived at St. John's, his church was located in a community in Gloucester County that included so many German settlers that its public school was called "Germania." St. John's Church was affiliated with the German Conference of the Ministerium of Pennsylvania. As was expected, Krepper conducted church services there in German. A photograph survives of Pastor Krepper as a newly ordained clergyman. He is shown as clean cut, with a determined look on his face, and wearing the traditional black preaching gown and white bands of German Lutheran pastors of the time.

In a later brief history of the St. John's congregation, Krepper was included in the list of clergymen who were characterized as among a "rapid succession of pastors and seminarians [that] proved difficult at times."[5] Krepper served at St. John's a little less than 22 months. Despite his brief pastorate in Williamstown, Krepper experienced a major change in his life there—he married his first wife, Marie Tessen. Krepper was then 26 years old, and Marie was 21. She was born in 1890 and was a Blankenese resident who had arrived in Philadelphia on June 3, 1911, aboard the SS America, which had sailed from Hamburg on May 25.

THE PATHWAY TO CITIZENSHIP: PHILADELPHIA, PENNSYLVANIA

On October 4, 1911, Krepper was called by the German Evangelical Lutheran Friedens Church in Philadelphia to become its pastor. Friedens Lutheran Church, as it came to be called, was organized in 1897, and was an offshoot of St. Michael's Lutheran Church (which is still located in the Kensington section of the city).

After existing for a little more than a decade, Friedens Church experienced a major controversy over an attempt to institute English-language services within the congregation. While not desiring to discontinue German church services, the congregation's first pastor, the Rev. Reinhold Schmidt, tried to inaugurate services in English to meet the growing needs of his community. In 1911, Pastor Schmidt proposed and seriously encouraged his congregation to offer English-language services in addition to the regular German services. He was refused permission to do so, and in August 1911, Schmidt left the congregation to become pastor of a Lutheran church in Harrisburg, Pennsylvania. The English-language controversy became a dividing issue, as a number of parishioners who sided with the pastor left the congregation over the matter,[6] and they organized another nearby congregation, the Lutheran Church of Our Savior, which offered services in English. When Pastor Krepper was called from St. John's Church in Williamstown, New Jersey, to become pastor of Friedens Church, it was stipulated that he conduct services solely in German. Krepper was very happy to comply. In the congregation's 15th anniversary booklet, his congregation glowingly celebrated Krepper's allegiance to German language and culture. Five months after his installation as pastor, the German-language booklet stated, "He is a man who preserves and maintains Germandom (*Deutschtum*) in our community with true seriousness."[7]

Krepper was installed as pastor of Friedens Church on December 5, 1911, by two well-known German Lutheran pastors in Philadelphia, Pastors Georg von Bosse and Andreas Biemüller.[8] Pastor Krepper's ministry flourished at Friedens Church. During his pastorate, the congregation paid down $12,000 of a $19,000 debt. Another change in Krepper's life occurred in Philadelphia when his wife Marie gave birth to their son, Ernst Wilhelm Carl Krepper, on October 10, 1913. During his ministry at Friedens Church, Krepper served as the conference statistician for the German Conference of the Ministerium of Pennsylvania.

With the United States at war with his homeland in 1917, Pastor Krepper nonetheless led his congregation in the parish's 20th anniversary celebrations, which coincided with the 400th anniversary of the start of the Reformation. As they looked to the celebration of the 400th anniversary of the Reformation, it would have seemed very fitting to Pastor Krepper and his congregation that the opening words of Martin Luther's "Battle Hymn of the Reformation" were painted on the chancel arch over the altar: "*Eine feste Burg ist unser Gott*" ("A mighty fortress is our God").

Krepper kept meticulous parish records at the church, and he recorded his own son's baptism there on All Saints Sunday, November 2, 1913. Ernst W. C. Krepper was baptized by his father. His baptismal sponsors were Max Krepper and Emma Tessen. Marie Krepper is recorded in the parish register as being a regular witness at many parish weddings in Friedens Church. The Krepper family lived at 3087 Emerald Street in Philadelphia.

In 1918, while the First World War was drawing to a close, and while Krepper was pastor of Friedens Church, he was investigated by the Bureau of Investigation for pro-German activities. He had stated to the agent who interviewed him that he was proud to be a German and he had no interest in becoming an American citizen. Nonetheless, on September 12, 1918, Krepper had registered for the draft as an "alien," and less than four years later, on June 28, 1922, Krepper became a citizen of the United States of America.

Krepper served as pastor of the Friedens Lutheran Church until 1924. Despite his 13 years of German-language ministry in that congregation, when Pastor Krepper left the Friedens Church, the congregation decided to once again call Krepper's predecessor, Pastor Reinhold Schmidt, to become its pastor. He introduced English-language church services to "keep the congregation from falling apart altogether."[9] The congregation was not the only thing that was falling apart at the end of Krepper's ministry in Philadelphia. His marriage to Marie ended in divorce, and he married the ex-wife of Charles Frey on October 3, 1923. Within four months of his marriage to Bertha, Krepper's ministry in Philadelphia came to an end. This was not unusual at the time. Divorce often ended a pastor's ministry in that day and age, as he was seen by many as unfit to conduct pastoral work if he could not maintain his household.

BACK IN NEW JERSEY: CARTERET AND RAHWAY

After he left Friedens Church, Krepper returned to New Jersey, where he had begun his parish ministry 14 years earlier. Krepper briefly served as interim pastor of the German St. John's Lutheran Church in Bridgeton, New Jersey, prior to accepting a call to a two-point parish in Middlesex County in central New Jersey.[10] This two-point parish included Zion Lutheran Church in Carteret and Zion Lutheran Church in Rahway. Krepper served as pastor of these parishes for eight years, from 1924 to 1932. When he moved to take this combined parish call, Krepper transferred his pastoral credentials to the second-oldest Lutheran ecclesiastical body in North America, the Ministerium of New York (initially organized in 1786).[11] While he was serving these two churches, Carl and Bertha, along with her son Eugene, lived in Carteret, but he presided over and preached at services in both congregations every Sunday. Each week he led meetings and taught confirmation classes in both Carteret and Rahway. In many ways, Krepper served his two-point parish well. He visited the sick, baptized the young, and buried the dead. He did what Lutheran pastors do. Furthermore, Krepper actively participated in the life of the two communities. When the country was preparing to celebrate the bicentennial of George Washington's birth in

1932, Krepper participated in the community celebrations that were held in both Carteret and Rahway.[12]

The German language issue that almost tore apart the Friedens congregation in Philadelphia was also being faced in different ways by his two congregations in central New Jersey. The older of the two congregations that Pastor Krepper served was Zion Lutheran Church in Rahway, which was founded in 1852. This congregation was originally organized as "the German Presbyterian (Reformed) Church in Rahway." In 1874, the congregation decided to become Lutheran, and it was reconstituted as the "German Independent Evangelical Lutheran Zion's Church of Rahway, New Jersey." The First World War brought changes to Zion, as the church introduced English-language worship services. When Krepper arrived, the congregation had dropped the word "German" from its name and the church became known simply as "Zion Evangelical Lutheran Church of Rahway," by which name the congregation is known today. During his time in Rahway, Krepper conducted services in German, while the Sunday School classes were held in English. Bertha Krepper was the head of the Ladies Aid Society. On August 27, 1927, the congregation marked a special event in its seventy-fifth anniversary year, as Krepper presided at the groundbreaking for the expansion of the church building, which was located on Campbell Street in Rahway. This expansion cost the congregation $15,744. On All Saints Sunday of 1927 (November 6), Krepper presided at the laying of the cornerstone of the renovated worship space. This cornerstone is still visible, even though the building is now the Veterans of Foreign Wars hall. As of All Saints Sunday, 1927, there were 245 members of Zion Church in Rahway. Nonetheless, by the time Pastor Krepper left the congregations in Rahway and Carteret to become pastor of the First German St. John's Evangelical Lutheran Church in Newark in 1932, the Rahway congregation was moving quickly to English-only services.

Zion Lutheran Church in Carteret was the younger of the two congregations making up Krepper's two-point charge in Middlesex County. Incorporated in 1903, the congregation was "an outgrowth of Zion, Rahway, and served by Zion's pastors until 1934."[13] In 1925, Krepper oversaw the building of a parish hall for the Carteret congregation. During Krepper's pastorate of the Carteret congregation, English services were offered along with German services. The parish continued offering German services until 1961.

As he lived at 710 Roosevelt Avenue in Carteret during his tenure in his two-point parish, Krepper became deeply involved in the Carteret community. He was said to be "quite active in politics during his time in Carteret."[14] Interestingly, this bit of information was contained within one of the files that the FBI compiled on Krepper during the course of its investigation of him on a charge of being an enemy agent for Nazi Germany. The fact that Krepper was involved in local politics in Carteret was noted by the FBI, as was the fact that while in Carteret, Krepper organized the town's "German-American Club,"[15] and that he purchased his own property while living in that town. In and of itself, there was, of course, nothing suspicious in Krepper's involvement in local politics. Krepper served as an assistant tax collector in the town, and he was treasurer of the Reliance Building and Loan Association in the town.[16] Prior to his departure from Carteret in 1932, Krepper had even applied to be a teacher in the town.[17]

What interested the FBI was the fact that after he returned to the United States in December 1941, Krepper did not pick up those local associations again. Rather, outside of his stepson Eugene and Eugene's wife Hilda, with whom he occasionally spent the weekend back in Rahway, Krepper seemed to shun his previous connections in Rahway and Carteret. When he was arrested in Newark in December 1944, his neighbors in Newark had no idea that he had served as a pastor of a Lutheran congregation in that city for years in the mid-1930s. Both Rahway and Carteret would play a role in the FBI investigation of Carl Krepper from 1942 to 1944, and in Krepper's work as a Nazi agent. In particular, the name of Pastor Krepper and an address associated with his stepson were both found on handkerchiefs brought over from Germany by the Operation Pastorius saboteurs. The handkerchiefs read, in part, "Pas Krepper, c/o E. Frey, R. RDF 2, Box 40 F, Rahway." This continued connection with Rahway would eventually be Krepper's undoing. When the FBI put two and two together and connected "Pas Krepper" with Carl Krepper, they began a surveillance of Krepper and Eugene Frey that in 1944 landed Krepper in jail on federal charges of being a "Nazi spy aide."

In 1928, when he was 44 years of age, Krepper traveled alone to Germany for a two-month visit with his family. The Weimar Republic had just held federal elections in May 1928, and former general and hero of World War I Paul von Hindenburg was serving his third year as the republic's second president. Hitler's National Socialist German Worker's Party (NSDAP) had only received 3 percent of the vote in the federal election. The Nazis were only able to garner enough votes to place 12 seats in the Reichstag. Hitler's *Mein Kampf* (*My Struggle*) had been published in 1925, and the third Nazi Party rally had been held in 1927, the year prior to Krepper's journey, in Nuremburg (the previous two Nazi Party rallies had been held, respectively, in Munich and Weimar). Every other National Socialist party rally thereafter would be held in Nuremburg (1929, and then yearly from 1933 to 1938). When Krepper visited his homeland in 1928, the country's economy had stagnated, and 650,000 people were unemployed. By 1930, the year after the stock market crash in the United States (1929), 3 million people would be unemployed in the German Republic.

When he returned home, Krepper's welcome made the front page of the local Carteret newspaper, the *Carteret Press*. The story detailed how the directors of the Building and Loan Association fêted Krepper with a dinner in his honor, during which he was presented with a wallet.[18] The *Rahway Record* also covered this welcome with a front-page story entitled "Lutherans Greet Returning Pastor: Surprise Rev. Carl Krepper, Home from Germany."[19] This was not Pastor Krepper's last trip before he moved back to Germany in 1935. Even after he and Bertha moved back to Germany on what they believed was a permanent basis, the two traveled back and forth between Germany and the United States multiple times, both together and individually, between 1936 and 1939. When, within months of returning home from another trip back to the Fatherland, he tried to take a leave of absence from his Newark, New Jersey, congregation for what he announced was a multiyear trip to Germany, Krepper was denied permission. He had a history of taking extended vacations to Germany, but his congregation in Newark had had enough. He then handed in his resignation and brought his ministry in the United States to an end.

Bertha Krepper herself took a trip to Germany in 1930 to visit family. She left Germany for the United States five days after that year's federal elections, and she arrived home in New Jersey on September 27. Germany was sliding into an economic crisis, but Hitler's Nazi Party was on the rise. Bertha Krepper would have witnessed something that would have caught her attention, as well as that of her husband—the Nazi Party had received over 6 million votes in the federal elections, taking 107 seats in the Reichstag. Within four years, Carl Krepper was not only an active member of the Friends of New Germany in America. He was flying the swastika flag in his church in Newark.

In the 1930 U.S. census, Carl Krepper is listed as living with his wife Bertha and stepson Eugene in Carteret. Krepper's 16-year-old son "Ernest" is listed as an inmate of the Annandale Reformatory of Men and Boys, working as a farm laborer. Ernst Krepper would have more run-ins with the law over the years, and when Krepper came back to the United States as a Nazi agent, the dealings of the father who had been questioned for "pro-German" activities during the First World War, and the son who had been convicted on multiple counts of criminal activity, were carefully noted by the FBI.

On June 5, 1931, Krepper marked a significant educational achievement when he graduated from Rutgers University with a BA in political science. He received his degree with honors. Krepper would continue his studies in New Brunswick by enrolling in the master of theology program at the New Brunswick Theological Seminary, a seminary of the Reformed Church in America, which, at the time, was affiliated with Rutgers University.[20]

A final note on Krepper's work in Rahway and Carteret comes from a 1944 newspaper account after his arrest for espionage. This very telling reflection came from an article in the *Newark Evening News* from December 21, 1944, entitled "Suspicious of Krepper: Neighbors Tell of 'Old Man with Satchel.'" The article stated, "Rahway and Carteret people who remember Krepper hold varied recollections of him, ranging from 'hard and domineering' to 'a nice man.'" The piece continued:

> Rev. Arthur B. Renschler, pastor of Zion Lutheran Church in Rahway, said his congregation still suffers from the Nazi stigma with which certain groups labeled the church some years ago. He said Krepper was "arrogant, dictatorial and rode roughshod over his congregation." Adolph Nearing of Carteret, trustee of Zion Lutheran Church of Carteret, recalled Krepper as reasonable and friendly and said he never indicated Nazi leanings.[21]

These differing opinions of Carl Krepper are fascinating on multiple levels. It can be noted that while Krepper was active in both congregations and communities in which he served, he was more deeply rooted in Carteret, and he was involved in more aspects of the civic life of that community than he was in Rahway. It can be said that his neighbors in Carteret knew Krepper better than did the residents of Rahway. His former congregation in Rahway remembered Krepper with a rougher edge to him than his former parishioners in Carteret. It is also interesting to note that the tougher assessment of Krepper's ministry came from another Lutheran pastor who was a successor to Krepper in Rahway, and might have been aware of the inner workings of the

Rahway congregation. The gentler assessment of Krepper in Carteret came from a lay leader who may have had more of an idealistic and prosaic reflection to offer, either out of deference to the pastor who had otherwise served faithfully within that church community, or out of respect for a church leader to whom respect and deference were owed. It needs to be remembered that these two different estimations of Krepper's ministry were expressed after his arrest on a charge of espionage, and at a time during World War II when the outcome of the Battle of the Bulge in Europe was still in question. Nonetheless, these two differing appraisals of Krepper's ministry and his personal character are also very telling in terms of the very real dichotomy in Krepper's life. There were two sides to this German-American pastor. Carl Krepper was in many ways a good parish pastor; he was also an enemy agent who betrayed his adopted country in a time of war.

CHAPTER THREE

Evolution of a Nazi: Pastor Krepper in Newark, New Jersey

ST. JOHN'S CHURCH: "THE COLONY IN NEWARK"

Despite Carl Krepper's busy pastoral and civic life in Rahway and Carteret, he resigned as pastor of his two-point parish in Middlesex County, New Jersey, and on September 1, 1932, he became pastor of the First German Evangelical Lutheran St. John's Church in Newark. St. John's Church had extended an official "letter of call" to Pastor Krepper on April 25, 1932. He accepted this call on May 4, and over the summer months he and Bertha prepared for their move to Newark. Krepper would only spend three years as pastor in Newark, but those three years would be quite busy for him, both personally and professionally.

The roots of the First German Evangelical Lutheran St. John's Church are complex. The parish was organized as a mission of the Ministerium of New York on October 10, 1833. The organizing pastor was the chair of the Ministerium's mission committee, the Rev. Frederick W. Geissenhainer. Starting in 1850, a decade-long controversy arose within the St. John's Church community that resulted in both a legal battle over the possession of the church property and a congregational split. It seems that some members of St. John's rejected a move by the New York Ministerium to introduce English into meetings of the Ministerium, and in 1852, the St. John's congregation left the New York Ministerium to join the more German-oriented and theologically conservative Buffalo Synod. Concurrent with the rise of this conflict within St. John's congregation, there was a growing movement among the Lutheran congregations in New Jersey to separate themselves from the New York Ministerium over the German language issue.[1] Many pastors in New Jersey wished to use English for the business of the Ministerium, as many of their members did not speak the mother tongue. In fact, in 1855, these New Jersey pastors created a New Jersey conference within the Ministerium, followed in 1861 by a separate synod in New Jersey that affiliated with the larger General Synod. German-speaking congregations in urban communities in New Jersey, such as St. John's in Newark, tended to affiliate with the Buffalo Synod or remain connected to the Ministerium of New York, rather than join the New Jersey Synod.

As a result of the congregation's association with the Buffalo Synod, the dissensions within the St. John's congregation grew. Two lay leaders fought for control of the parish. One, John Disch, a former church council president who had been deposed because only pastors could be presidents of church councils in the Buffalo Synod, argued that the congregation should remain within the New York Ministerium. The other, Johann F. Laible, was a newer member who advocated a more traditional German service and polity. The group that supported Disch seized the St. John's Church building, while the congregation's pastor (the Rev. Frederick G. Maschopp) and the group that supported Laible broke off from the original congregation and asserted that they were the legitimate St. John's Lutheran Church. Both congregations claimed the name St. Johns' Lutheran Church and both congregations claimed the distinction of being the oldest Lutheran church in Newark. The splinter group took with it the original parish records of the 1833 congregation and called itself the First German Evangelical Lutheran St. John's Church. In 1855, it called its own pastor, the Rev. George Tuerk, and in 1858 it erected a church building on West Street in Newark. The congregation built another new church on Court Street in Newark in 1867. Prior to his arrival, Krepper's predecessor, the Rev. Dr. A. C. Redderoth, had fought what was at the time an unsuccessful battle to introduce English-language church services at St. John's. In an unusual turn-around from his previous experiences, during Krepper's three-year ministry in the congregation, he conducted some English-language services.

Carl Krepper was this congregation's 11th pastor, and he preached his first sermon at St. John's Church on the Sunday of Labor Day weekend, September 4, 1932. He was installed by the president of the United Lutheran Synod of New York (a successor church body to the Ministerium of New York), the Rev. Dr. Samuel G. Trexler. Samuel Geiss Trexler was born October 19, 1877, in Bernville, Pennsylvania. He served churches in Brooklyn and Buffalo, New York. In 1920, he was elected president of the New York and New England Synod, then in 1929, he was elected president of the United Synod of New York. In 1946, he was made commissioner for Russia of the Lutheran World Convention (predecessor body of the current Lutheran World Federation). He died on May 30, 1949. Pastor Trexler was very much opposed to Nazism and he would play another important role in Krepper's life when he was interviewed by the Federal Bureau of Investigation concerning Krepper's whereabouts in 1942. Ten years after presiding at Krepper's installation as pastor of St. John's in Newark, Trexler told the FBI that he would not appoint Krepper to serve another congregation "under any circumstances," because the Lutheran Church would not benefit from Krepper's "pro-German sentiment."[2] By 1942, with the United States at war with Germany, Krepper's Nazi leanings would preclude him from serving another parish in America.

Taking part in Krepper's 1932 installation at St. John's was the Rev. Carl Edward Poensgen, the president of the Lutheran Conference of New Jersey and pastor of St. Paul Lutheran Church in Jersey City. Another pastor who assisted in the installation service was the son of an old friend, the Rev. Sigmund von Bosse, who was the son of Georg von Bosse, the pastor who had installed Krepper in his Philadelphia congregation in 1911. Sigmund von Bosse was the director of the Wartburg Lutheran Home, in Mount Vernon, New York. Sigmund was born in 1893, while his father was pastor of Zion Lutheran Church in Egg Harbor, New Jersey. Like his father, Sigmund von Bosse was proud of his German heritage. Like his father, Sigmund advocated for neutrality on the part of the United States during the First World War and he served as president of the National German-American Alliance that promoted that goal.[3] He also became a prominent member of the German Society of Pennsylvania. While Sigmund did not join the Friends of New Germany or the German-American Bund, he was a known sympathizer of these organizations. Sigmund von Bosse not only attended the February 20, 1939, Bund rally at Madison Square Garden, which attracted 20,000 Bund supporters. He was also a speaker at the rally, where he claimed that if George Washington were alive in 1939, "he would have been a friend of Hitler." When he finished his speech, von Bosse was acknowledged with shouts of "Heil Hitler" and the Nazi salute.

The evidence of Krepper's ministry in Newark comes from the "Protocoll," or church council minutes, as well as other archival materials that were maintained by the now-closed Redeemer Lutheran Church in Irvington, New Jersey. This church was a merged congregation that was organized in 1955, and included St. John's Church in Newark together with nearby St. Paul's and Trinity Lutheran Churches. Within the St. John's Church archives is a record of Krepper's active parish ministry in Newark. These records also bear witness to the evolution of Krepper's interest in Nazism. Krepper did not keep his political sentiments to himself in his role as pastor in Newark, but he publicly espoused his fascination with, and loyalty to, the ideology of Adolf Hitler.

It was in Newark that Krepper would become heavily involved with the pro-Nazi Friends of New Germany. While serving in Newark, Krepper would, furthermore, meet the man who would eventually recruit him as a Nazi agent and as a contact person for the Operation Pastorius saboteurs. The St. John's Church Protocoll provides insight into Krepper's support of the Friends of New Germany that eventually led to the pastor's entrance into the world of espionage.

The St. John's Church parish council (*der Kirchenrath*) met each month. Its meeting records were recorded on sheets of lined notebook paper, and each month's record was signed by Krepper, as presider or council president (*Vorsitzender*), and the parish council secretary (*Secretaer*), named John Betschinger. The parish council meetings were conducted in German, and routinely concluded with the Lord's Prayer (*Vaterunsers*). Among the mundane recitation of activities from month to month there are listings of German and English services and dates when the congregation would celebrate Holy Communion, summaries of committee reports, property reports of work done on the church and parsonage, and various donations received. These records indicate an active and lively parish that was focused on meeting a variety of needs within the parish community. Listed in the church's 100th anniversary booklet was the fact that Pastor Krepper instituted a "branch Sunday School," which was an expansion of the parish's regular educational program for children in the community, located at a distance from the church. Bertha taught in this branch Sunday School program, and was also a member of the Ladies Aid Society.

The parish council records report that a little over a year after his arrival in Newark, Pastor Krepper presided at a very significant event in the life of his congregation, as he led St. John's Church in their 100th anniversary festivities. Taking its anniversary date from the organization of the old St. John's Church in Newark in 1833, the congregation started the celebration on Sunday, October 8, 1933. There were two special anniversary services that day. Preaching at the morning service was the Rev. Paul Kirsch, the mission superintendent of the United Synod of New York and New England. At the evening service were Krepper's two friends who participated in his installation in Newark, Sigmund von Bosse and Carl E. Poensgen. Special music accompanied both of these anniversary services. The oldest choral society in Newark, the Arion Singing Society, of which Carl Krepper was a member, sang at both liturgies. This German singing society was celebrating its own 75th anniversary in 1933. A second choral society, the male choir of the Friedenslodge, the Newark branch of the German Masonic society (*verein*), the Franz Sigel Order,[4] sang at the evening service.

A singular part of the St. John's anniversary was the arrival of what would have been seen as an amazing gift from the Fatherland—a copy of the German Luther Bible that came from German president Paul von Hindenburg. The presentation Bible had a personal inscription from President von Hindenburg for the church as it celebrated its 100th anniversary. The inscription was written in dark blue ink in a careful German script, with capital letters decorated in gold leaf. The greeting from the German president read:

The First German Evangelical Lutheran St. John's Church in Newark, On the occasion of the celebration of the 100th anniversary of the colony (*der Kolonie*) dedicated to the desire that, mindful of the heritage of the fathers, you would always inspire and guide the parish in Christian conviction and fraternal concord! Berlin, October 13, 1933 [signed] von Hindenburg[5]

That the Newark congregation was referred to as a "colony" by the German president is fascinating. It doesn't so much harken back to Pastorius's seventeenth-century Germantown or other German settlements in the New World prior to the nineteenth century, all of which, to one degree or another, had been assimilated into the American cultural landscape well before 1933. For that matter, German-American Lutheran congregations in the first decades of the twentieth century did not necessarily think of themselves as literal "colonies" of the Fatherland. Germany had lost its colonial possessions after World War I as the nation evolved from an empire to a republic. There were, nonetheless, many Germans still living in parts of Europe lost to Germany after the Treaty of Versailles (including Alsace and Lorraine, which reverted to France; the Sudetenland, in western Czechoslovakia; and Pomerania and Upper Silesia, which went to Poland). Along with other German-Americans who were living in the United States at the end of the First World War, Carl Krepper would have been aware of all these losses, both in terms of the landmass and the population of the old German Empire.

As President von Hindenburg addressed the St. John's Church community with his presentation Bible in October 1933, Hitler had been chancellor of Germany for less than nine months. Von Hindenburg would be dead in less than a year, and Hitler's international ambitions would soon make the front page of newspapers all over the world. It may be that President von Hindenburg's reference to the Newark congregation as a "colony" spoke more to the German world of the later nineteenth century. This was the Germany in which Carl Krepper was raised, a Germany that was an empire, and that had real colonies all over the world. Carl Krepper may have looked upon his Newark congregation (and the other German-American churches he served in New Jersey and Philadelphia) as a remnant of the German world he knew as a boy, but which had otherwise disappeared. On the other hand, the reference to St. John's Church as a "colony" was also a quaint way of reflecting back on the immigrant experience of a congregation that had deep German roots and that was proud of its connections to the Fatherland.

The parish council and Pastor Krepper had a special photographic portrait taken on the occasion of the church's 100th anniversary. Front and center in this photograph is a seated Carl Krepper, holding the Hindenburg Bible, among seven parish councilmen. The inscription on this photograph reads, "The church council during the centenary of the First German Evangelical Lutheran St. John's Church, Newark, New Jersey." On either side of the caption are the dates 1833 and 1933. This Bible was an important link for Krepper to his homeland, and it continued to hold an important place in the St. John's parish even after Carl Krepper left for Germany in 1935.

NAZIS IN GERMANY AND AMERICA

As their 100th anniversary year drew to a close, Krepper and the German "colony" in Newark would have heard the news coming from their homeland. Throughout the crucial year 1933, all the major

American newspapers covered the rise of Nazism, and Krepper and his fellow German-Americans would have known that Hitler had become chancellor on January 30, 1933. Throughout the year, Hitler's Nazi policies would soon begin to irrevocably change Germany from a republic into the Third Reich. The pastor of the First German Evangelical Lutheran St. John's Church in Newark was very much aware of the changes taking place in the Fatherland, and he was supportive of the Führer's policies. Krepper would have read the news that as a response to the Reichstag fire of February 27, the next day President von Hindenburg signed the "Reichstag Fire Decree," which curtailed civil liberties across a broad spectrum of German society. The freedom of the press, freedom of expression, and freedom of assembly were suspended. The decree also suspended the right of privacy for enemies of the Nazi Party. Mail to or from suspected enemies could be opened and examined. Private telephone conversations could be listened to by the Nazi authorities, and telegrams could be opened and read. Private property could be confiscated, and the decree provided the basis for the arrest of many of Hitler's political opponents. The tide continued to turn for the Nazis as they received a majority of the seats in the Reichstag in the March 5 federal elections. Under pressure from the SA (Hitler's Storm Troops, the *Sturmabteilung*), who positioned themselves in and around the Kroll Opera House (where the Reichstag was temporarily meeting), on March 23, the Reichstag approved Hitler's "Enabling Act." Officially called the "Law to Remedy the Distress of the People and the Reich," Hitler personally addressed the Reichstag with an oversized Nazi flag hanging in the background and promoted the law, while also publicly berating the Social Democrats, who opposed it. The law passed, with the only opposition coming from the Social Democrats. The law basically gave Hitler dictatorial powers, and enabled him to pass laws without the approval of the Reichstag.

Buttressed by Nazi victories, the SA targeted German Jews in the business and legal professions and subjected them to humiliating public spectacles. Synagogues were defaced and Jews throughout Germany were beginning to be isolated by the Nazi government.

In response, the Jewish community in the United States urged a boycott of German products. Starting in the summer of 1933, a number of groups publicly promoted the boycott of German goods, including the American Jewish Congress, the American League for the Defense of Jewish Rights and its successor organization, the Non-Sectarian Anti-Nazi League, the American Federation of Labor, and the Jewish War

Veterans.[6] Between 1933 and 1939, these groups sought to hit the Nazi regime economically as a means of protesting the treatment of German Jews. Picketers handed out circulars in front of stores that sold German-made products, encouraging shoppers to not buy German goods and encouraging stores to not sell them. The boycott drew the attention of the press, and to a degree it negatively impacted public opinion of Nazi Germany. U.S. trade with Germany decreased as a result of the boycott.[7] The American boycott of German goods impacted Germany at a number of other levels as well. German authorities claimed that if American Jews would lift the boycott, conditions for German Jews would improve.[8]

The American boycott provoked a counterpunch by the German government. A nationwide German boycott of Jewish stores was put into effect from 10 a.m. to midnight of April 1, 1933. Signs instructing buyers to not buy from Jews were placed on the windows of Jewish-owned stores by the SA. Despite the best efforts of the SA, the German boycott was not very effective. Nonetheless, Hitler's anti-Jewish agenda gained momentum. On April 7, the Nazi government enacted the "Law for the Restoration of the Professional Civil Service," which restricted civil service employment to those who were considered to be true "Aryans"—that is, those whose parents and grandparents were German Christians. This was the so-called "Aryan paragraph," which stipulated that even if a grandparent had converted from Judaism to Christianity, the grandchild of such an individual would not be considered to be a true Aryan, and thus would be excluded by law from working in the German civil service.

The "Law for the Restoration of the Professional Civil Service" was soon expanded to include those working in the medical, legal, and ecclesiastical fields. Lutheran pastors who had Jewish grandparents, even if those grandparents had converted to Christianity, were excluded from office. Some of those pastors who had Jewish ancestry were able to migrate to the United States to serve in German-American congregations. Such was the case with Krepper's successor at the First German Evangelical Lutheran St. John's Church in Newark, the Rev. Heinz W. H. Kugler. Pastor Kugler had left Germany in 1934 to complete his theological studies at the Lutheran Theological Seminary at Philadelphia. He left Germany at a time when seminarians who had any Jewish ancestry were precluded from serving in the German Lutheran Church by the "Aryan paragraph." Kugler completed his theological preparation in 1936 and was called to serve St. John's, Newark, where he succeeded Carl Krepper. Kugler served St. John's until 1942, when he was called to serve at First Lutheran Church in Poughkeepsie, New York. During his time in Poughkeepsie, Kugler would be appointed by the U.S. Army as a chaplain to the German prisoners of war who were interred at the Green Haven United States Disciplinary Barracks in Dutchess County, New York. Kugler would come back to New Jersey in 1945 to become pastor of St. Mark's Lutheran Church in Elizabeth. At the same time that Krepper was working to subvert the United States as an enemy agent, Krepper's successor in Newark, who would have been precluded from serving in the German church, had not only accepted the call to serve his adopted country at a time of war, he also served his fellow Germans who were in the United States as prisoners of war.

When Krepper left the United States for Germany in 1935, he complained to the German church and governmental authorities about what he called the "plutocratic Jewish" influences in American society. He would probably not have been happy that a pastor whom he would not have considered an "Aryan" was serving his old German congregation in Newark. On at least one of his trips back to the United States prior to 1941, Krepper investigated the possibility of resuming his service at St. John's in Newark. By then, Pastor Kugler was serving the congregation, so Krepper went back to the Fatherland to continue serving there.[9]

Even though he undoubtedly supported the application of the "Aryan paragraph" to the church, as a naturalized American citizen serving in Nazi Germany, Krepper had his own issues with which he would have to contend. Krepper was indeed an "Aryan" in the Nazi sense. He was German born, and he did not have grandparents who were Jewish. Nonetheless, he had renounced his German citizenship years earlier when he became an American citizen. The issue of his citizenship plagued Krepper during his years in Germany. The fact that he had relinquished his German citizenship would have precluded him from serving in many capacities within and outside Germany. Had he not been recruited by Lt. Walter Kappe for his work as a Nazi agent in America, Krepper most likely would not have received the blessing of the *Auslands-Organisation*, which promoted support of Nazi Germany in foreign lands by German nationals, because it only accepted German citizens. It can be asserted that it was only because he was coming to play a key role as a contact person for Nazi agents and saboteurs that he had the support he received from various levels of the German government for his trip back to the United States in December 1941.

The Pastors' Emergency League was organized on September 11, 1933, as a direct result of this application of the "Aryan paragraph" to the life of the German church. This association united Lutheran clergymen through-out Germany against the attempt of Hitler and Reich Bishop Müller to co-opt the church and force German pastors into the Reich Church.

As these developments were transforming Germany into Hitler's image of an Aryan nation, in the United States the "Association of the Friends of the New Germany" (*Bund der Freunde des Neuen Deutschland*) was organized. With headquarters in New York City, the group formed between April and May of 1933 to support the "New Germany" that Hitler was creating. It openly supported Nazi ideology and the Nazi agenda. It raised the swastika flag at meetings and members sang the song of the Nazi Party, the *Horst-Wessel-Lied* or "Horst Wessel Song," as well as the national anthem of Nazi Germany, *Deutschland Über Alles*. When they joined the organization, members pledged themselves to be Aryans, with no "Jewish or colored racial admixture."[10]

The Friends of New Germany were first led by Heinrich (Heinz) Spanknöbel, who was appointed to lead this new organization in 1933 by Rudolph Hess, Hitler's deputy Führer. Spanknöbel was born on November 27, 1893, in Homberg, Germany. He had served as a Seventh Day Adventist clergyman in Germany and the United States, making previous trips and being listed in various ship records as a "missionary," a "preacher," and a "journalist." Like Carl Krepper, Heinz Spanknöbel would see no conflict between his vocation as a clergyman and his sup-port of Nazi ideology.

After briefly working for the Ford Motor Company in Detroit, Spanknöbel labored full-time for the pro-Nazi "National Socialist Association of Teutonia," which he brought into the Friends along with another pro-Nazi group, the Gau-USA (organized in 1931). Unlike the later German-American Bund, the Friends of New Germany welcomed both German-American citizens and noncitizens among its members. Spanknöbel sought to infiltrate the various German societies in the United States, including the United German Societies of New York, and thus bring them into the Friends. Representatives of the Friends were sent around the country in an unsuccessful effort to unite German-Americans under the Friends' pro-Nazi umbrella. As leader of the Friends, Spanknöbel spoke at a number of rallies, many of which led to riots. Spanknöbel found himself in serious trouble with both American authorities and with German-Americans who thought his tactics and goals were too violent. Within less than six months of assuming leadership of the Friends, he was indicted in New York as an unregis-tered foreign agent (after an open conflict with the mayor of New York

City), and he escaped back to Germany on October 29, 1933. Back in Germany, Spanknöbel became an officer in the SS, and died in 1947 in Soviet custody.[11] Fritz Gissibl stepped into Spanknöbel's shoes as leader of the Friends, along with a German-American, Herbert Schnuch.

Carl Krepper became an active member of the Friends while he served his church in Newark. He hosted a church service for the organization in 1934, and he later proudly boasted to his ecclesiastical superiors in Germany and to the German Foreign Office that he flew the swastika flag in his church. The Friends of New Germany flew the swastika at meetings, and tried to force the flying of the flag at other gatherings of German-Americans as well. Carl Krepper did his part to follow that part of the Friends' agenda within his own congregation.

Prior to the organization of the Friends, Nazis were already active in the United States. The Nazi leadership in Germany knew that there were large clusters of German immigrants in urban areas between New York and Los Angeles, and that roughly half a million Germans had come to the United States from the end of World War I to 1930. The Nazi foreign policy specialists in Germany believed that nearly 7 million German-American homes used German as their primary language,[12] and hoped that they would therefore have a good base of support in the United States.

THE KOHLER LETTER: CARL KREPPER AS A FRIEND OF NEW GERMANY

A unique assessment of how the Friends of New Germany viewed Carl Krepper is found in his FBI file.[13] On January 5, 1942, a spot search by the FBI at the home of the New Jersey state treasurer of the German-American Bund, Matthias Kohler, uncovered a carbon copy of a letter "to the National Directorate of the German-American Bund." Kohler would have known Krepper personally, as he was a leader of the Newark Friends. Kohler was born in Germany on June 10, 1896. He had come to America in 1927 and worked as a watchmaker in the Newark area for many years. Koehler became the leader of the Newark Friends' *Ordnungs-Dienst* (O.D.), which was a "uniformed service" fighting unit (often called the "Order Service") based on the example of the SA in Germany. As New Jersey state treasurer of the German-American Bund, Kohler was a supporter of Camp Nordland, one of a number of Friends' outdoor camps that were established throughout the United States. Nordland was located in Andover Township, New Jersey. In June 1940, along with August Klapprott, the head of Camp Nordland, and Wilhelm

Kunze, the national Bund leader, Kohler was accused of violating New Jersey law by advocating "race hatred and hostility against people of the Jewish religion."[14] Along with these three, a total of eight Bund leaders were found guilty and fined from $1,000 to $2,000, and sentenced from 12 to 14 months in jail. Kunze and Kohler were both indicted for making an anti-Jewish speech and were each fined $2,000.

Kohler registered for the draft on April 26, 1942; the following year, the United States Immigration and Refugee Service considered revoking his citizenship on the basis of a "lack of attachment to the Constitution of the United States." Since he had registered for the draft, Kohler was not, after all, "denaturalized." He continued to work as a watchmaker in Belleville, then in Irvington, and finally in Bloomfield, all in New Jersey. He died in 1973 in Long Valley, New Jersey.

As the New Jersey treasurer of the Friends of New Germany, Kohler was in a unique position to attest to Pastor Krepper's pro-Nazi allegiance. The letter that was found in his possession by the FBI was headed "The Friends of New Germany," and was apparently a reply to a letter from Germany from a Pastor O. Mordhorst,[15] who had enquired about Krepper's Nazi bona fides.

According to Krepper's church personnel record, Pastor Mordhorst was an American Lutheran colleague of Krepper who went back to Germany to serve in a Lutheran parish in the Fatherland. There was clearly a personal animosity between Pastor Mordhorst and Pastor Krepper. Not only did Mordhorst inquire of the German-American Bund about Krepper's support of the Nazi cause, back in Germany he leveled what were considered to be serious accusations in regard to Krepper's personal morality. While it is not explicitly stated what Krepper was accused of, this charge of immorality was likely related to Krepper's divorce from his first wife and his remarriage to Bertha Frey. Krepper's personnel record indicates that the charges against Krepper made by Pastor Mordhorst were severe enough that they were investigated by the German church. With the cooperation of the New York and Pennsylvania Ministeriums, it was ascertained that Krepper was not guilty of the charges, and it was noted that the president of the Ministerium of Pennsylvania considered Krepper to be "honorably discharged" from that ecclesiastical body into the care of the New York Ministerium, and that honorable discharge was considered to be "irrevocable." Furthermore, it was noted in Krepper's personnel record that "[o]n June 1, 1937 pastor Krepper received an honorable discharge from . . . the United Lutheran Synod of New York." Krepper apparently brought charges of slander against Mordhorst in a German district court, which fined Mordhorst 200 Reichsmarks for defaming Krepper. Krepper's ecclesiastical superiors believed that Mordhorst acted out of jealousy, and after their investigation they considered the matter to be concluded.

Nonetheless, it is clear that either on his own or at the behest of others, Mordhorst had also contacted the Bund in New Jersey with a question regarding Krepper's support of National Socialism. Matthias Kohler's letter was apparently written without any regard to the personal conflict between Mordhorst and Krepper, and Kohler simply stated what the Friends of New Germany thought of Krepper's pro-Nazi stance back in the United States.

The FBI included a transcript of the Kohler letter in his file:

Efdende

(The Friends of New Germany)

P. O. Box 65, Irvington, NJ

To the National Directorate of the German American Bund: I herewith make a truthful report in answer to inclosed [sic] letter of Pastor O. Mordhorst from Ihlsburg Post, Parchau, Germany.

Reverend Krepper, whom we have known for many years, was the former minister of a small congregation in the heart of the Jewish District in Newark. In 1934 he was one of the few persons in Newark who stood up for his Fatherland, and even at the time we celebrated the memorial services for the dead in his church with flags and with the Order Service.

He belonged to the German American League as a representative from his congregation, and there also he publicly stood up for his pro-German views. Success was of course forthcoming. He received no support whatever from our opponents nor from any of his own "German" supporters, and after it became impossible for him to earn his own bread, he went back to Germany. We, the members of the Bund of this Unit, know him and value him as a German man who always upheld his own convictions at all times, and we can only wish him the best of everything.

Sieg Heil!

M. Kohler

Unit Leader[16]

The Order Service referred to in the Kohler letter was the Friends of New Germany's Ordnungs-Dienst, the OD. The references to Krepper's time in Newark are fascinating on a number of levels. First, the characterization of the neighborhood around St. John's being "a Jewish District" was clearly meant to underline Krepper's dedication to the anti-Semitic ideals of the Nazi party. The Kohler letter attempted to underscore that Krepper was steadfast in his "pro-German views" in the midst of what the Friends of New Germany, the Bund, and the Nazi leadership in Germany would have seen as a difficult situation. To serve in and be faithful to the Nazi racial ideals in a "Jewish district" would undoubtedly have given Krepper credibility with the Reich Church leadership back in Germany. Even though he served in a "Jewish District," Krepper stood up for the Fatherland. When he returned to Germany, Krepper would complain about the "plutocratic Jews" back in America, and how Germans were being persecuted by them. At his federal trial in 1945, Krepper would admit that one of his missions in America was to provide refuge for Bundists who were "persecuted" by the Jews. Kohler's letter furthermore bore witness to what Krepper told the German church authorities, that he proudly raised the swastika in church. The celebration of "memorial services" with "flags" is a clear indication of what Krepper indicted to his ecclesiastical superiors in Germany—that he proudly flew the swastika flag in his church many times. He also had the Order Service men in uniform with the swastika flags in his church. It could be presumed that when Krepper hosted his services with the Friends of New Germany in his church in Newark, there were uniformed Order Service men carrying the flag of the Nazi Party into the church itself.

Kohler's letter also stated what Krepper would proudly boast about in his letters to church authorities in Germany, namely that he was known to fellow German-Americans who were members of the Bund, and that, despite any antagonism, Krepper was a man who "stood up for his convictions."

The FBI report speculated about the purpose of this assessment of Krepper's fidelity to the Nazi ideals:

It is possible that the information contained in Kohler's letter was forwarded to Germany at the request of German authorities who were checking into Krepper's background to determine his sympathies toward Germany while he was in the United States. This may have been used for the purpose of giving him employment as a minister or in connection with sabotage or espionage activities.

This letter was written and discovered by the FBI prior to the arrival of the Pastorius saboteurs in the United States. When the FBI first discovered this letter in January 1942, the war was not even a month old, and while agents posited the possibility that Pastor Krepper may have been recruited for "sabotage or espionage activities," they did not know who he was. When the FBI found this letter, it did not know that Pastor Krepper had returned to the United States the previous month, and until the capture of the Pastorius saboteurs, agents would have had little idea that Pastor Krepper had been vetted for his role as a Nazi agent in what would be the most wide-ranging terrorist attempt on American soil during World War II. As time went on, the FBI would discover much more about Carl Krepper's role in the Pastorius sabotage plot.

The Kohler letter described Carl Krepper's pro-German activities in 1934, while he was pastor of St. John's in Newark, and while he was an active member of Friends of New Germany. Whether he knew it or not, in 1934, Krepper was earning a credibility that would, in five years' time, give him a part in a plan that the German military intelligence network believed could help win the Second World War and bring the United States into the Nazi Reich.

Whether Pastor Mordhorst was impressed by this response or not, the pro-Nazi references in the Kohler letter would indeed have made a difference for the Reich Church leadership as they assessed Krepper's fitness to serve a church back in the Fatherland. While other Lutheran, Roman Catholic, and Reformed clergy would have trouble subscribing to the "Aryan paragraph," after serving in a "Jewish district" in Newark, Krepper would have no qualms about supporting the application of the Nazi racial agenda within the church. Thus it was that, despite the troubles that Krepper had with some German clergy because he had renounced his German citizenship after the First World War, Krepper was given significant support by the Kohler letter that would have enabled him to both serve as a pastor in Germany, and to be recruited as an agent of the *Abwehr* (German military intelligence).

The FBI realized that since Krepper's name appeared as a contact person on two different sets of handkerchiefs issued to the two groups of Pastorius saboteurs, Krepper was a person of some significance in the attempted terrorist attacks on the American mainland. Having pro-Nazi credentials would have helped Krepper in both of the ways suggested in the FBI file. First, the Reich Church would be interested in whether or not, as an American citizen who had been ordained in the United States, Krepper could realistically support the Reich Church or work to undermine it. Secondly, as he was recruited to work as a Nazi agent in the United States, Krepper would need to be vetted for such a significant task. His Nazi credentials would need to be, and indeed were, checked back in America.

Another significant feature of the Kohler letter is its statement that, along with Francis Just, Krepper was a member of the pro-Nazi German-American League. This link demonstrates that Krepper had contact with many future leaders of the Bund, and lends credence to the claim that Krepper made after his arrest that he was sent over to the United States in December 1941 with a mission to aid "Bundists persecuted by the Jews." This claim only makes sense if he indeed had connections with these soon-to-be Bundists in the United States prior to his departure for the Fatherland in 1935.

In the same year referred to in the Kohler letter, Krepper worked with his German-American League colleague, Dr. Just, in organizing an Essex County chapter of the German-American Business League (*Deutscheramerikanischer Wirstschaftsausschuss,* or DAWA). Formed in New York City in 1934, DAWA promoted a boycott of Jewish-owned stores in the United States, in an effort to counter the Jewish boycott of German goods. DAWA concurrently encouraged Americans to purchase goods from German-owned businesses. As he organized a DAWA chapter in Essex County in April 1934, Krepper worked closely with Just, and the two would have helped facilitate the distribution of stickers that were placed in windows of businesses that supported the DAWA in Newark and nearby Irvington. Later in 1934, a directory of stores in Hudson and Essex County that sold German goods was published and distributed as well.

DR. FRANCIS JUST: KREPPER'S NAZI FRIEND

Francis Just was born Franz Just in Wechselburg, Germany, on December 1, 1884. Just and Krepper were contemporaries, having been born less than nine months apart. Just immigrated to the United States in 1914, and was naturalized in New York on December 11, 1919. Like Pastor Krepper, Dr. Just had been born into a Germany that was an empire with a kaiser at its head. Like Krepper, Just had lived through the Great War as a resident alien while his adopted country was at war with his homeland. Like Krepper, Just became a naturalized citizen of the United States after the German Empire was defeated. After meeting his future wife Hildegarde in Texas, Dr. Just moved to New York, and from thence to Newark, New Jersey, where he lived and worked as a physician, and where he met Carl Krepper. Just became a fixture in German-American life in Newark and throughout Essex County, supporting a school that taught the German language, called the *Deutscher Sprachschule* (organized in 1935), as well as other German-American organizations.[17] Like Krepper, Just became a member of the Friends of New Germany, which supported Hitler's racist and fascist agenda in the United States. As an active leader of the Newark Friends, Just was involved in a number of attempts to bring the Friends into the mainstream of New Jersey German-American societies. Just became the president of the German-American League of Essex County, and he promoted the flying of the swastika flag at a number of functions, including German Day celebrations in Newark. Krepper was also a member of the German-American League. Together with Francis Just, Krepper and other DAWA supporters encouraged the placement of stickers in windows of businesses that supported the DAWA in Newark and nearby Irvington. After the Friends of New Germany morphed into the German-American Bund, Dr. Just became an active member of that organization.

Due to his support of the German-American Bund, the successor organization to the Friends, Francis Just came to the attention of both the Immigration and Naturalization Service and the FBI. Just was one of many German-born members of the Bund whose citizenship was put in jeopardy by their participation in the Bund. The Immigration and Naturalization Service and the FBI enacted what was called the "Denaturalization Program," whereby naturalized American citizens could have their citizenship "canceled" if their loyalty to the Constitution was in question. While denaturalization of German-Americans took place during the anti-German hysteria of World War I, the Word War II–era Denaturalization Program was initiated in October 1941 several months prior to the U.S. entry into World War II, and as a direct result of the investigation of the Bund by the Immigration and Naturalization Service. By 1944, all the investigative effort in the Denaturalization Program was concentrated in the FBI. While "mere membership in a national socialistic organization, such as the German American Bund, [was] not sufficient indication of the subject's lack of attachment to the principles of the Constitution," nonetheless, if it could be "shown that he knew of and subscribed to the national socialistic principles of that organization," a Bund member could be subject to having his or her citizenship "canceled."[18]

Lists were drawn up of naturalized German-Americans whose loyalty was considered to be in question, and who became part of the

Federal "Denaturalization Program." Francis Just's name was placed on that list on October 12, 1942. Often these German-Americans were given the choice of registering for the draft or having their citizenship revoked. The FBI and the Immigration and Naturalization Service considered that "a mental reservation as to willingness to bear arms is fraud which will warrant revocation proceedings."[19] On April 27, 1942, a little less than six months prior to his being placed in the Denaturalization Program, Dr. Just had registered for the draft, and thus his citizenship was not canceled.

The names of Carl Krepper and Francis Just were later linked together in Krepper's FBI file. An anonymous letter to the FBI dated January 10, 1942, suggested that the bureau look into the recently returned Carl Krepper. Then, in June 1942, Krepper's name was linked to the Pastorius saboteurs on the handkerchief given to them prior to their landing in the United States. They were told that Krepper was a man they could contact for rooms and other support. Shortly after the FBI caught the saboteurs, the bureau gathered what information on Krepper it could from the State Department and the Immigration and Naturalization Service. The FBI found that Krepper was an American citizen, and that among the references on his June 22, 1935, passport renewal, Krepper had listed the Rev. Georg von Bosse of Montgomery County, Pennsylvania, together with his "son-in-law" (actually his stepson) Eugene Frey of Rahway, New Jersey. Topping this list of references was none other than Dr. Francis Just of Newark, New Jersey. This information was recorded on page 12 of a 16-page FBI report from the Newark Field Office dated July 14, 1942, just a little over two weeks after the last Pastorius saboteur was apprehended. This report succinctly stated what the FBI knew about Krepper up to that point, and was entitled "George John Dasch, with aliases; et al." As the FBI tried to put together a picture of who Krepper was in July 1942, the names of Carl Krepper and Francis Just were once again linked.

Pastor Krepper rubbed elbows with many pro-Nazi Friends of New Germany during his ministry in Newark. Another significant contact among the Friends of New Germany was Walter Kappe. Krepper's meeting with Kappe took place in New York City at a memorial service for German president Paul von Hindenburg. Kappe was the man who would eventually recruit Krepper as a Nazi agent and a contact person for the Operation Pastorius saboteurs. The St. John's Church Protocoll provides insight into both Krepper's support of the Friends of New Germany and the memorial service for President von Hindenburg in

New York that eventually led to Krepper's entrance into the world of espionage.

WALTER KAPPE: MEETING A FUTURE SPYMASTER

The year that Krepper moved back to New Jersey to become pastor of his two-point parish in Rahway and Carteret, the "National Socialist Association of Teutonia" (*Nationalsozialistische Vereinigung Teutonia*) was founded in Detroit. Teutonia was organized in Michigan in 1924 by three Hitler supporters who had immigrated to the United States from Germany, brothers Fritz and Peter Gissibl, and a man who would significantly influence Carl Krepper's life, Walter Kappe. Kappe would later return to Germany to serve in the *Abwehr* (German military intelligence), and attain the rank of lieutenant in the German Navy. Most significantly, Kappe would hand pick and oversee the training of the Pastorius saboteurs, and he would recruit Carl Krepper as their contact man in the United States.

Kappe was from the Saxon town of Alfeld, and was born January 12, 1905. He had been one of the first 1,000 members of the Nazi Party, but along with other disillusioned supporters of Hitler, he had decided to come to the United States after the failed Beer Hall Putsch in 1923. He left Germany from Hamburg aboard the SS Orduna, which arrived in New York on March 8, 1925. Kappe was 19 years of age when he arrived. His occupation on the ship's register was listed as a "banking clerk," and his final destination listed as Lockport, Illinois. He already spoke both German and English. Kappe married another German immigrant, Hilda Kauffman, who had come to America as a 16-year-old with her family in 1923. After a stint in a factory in Illinois, Kappe's English skills would eventually land him a job as editor of several German-American newspapers in Illinois and in New York. In addition to editing German newspapers, Kappe was instrumental in helping to establish the pro-Nazi Teutonia organization, which in 1933 led to the formation of the Friends of New Germany.

Kappe made a name for himself as editor of the newspapers the *Deutsche Zeitung* and its successor, the *Deutscher Weckruf und Beobachter*, both published out of New York. Kappe's outspoken attacks on Communists and Jews in print and at the meetings of the Friends of New Germany throughout the United States made headlines. Kappe protested any and all real or perceived slights to Nazism in the United States, and he railed against what he called the "world-wide Jewish conspiracy." He bragged that under Hitler, Communism had been rooted out of Germany, and that if the Friends had their way, it would similarly be rooted out of America. Some of Kappe's speeches led to violence as riots broke out, and Kappe himself was injured.

Kappe's newspaper work in New York, along with his labors as a spokesperson for the Friends, brought him into contact with Pastor Carl Krepper at the memorial service for von Hindenburg in New York City. Von Hindenburg died on August 2, 1934, and that same day, the Reichstag enacted a law that declared Hitler to be the Führer, with the authority of the combined offices of Reich chancellor and Reich president vested in the office of Führer. At the moment that Germany mourned the loss of its president and national icon, the nation transformed itself into a dictatorship with Hitler as Führer and supreme commander of the armed forces.

In the United States, the German-American community mourned von Hindenburg's passing. Even as it celebrated Hitler's elevation as Führer, the American Nazi community also mourned the death of the last president of the Weimar Republic. Thus it was that, along with other German-Americans, leaders of the Friends of New Germany took part in the New York memorial service for von Hindenburg. Pastor Krepper not only attended the service, but he also chaired a committee that planned what was to be a Hindenburg memorial church in the United States.

While the church was never built, Krepper's work in planning it is recorded in the October 9, 1934, parish council minutes of First German Evangelical Lutheran St. John's Church in Newark. Krepper reported to his parish council that he was busy negotiating the particulars of this proposed church, and he secured their agreement to support this work. His work as chair of that committee would otherwise conflict with the evening service at the church on the first Sunday in November, All Saints Sunday, and Krepper received the support of his parish council for his extracurricular work to memorialize the late German president. Krepper seemed to be proud of his attempts to memorialize von Hindenburg, and he mentioned it again in a May 4, 1937, letter to his regional church office in Kiel (the *Landeskirchenamt*).[20] In this letter to his ecclesiastical superiors, Pastor Krepper stated that while pastor of St. John's Church in Newark, New Jersey, he was also director of an institute promoting "German Understanding," which, Krepper claimed, was personally supported by both President Franklin Roosevelt and Reich Bishop Müller.[21]

When Krepper attended the Hindenburg memorial service in New York and planned for the ill-fated Hindenburg Memorial Church, Walter Kappe was a nationally recognized leader of the Friends of New Germany, as well as the editor of a nationally significant German-American newspaper, while Krepper was an enthusiastic member of the Friends in Newark.

Walter Kappe returned to Germany in 1937 as a result of a failed attempt to take control of the German-American Bund, the successor body to the Friends (which had been shut down by order of Rudolph Hess in December of 1935).[22] Fritz Kuhn,[23] who was known by Krepper, would take over the leadership of the Bund, while back in Germany, Kappe would join the *Abwehr* and eventually be given leadership of Operation Pastorius, a very daring and potentially a very deadly terrorist plot to undermine American support of the war. Kappe survived the war, dying in 1958 near Frankfurt, Germany.

While he served as pastor of St. John's Church in Newark, Krepper had become quite embedded in the American Nazi movement. He rubbed elbows with a number of individuals who helped shape the course of the pro-Nazi organizations in the United States, and he ardently supported this cause. Krepper had been proud of the empire that he had known as a boy, and he had a growing pride in the new Germany that Hitler was creating in the Fatherland.

CHAPTER FOUR

On the Road to the Reich

CARL KREPPER, MASTER OF THEOLOGY

May 1934 was a busy month for Carl Krepper. He and Francis Just organized the Essex County branch of DAWA, and he completed his master of theology degree at the New Brunswick Theological Seminary in New Jersey. His thesis was entitled "Protestant Churches and Slavery," and was dated May 7, 1934. Krepper's advisor was the Rev. Dr. Milton Hoffman, professor of ecclesiastical history at the seminary.[1] Krepper's thesis consisted of a 53-page survey of various reactions to slavery among the Protestant denominations of the United States, with some emphasis, understandably, on the Lutheran reactions to it, and concluded with the end of the Civil War and President Lincoln's assassination. While it had a decent organization and breadth of topic, Krepper's thesis was clearly written by a non-native English speaker and, among other things, there were numerous unedited grammatical errors, as well as a number of page-long quotations without indentation and other stylistic matters. The following year, Krepper would leave the United States and return to his homeland, and there he would strongly criticize the plurality and diversity of American society. The conclusion of his thesis is, therefore, somewhat ironic:

The slavery issue was settled by the outcome of the Civil War and the Emancipation of the slaves by President Lincoln. The success of the North was won at a fearful cost; but the result of the victory compensated fully the expenditure of blood and treasure it involved. Public life was freed from a noxious incubus and source of corruption; the possibilities of intellectual and moral development were opened to millions of human beings; and the formation of a great slave empire was decisively and for ever [sic] prevented.[2]

The irony of this conclusion in his master's thesis is the fact that when Krepper wrote these words, he was an active member of an organization that excluded Jews, Masons, and "coloreds." As a member of the Friends of New Germany, Krepper had to swear that he had pure Aryan blood, with no racial "admixture." When he co-organized the Essex County branch of DAWA, he believed that the financial well-being as well as the intellectual and moral development of millions of Jewish-Americans should be subjugated to the fascist agenda of Nazi Germany.

Krepper's master's thesis topic is also interesting from another standpoint. During the First World War, Kropp Seminary graduates were accused of provoking racial unrest in the Southern states as a means of keeping the United States out of the war. While Krepper's reflections on the damaging effects of slavery in the United States cannot in any way be seen as encouraging racial unrest in New Jersey or elsewhere, they can certainly be seen as delving into the theme of national turbulence over racial issues that Hitler's Germany believed they had solved. Krepper and his colleagues in the Friends of New Germany believed that Hitler had removed from German society the possibility of the kind of racial unrest that was experienced prior to and after the American Civil War. If not for the fact that he was a member of an organization that promoted racial unrest and bigotry, the topic of Krepper's master's thesis would not seem unusual in any way. As a member of an organization that espoused racial hatred and isolation, the topic of Krepper's master's thesis provides a fascinating glimpse into the mind of a man who would soon leave his adopted country to return to his homeland, where death camps were being built to not only destroy the "intellectual and moral development" of millions of people, but would endeavor to exterminate an entire race. Krepper's thesis sits in the Gardner A. Sage Library of the New Brunswick Theological Seminary, and it remains an ironic testament from a man who would, within seven years of writing it, merge his calling as a Lutheran clergyman with a new calling to become an enemy agent against the very people he had previously felt called by God to serve. When Krepper returned to the United States as a Nazi agent in 1941, he would live within and work against the American Republic less than an hour's drive from the library that contained what in 1934 he had believed was an insightful analysis of American society.

As Krepper completed his master's thesis in church history at the seminary, the Lutheran Church in Germany was undergoing a major challenge with the struggle between the "German Christians" of the Reich Church on the one hand and the Confessing Church on the other. Just three weeks after Krepper presented his thesis, the "Barmen Declaration" was signed by pastors in Germany denouncing the merger of the church and the state in the Reich Church. In his thesis, Krepper had articulated a classic American understanding of the nature of the church and its relationship to the state:

> The Lutheran Church, believing that political and social issues are the province of citizens in their civil capacities and not in their ecclesiastical organizations, has persistently refused to permit itself to be drawn into the arena of affairs of the state, whether they be political or so-called "social reforms."[3]

Krepper was articulating an American understanding of the separation of church and state that was very different from what he would experience back in Germany. As he completed his thesis, Krepper had served his entire pastoral career in the United States. He had spent 25 years serving in a country that had a distinctive separation of church and state relations and that differed in many significant ways from what Germany had experienced prior to the rise of Hitler, and would be diametrically opposed to what was espoused by those who organized the Reich Church in Germany. Krepper's German personnel record is rife with evidence of struggles between fellow German clergy who seemed to doubt the real German nature of their German-trained but American-ordained colleague. There were also questions about his loyalty to the Nazi ideology, as well as regarding the style and substance of Krepper's ministry in Germany. While he was prepared for his pastoral work in Germany, he had only served congregations in the United States.

There was no reference in his thesis to the "church struggle" (*Kirchenkampf*) that was playing out within the German Lutheran Church. Even though there are clear parallels between the German church struggle of the 1930s and the ruptures faced by some American Protestant denominations over slavery up to and during the American Civil War, there was no connecting of the dots in Krepper's mind. Yet, as with other German-American pastors, Krepper would have known of this struggle for the heart and soul of German Lutheranism, as Hitler tried to merge church and state into a Reich church that was in conflict with the classic image of the church/state relations of which Krepper wrote.[4]

During his 1945 federal trial, it was clear that Krepper knew where these ecclesiastical battle lines were drawn,[5] and he had sided with those who supported the Reich Church. Some years later, a leading American Lutheran leader, Franklin Clark Fry, would get to the heart of the matter: "Krepper was strongly pro-Nazi in sentiment. . . . God and the Reich were closely identified in his mind."[6]

Later in 1934, as he worked on the committee for the proposed Hindenburg memorial church, Krepper and the other Friends of New Germany would know that in the United States, the tide of public opinion was turning against Adolf Hitler and the Nazi movement.

AMERICA AT ODDS WITH NAZISM

There was trouble in the American Nazi camp in 1934 on a number of fronts. When the McCormack-Dickstein Committee began its work investigating Nazism and other forms of fascism, there was growing unrest with the extremes of Nazism within German-American society in general.

Starting in 1933, New York congressman Samuel Dickstein began investigating the Nazi infiltration of American society. Dickstein's work led to the formation of what was called the McCormack-Dickstein Committee, or the House "Special Committee on Un-American Activities Authorized to Investigate Nazi Propaganda and Certain Other Propaganda Activities," which focused on investigating the threat of Nazism within the United States. Its work helped support the seizure of Nazi propaganda that was sent from Germany to America. It held hearings that uncovered evidence that the German government was financially supporting the Friends of New Germany, and it charged that Berlin was directing the group's anti-American propaganda work on behalf of the German government. The McCormack-Dickstein Committee furthermore called attention to the string of Friends-sponsored Nazi camps that were spread across the United States. These camps were seen by the committee as indoctrination centers for young people and families, and thus were considered as centers that promoted both racial unrest and subversion of American freedoms.

The committee released its 4,800-page report on February 15, 1935. One of the most significant results of this report was the passage of legislation that required foreign agents to be registered with the United States government. This June 8, 1938, act was an effort to control the spread of foreign propaganda (i.e., propaganda from Soviet Communists and German Nazis) that could be construed as un-American. The significance of what was called the "Foreign Agents Registration Act" (FARA) was that it became a crime to be an agent or representative of a foreign country without first registering with the U.S. attorney general. The act required that agents of a foreign government had to complete a registration statement that identified them as foreign agents. Excluded were diplomatic and consular staff as well as foreign newspapers. Foreign agents were required to make "periodic public disclosure of their relationship with the foreign principal."[7] Originally foreign agents had to register with the secretary of state, but this was changed by President Franklin Roosevelt in 1942 under Executive Order 9176, so that the registration of such agents would be conducted under the authority of the attorney general. Among other things, when Carl Krepper was arrested in December 1944, he was charged with violating FARA.

Carl Krepper would have been aware that, as 1935 progressed, there was trouble brewing for the Friends of New Germany.[8] Many communities in New Jersey banned meetings of the Friends, as riots were not uncommon during or in the aftermath of their meetings. While there were many supporters of the Friends in Hudson County, New Jersey, only one community, Guttenberg, allowed them to meet. The Newark branch of the Friends had to meet in Irvington because the city of Newark banned the meetings there. The larger gatherings of the Friends were held in Springfield, as that community had both the space for such meetings and the support of the local government.

Recognizing the growing threat of Nazism in the Garden State, the New Jersey legislature passed the "Anti-Nazi Act." The New Jersey House passed the act on March 17, 1935, and the New Jersey Senate passed it on April 9. While it was eventually overturned as unconstitutional by the U.S. Supreme Court on December 5, 1941, the very fact that New Jersey enacted such a bill in the first place demonstrates the growing concerns that many had about the spread of Nazi propaganda.

Within the German-American community itself, alarm bells were being sounded on a number of fronts as the Friends had tried to infiltrate German-American clubs and organizations. Despite some success within Essex County, New Jersey, in Manhattan, and elsewhere, their efforts were, for the most part, unsuccessful. At their meeting in Union City, New Jersey, on July 17, 1934, the gathered delegates from the various lodges of the Franz Sigel singing society banned the flying of the swastika flag at their gatherings. The society, which had its head-quarters in the Manhattan neighborhood of Yorkville, ruled that as the flying of the swastika was a political statement, the Nazi flag would have no place in their clubhouses. This decision was seen as a sea change within German-American society. It was described as

> one of the most significant signs of the waning power of Nazis in New York. . . . It is believed to mark the turning point—the Water-loo of the up-to-now successful march of Nazis throughout America's Germandom.[9]

With its assertions that Nazi Germany was directing the work of the Friends of New Germany, the McCormack-Dickstein Committee report in particular caused some apprehension within the German govern-ment. It was assumed in Berlin that the United States' problems with the Friends stemmed from the fact that there were many members who were still German citizens.[10] There was a growing awareness within the Nazi leadership in Berlin that their cause in the United States could best be achieved by native-born or naturalized American citizens who had embraced the Nazi cause. By December 1935, the decision was made by the German government that its interests would be furthered most effectively by the disbanding of the Friends organization. Thus it was that the order came from Deputy Führer Rudolph Hess that as of the end of December 1935, the Friends would cease to exist.

A month earlier, Carl Krepper had left the United States behind. By the time the Friends disbanded, Krepper was already in Germany and serving as an assistant pastor of the St. Johannes Kirche in Oldenburg.

BACK TO THE FATHERLAND

The year 1935 was significant for Carl Krepper for a number of rea-sons. On January 5, 1935, Krepper marked a milestone in his American odyssey. On that date he marked the 25th anniversary of his ordination. In the St. John's Church Protocoll for December 5, 1934, it was noted that on January 5, Pastor Krepper would celebrate his "twenty-five year

Pastoral Jubilee." It was noted that there would be a "solemn service" to mark the occasion.

Five months after Pastor Krepper celebrated his 25th anniversary of pastoral service in the United States, he prepared for a significant trip. He would once again travel to Germany. After 25 years in America, Krepper would take a two-month trip back to the Fatherland, and during that trip he would investigate the possibility of securing a Lutheran parish in Germany. This journey would be pivotal for Krepper, as it would help him make up his mind to leave the United States and go back to the Fatherland. That decision would have monumental consequences for Carl and Bertha Krepper.

The June 5, 1935, parish council minutes record that Krepper informed his lay leaders that he would take this months-long journey. The July 7, 1935, Protocoll recorded that the pastor would be away from July 11 to September 20. During that vacation he was employed in a parish in the Schleswig-Holstein Territorial Church, employment that would bear fruit for Krepper later that year as he began serving as a pastor in the German Lutheran Church.

Krepper arrived back in New York on October 4 aboard the SS New York, which had sailed from Hamburg, Germany, on September 26. Krepper was in Newark for his October 8 parish council meeting. Four days later, Krepper sprang some big news on his congregation. Under "new business," he requested a two-year leave of absence in order to serve a new congregation back in the Fatherland. He would assume the position of assistant pastor of St. John's Church in Oldenburg, Holstein. He expected to start this new position on All Saints Day, November 1, 1935.

Krepper had only been home four days from his nearly three-month trip, and it is not surprising that the parish council did not grant him the two-year leave he requested. Pastor Krepper submitted his resignation there and then. The parish council wished their pastor luck and blessings in his new field of labor. After some minor financial business, the meeting concluded, as was their custom, with the Our Father.

Pastor Krepper's last official day at St. John's in Newark was Tuesday, October 15, 1935.[11] This was less than a month from the 26th-year anniversary of his arrival in the United States. He was to start his new church in Germany one day shy of the 26th anniversary of his departure from Germany in 1909. Krepper would have seen this as a very fitting conclusion to his pastoral ministry in the United States, as he reflected on that date when more than a quarter century earlier, the 25-year-old Kropp

Seminary graduate had arrived in the United States. That October, Carl and Bertha Krepper returned to the land of their birth, and Krepper became assistant pastor of St. John's Church in Oldenburg, serving there from November 1, 1935, to July 1, 1937.

OLDENBURG: TO BE OR NOT TO BE A GERMAN

While Krepper served in Oldenburg, he was plagued by questions regarding his American citizenship. It seems that the fact that Krepper had renounced his German citizenship during his ministry in Philadelphia became a thorn in his side while in Oldenburg. The residents of Oldenburg only wanted a German citizen as their pastor. Even though he had been born and educated in Germany and had only served German-speaking parishes in America, the fact that he retained his American citizenship became a stumbling block to securing a full-time position as a pastor in Oldenburg. A January 22, 1937, memorandum addressed the issue of Krepper's "nationality."[12]

Krepper reported to the church authorities in Germany that a "teacher" in America had made it clear that when the United States entered the war he "had to acquire American citizenship," or else "he could not keep his position." It is fascinating to note that even though he became an American citizen in 1922, Krepper used the First World War as an excuse for his decision to become an American citizen. According to his FBI file, Pastor Krepper was defiant during World War I and stated that he would never give up his German citizenship. While in America during the Great War, Krepper had lived as a citizen of the German Empire. It was only after the war, when the German Empire ceased to exist, that following the example of Lutheran pastors like Georg von Bosse, Krepper made the decision to renounce his German citizenship. When he told his ecclesiastical superiors in Germany in 1937 that he was basically forced to become an American during World War I, he lied. He had become an American citizen in 1922, after the First World War was over, making a strategic decision to live as an American citizen. As an American citizen, he had served German-speaking congregations in largely German neighborhoods in New Jersey and Philadelphia. As an American citizen, he had served the German-American community for two-and-a-half decades, and he had the freedom to join pro-Nazi organizations. In the United States, he had no reason to apologize for becoming an American citizen and renouncing his German passport. Yet in Germany, Krepper felt constrained to lie to his church superiors about when and why he had become an American citizen. Perhaps Krepper felt that this claim made him look more like a martyr who suffered in the *Ausland* in order to serve his countrymen—or maybe Krepper lied because he hoped it would help him keep his job. Whatever his motivation, Pastor Krepper was told by his superiors in the January 22, 1937, memorandum that he had "to strive for the acquisition of his German citizenship."

Apparently, as a German-born American pastor, Krepper believed that when he received a full-time position in Germany he would be able to once again become a German citizen.[13] He had expressed a clear desire to live and work in his homeland within the German Lutheran Church. Krepper knew, furthermore, that there was a shortage of Lutheran pastors in some portions of Germany, in part due to the fact that some clergy were thrown into jail for being members of the Confessing Church, and others, who did not swear the oath of allegiance to Hitler, were drafted and sent to fight in the army. As a supporter of National Socialism and Hitler's "national community," Krepper hoped that he could offer support to this new Germany in his role as pastor.

Krepper found himself in a difficult position in 1937. He had been removed from the clerical roster of the New York Synod of the United Lutheran Church in America, and his clerical status was officially "transferred" to the German Lutheran Church.[14] This transfer was effective June 1, 1937. Nonetheless, because he retained his American citizenship, from his arrival in December 1935 until 1940, Krepper was denied the status of being permanently employed within the German Church. In May 1937, Krepper filed a rambling complaint about this situation to the regional church headquarters in Kiel:

> May I point out that without the confident assurance of the Lutheran Church Office regarding my permanent job I would never have abandoned my flourishing congregation in Newark, a city with a very strong German presence; I would never have exposed myself to the risk of being removed from the Pastoral List of New York— which actually happened—I have lost my pension entitlement from the New York Synod—and would never have broken up my household, and with great loss, spent the substantial cost for a move to Germany.

Needless to say, Krepper had a reasonable complaint. He seems to have felt that he had the promise of a permanent position within the German church when he was offered the position of assistant in Oldenburg. He was, however, dealing with a bureaucracy with which he had no real experience prior to his hasty move to Germany in 1935. Even though he had met with the then friend and confidant of Hitler, Dr. Ernst Hanfstaengl, a graduate of Harvard University and head of Hitler's Foreign Press Department, Krepper had problems related to his American citizenship until 1940. When he arrived in Germany in 1935, Krepper said that he first informed Dr. Hanfstaengl of his membership in the Bund of the Friends of New Germany, but he was told that issues around his employment would have to be handled through the church leadership.

When Krepper was in Germany for his summer trip to the Fatherland in 1935, the Nuremberg Laws were enacted within the Reich. On September 15, 1935, the "Reich Citizenship Law" and the "Law for the Protection of German Blood and Honor" were decreed. These laws denied Jews citizenship within Germany and outlawed marriage and sexual relations between Jews and Aryans. While these laws did not immediately affect Krepper, as he was considered a full-blooded Aryan according the Nuremberg Laws, nonetheless the questions raised about his renunciation of his German citizenship could not have come at a worse time for him. Krepper came back to his homeland as a noncitizen at a time when the Reich was defining issues of citizenship (i.e., who was an Aryan and who was not, and who could be a citizen of the Reich and who could not). Even though he had been an active member of the Friends of New Germany and supported its strict membership rules that excluded non-Aryans, and had organized a branch of the DAWA that promoted a boycott of Jewish stores, Krepper was looked upon as less than fully German by his community in Oldenburg.

According to his German church personnel record, Krepper worked in Oldenburg under the Rev. Julius Christian Loos,[15] who had arrived in Oldenburg as pastor in April 1931. Besides the issue of Krepper's nationality, one of the other main problems with which the American pastor had to contend was the inability of his congregation to support two pastors. Financial difficulties loomed large in the reports on Krepper's ministry in Oldenburg. Even though the work was too hard for Pastor Loos alone, St. John's Church could not afford two pastors.

According to the January 22, 1937, memorandum, another difficulty that Krepper faced in Oldenburg was a developing controversy with another former American Lutheran clergyman, a Pastor Mordhorst. The third issue that was addressed in the above-mentioned memorandum was the issue of Krepper's divorce and remarriage. The Lutheran Church leadership in Kiel, Germany, had "doubts" about Krepper's past. They knew that Krepper's wife was the former wife of a barber, and they had heard rumors that he was "sexually active" with her "before his divorce." Krepper had to be heard on the subject, they asserted, but if that doubt was not removed, Krepper would not find permanent employment in the Lutheran Territorial Church.

There were also other issues with which Krepper had to contend in Oldenburg that focused around issues of style and approach to his church work. While there were a number of parishioners at the St. John's Church who appreciated Pastor Krepper's work, there were others who disliked his approach to pastoral ministry. According to the January 22, 1937, memorandum, Krepper was accused of being too literalistic in his approach to the Bible. In particular, he was said to have used "too many Bible sayings" in his funeral sermons.

Nonetheless, it seems that Krepper used his time in Germany to advance himself, academically speaking. It was asserted by a confidential source in America that while in Germany, Krepper earned a PhD from Kiel University,[16] but it appears that the war interrupted his completing the degree.[17]

Overall, Krepper's time in Oldenburg does not appear to have been very fruitful, either for him or the congregation he served. In a June 6, 1937, report to the *Landeskirchenamt* (the regional church council) it was clear that Krepper's problems had come to a head.[18] In the report it was stated that, among others, Krepper was said to have met with leaders from both the Confessing Church and the German Christians (the Reich Church), and had planned to write a book about National Socialism in Germany, and about church conditions in particular. As an ardent supporter of National Socialism in the United States, Krepper obviously believed that he could assess the real thing in Germany. It was undoubtedly his proposed assessment of German Church life that worried his judicatory heads. Krepper actually claimed that his book "would make much money" and would help him "become a famous man." This proposed book would prove to be a breaking point for his relationship with his ecclesiastical judicatory heads in Kiel. Krepper had been told in January 1937 that he had better become a German citizen or not expect employment in Oldenburg. Yet by June of that year, Krepper had not become a German citizen, and he had to be urged to once again become a citizen of his homeland (he claimed in the June 25th report that no Lutheran pastor who was a German citizen could remain in office in America). Krepper also had problems with his congregation, and his church could not afford him. Finally, to round off the list of troubles, Krepper had been accused of questionable morality as well.

In the eyes of his clerical superiors in Kiel, Krepper and his book about German church life were seen as a "threat" to the German church, and they believed he should not receive any employment as a pastor in Germany.

Krepper was informed that as of July 1, 1937, he would be relieved from his position in Oldenburg. The excuse of the regional church council was that there was an "increasing number of our candidates." Nonetheless, the regional church expressed its thanks to Krepper for his services.

An interesting twist to Krepper's attempts to serve in the German Lutheran Church is that, as the FBI found in the course of their investigation of Krepper starting in 1942, in the summer of 1937, Krepper came back to America for the "purpose of securing [a] Lutheran congregation but was unsuccessful."[19] Krepper was actually in the United States when his tenure at St. John's, Oldenburg, concluded. He and Bertha had traveled back to the United States and stayed with her son Eugene and his family. This was undoubtedly the journey that Krepper made to try and return to St. John's Church in Newark, only to find the Rev. Heinz Kugler in place in his former parish.

Between 1936 and 1939, both Carl and Bertha Krepper traveled back and forth between Germany and New Jersey multiple times. Carl and Bertha traveled together in the summer of 1938, while Bertha traveled twice on her own in this period, in 1936 and 1939. Her 1939 trip lasted an entire year. She had arrived in New York aboard the SS Hamburg on April 28, 1939, and stayed into 1940. Bertha was actually staying with her son and daughter-in-law Hilda, and their daughter Ilsa, on April 26, 1940, when the census taker arrived to record the 1940 data. In that census Bertha was, strangely enough, listed as a "widow." At that moment, she was, of course, very much married to Carl Krepper, who was back in Germany.

RENDSBURG-NEUWERK: A SPY IS BORN

Despite the judgment of some within the church leadership in Kiel, Pastor Krepper continued with his ecclesiastical service in Germany. Starting on July 1, 1937, he was appointed to serve in Büdelsdorf, and on June 30, 1940,[20] Krepper became the Pastor of the Rendsburg-Neuwerk Church III (the Third Church). He would continue in that church until he left for the United States in December of the following year, and even during his sojourn as a Nazi agent in the United States, he would continue to receive his salary as pastor of that church.

Krepper's personnel records after his move to Rendsburg-Neuwerk detail not simply his curriculum vitae, but also his loyalty to National Socialism while in the United States. During his time in Büdelsdorf, there was an important correlation between Krepper's German personnel record and his FBI report. A March 11, 1940, report from the Evangelical Lutheran Church headquarters in Kiel (the *Kirchenamt*) to the Reich Minister of Church Affairs, Dr. Hans Kerrl, refers to two personal reference letters that were written for Carl Krepper from men in the United States who supported both the Reich and Carl Krepper. One letter was from his German-American clergy colleague, Georg von Bosse, and another was written by the New Jersey German-American Bund treasurer, Matthias Kohler, a copy of which was discovered in a spot search of his New Jersey home by the FBI on January 5, 1942. The Kohler letter is a reference for Krepper that testified to Krepper's real support for National Socialism. Kohler knew Krepper in Newark as a member of the Friends of New Germany, and as a pastor who served in a "Jewish" neighborhood, who, in that context, stood up for what the Bund considered to be German values (this would have meant that, among other things, he spoke against the Jews and promoted the boycott of Jewish-owned businesses). The letter found by the FBI stated that Krepper was known to the leaders of the Bund, and that they knew he had been an outspoken proponent of National Socialism within the United States.

The March 11, 1940, report to Reich Minister Kerrl referred to Matthias Kohler as an *Ortsgruppenleiter* (a local Nazi group leader). This is significant on several levels. First, it confirms something that has been suspected for many years, that Kohler was actually a member of the German Nazi party, the NSDAP (or *Nationalesozialistische Deutsche Arbeiterpartei*). Previously, historians have believed that "strong evidence"[21] suggests this connection between Kohler and the German Nazi party. The 1940 Krepper report to Hitler's Reich Minister of Church Affairs certainly confirms this belief. The report very specifically utilized the term *Ortsgruppenleiter* for Kohler, which was a word used by the Nazi Party as a title for leaders who organized party members in Germany and around the world in the *Ausland*. The *Ortsgruppenleiters* of Nazi Party groups in places like the United States were connected to the Nazi Party leadership in Germany first through the *Auslands-Abteilung* (the Foreign Department), and then through the *Auslands-Organisation* (the AO or Foreign Organization). The later organization would be a conduit for Carl Krepper's journey to the United States in 1941 for the ostensive purpose of promulgating pro-German propaganda, but which was secretly planned by Krepper's fellow Friend of New Germany in America, Walter Kappe, to enable Krepper to create a network of safe houses, and to be a conduit for financial resources to Nazi agents arriving in the United States.

Krepper's letter of reference from *Ortsgruppenleiter* Matthias Kohler is also significant in that it provides evidence of Krepper's deep connections to what would become the German-American Bund, and of his support of their efforts, even when he was serving his church in Germany. That the church authorities knew of this connection, and cited it in their recitation of Carl Krepper's curriculum vitae to the Reich Ministry of Church Affairs, speaks to a merging of church/state relations that would have been foreign to Krepper when he was in the United States. This was, nonetheless, a church that Krepper very much wanted to serve. His connections with the Bund in the United States would bear fruit when he was sent there as an agent of the Nazi government.

The March 11, 1940, report to the Reich Minister stated that Krepper had a healthier relationship with his congregation in Büdelsdorf than with his previous congregation in Oldenburg. On the basis of his two years of faithful service in Büdelsdorf, Krepper's immediate supervisor, Propst (Provost) Hugo Bender, recommended that Krepper be granted permanent employment within the German church. This ecclesiastical decision would have great significance for Krepper in later years. On the basis of this decision, Krepper would eventually request, and be granted, a full German church pension after his release from prison in the United States. Krepper would only serve as a permanently employed pastor in Germany for 21 months. Even though he spent the entire war in the United States, with the last five months spent in jail, he would continue to receive his church salary for the duration of the war. This money paid for an assistant to serve in Krepper's place in Rendsburg-Neuwerk, and the remainder went to his wife Bertha. It is something of an irony that on the basis of 21 months of permanent employment, after his release from prison in the United States, as an American citizen, Krepper received two decades of retirement pension payments from Germany, as he lived in retirement in the Berkshires in the state of Massachusetts until his death on June 21, 1972.

This report to the Reich Minister specifically requested two exemptions from the Reich Ministry of Church Affairs: that Krepper be allowed to continue serving as a pastor in Germany, with an exemption from the requirement of becoming a German citizen; and that he be granted an exemption from the education requirements for serving in the German church. The report detailed Krepper's theological studies in Germany and the United States, highlighting, among other things, his bachelor's and master's degrees from Rutgers University. In reality, Krepper more than met the equivalent of the German secondary degree requirement. It was his exemption from the legal requirement that he become a German citizen that is most interesting. Even though they had no idea of the *Abwehr's* plans for Krepper the following year, his ecclesiastical superiors had asked the Reich Minister to free Krepper from a basic requirement for permanent employment within the church. But in reality, this exemption freed Krepper to return to the United States the very next year as an agent of the Nazi government, and to do so with a full clerical salary of 60,000 Reichsmarks a year. Out of that salary, he paid an assistant 1,800 Reichsmarks, and the rest went to Bertha Krepper.[22]

The report to the Reich minister was written as Hitler's Germany was beginning its conquest of Europe. The two requests of the Reich minister of church affairs came six months and 10 days after Germany's invasion of Poland (September 1, 1939), which, in the eyes of many, marks the beginning of the Second World War. The Battle of the Atlantic had been raging since September and less than a month from the writing of that report, Germany would begin its invasion of Norway (on April 9, 1940). The Battle of France began on June 5, 1940, and in July, the Battle of Britain. The fact that Krepper was allowed to retain his American passport in the midst of these circumstances is somewhat unique, and it undoubtedly brought him to the attention of his old friend from the United States, Walter Kappe, who was now with the *Abwehr*. Kappe saw in Krepper a man who possessed all the necessary characteristics to become an agent for Nazi Germany. As an American citizen who was loyal to the Fatherland and who had a variety of contacts back in the United States, Carl Krepper was able to play a distinctive role in Kappe's daring Operation Pastorius. Within 16 months of the decision to allow Krepper to work in Germany without obtaining his German citizenship, a Nazi spy was born. Because of what transpired while Krepper was pastor in Rendsburg-Neuwerk, in December 1941, Krepper would be bound for the United States with a mission to, among other things, support Nazi saboteurs whose goal was to create havoc.

CHAPTER FIVE

Carl Krepper and His Mission in America

RECRUIT OF THE ABWEHR

It was while he was in Büdelsdorf that Krepper was recruited by the *Abwehr* for a special mission. As Krepper told the story at his federal trial in Newark in February 1945, he met his old acquaintance from the Friends of New Germany, Walter Kappe, in Berlin in 1941.[1] Within months, Krepper was on board a ship to the United States as an agent of Nazi Germany.

The version of the story that Krepper told at his trial is quite different from that presented by the evidence found in his German clerical personnel record and in his FBI files. According to his trial testimony, in June 1941, the United States Consul in Hamburg told Krepper that because of his five-and-a-half-year residence in Germany, his United States citizenship was about to be canceled. During his trial, Krepper claimed that the reason he came back to the United States in December 1941 was to ensure that his American citizenship would not be revoked. As he prepared for this trip, he claimed that he met up with Walter Kappe in Berlin after he sought to withdraw $2,500 of his own funds from the Reich Bank for his intended trip to the United States. This was money that Krepper claimed to have brought back to Germany with him when he left the United States in 1935. The Reich Bank, so Krepper said, denied this request to withdraw his money. The bank required that he find someone to "vouch" for him. According to his trial testimony in 1945, Krepper said that Kappe agreed to help him acquire his money from the Reich Bank, but for a price: Krepper was expected to "tell people [in the United States that] Germany was not responsible for the war," and "in every way possible present Germany's side in the best possible way"; finally, he was to "give aid to Bundists who might be persecuted by Jews."[2]

The reference to Germany not being "responsible for the war" is a reference to Germany's actions prior to the entrance of the United States into the war. According to Krepper, Kappe wanted him to tell the Americans that, among other things, Germany was not "responsible" for its invasions of Poland, Norway, and France, or for the Battle of the Atlantic or the Battle of Britain. It is not clear exactly what Kappe wanted Krepper to say about these military actions, but the one thing he wanted Krepper to state categorically was that Germany was not responsible for its military victories and incursions. Krepper was charged by Kappe with implementing the *Abwehr's* propaganda efforts in the United States. Krepper was to put a pro-German spin on the news of Germany's military expansion in Europe and, in effect, make the claim that Germany was forced into war. As Krepper claimed in his trial, his instructions were given to him prior to the commencement of the war with the United States, and so, as some of his fellow Kropp Seminary graduates had done during the First World War, Krepper was tasked with trying to keep the United States out of what was shaping up as a second World War.

The other two tasks that Krepper claimed he was charged with performing by Kappe were ideas and concepts that he readily accepted and promoted. While the stated goals of his trip to the United States (to promote German propaganda and to aid Bundists "persecuted by Jews") were tasks he publicly admitted to performing during his trial, there are several aspects of his claims to the jury that are suspect. First, Krepper's claim that his $2,500 was being held by the Reich Bank until he had someone to vouch for him seems rather dubious. Second, his claim that he met Walter Kappe as a result of this Reich Bank scheme is most certainly false.

By the time he visited the Reich Bank offices in Berlin during the summer of 1941, Krepper was permanently employed in Germany. Moreover, he had the official permission of the Reich minister of church affairs to remain in office as a full-time parish pastor without the requirement of maintaining German citizenship. His parish in Rendsburg-Neuwerk continued to pay his salary until November 1945.[3]

That salary not only paid for an assistant to serve in his stead in his church, but it also supported his wife Bertha while he was serving the Reich in the United States. Nonetheless, Krepper told an American jury in his trial that the only way he could retrieve his funds from the Reich Bank was to have someone who knew him testify to his identity. As he continued his tale to the jury in Newark in 1945, Krepper said that the Reich Bank sent him to the Propaganda Ministry (*Reichsministerium für Volksaufklärung und Propaganda*, the Reich Ministry of Public Enlightenment and Propaganda), which was headed by Dr. Joseph Goebbels. That a representative of the Reich Bank would send Krepper to the Propaganda Ministry for confirmation of his identity seems unusual. The Reich minister of church affairs was aware of Krepper's identity, as were the church authorities in Kiel who had pressed for Krepper's exemption from the requirement that he be a German citizen in order to serve his congregation. Krepper furthermore had an entire congregation in Rendsburg-Neuwerk who could vouch for his identity. That he would be told by the Reich Bank to go to the Reich Ministry of Propaganda instead of to the Reich Ministry of Church Affairs to confirm his identity does not make sense, nor does it match any of the other contemporary evidence. Nonetheless, this rather odd sequence of events does not seem to have been questioned in his American trial.

According to Krepper's testimony, it was at the Propaganda Ministry that he met Walter Kappe.[4] This too seems unusual. In the summer of 1941, Kappe was employed by the *Auslands-Organisation* (AO), among other things, interviewing English-speaking German expatriates returning to the Fatherland.[5] Kappe was soon recruited to work under Admiral Wilhelm Canaris for the *Abwehr*, German military intelligence, and by the summer of 1941, he had already made contact with at least one of the men whom he would later recruit for Operation Pastorius, George John Dasch.[6] In his work with the AO, Kappe in particular was tasked with interviewing English-speaking Germans who had returned to the Fatherland from the United States.

Kappe's cover with the *Abwehr* was working as the editor of a nonexistent publication entitled *Der Kaukasus* (*The Caucasus*). The address of the editorial office of this supposed magazine was Berlin W 15, *Rankenstrasse* 8.[7] It appears that Krepper met Kappe again through the AO, which required men like Krepper who had returned to the Reich from the *Ausland* to register and to remain in contact with it. Krepper, like George John Dasch and the other saboteurs recruited by Kappe, had taken on American citizenship, spoke English, and was well acquainted with American life. Even more significant for Kappe, Krepper was both an ardent supporter of National Socialism and the Reich and had contacts in the United States who felt the same way about the Reich. These were traits that would have made Carl Emil Ludwig Krepper a perfect recruit in view of Kappe's plans.

At some point after his arrival in Germany in 1935, Krepper would most certainly have had to register with the AO, and as he worked with the AO, Kappe would have been aware of the presence in the Reich of his old acquaintance from New Jersey. Krepper's meeting with Kappe in Germany was not a chance encounter based upon a suggestion from the Reich Bank. Pastor Krepper was intentionally recruited as an agent by the *Abwehr*.

This explanation of where and how Krepper met up with the man who would soon be the mastermind of the Pastorius sabotage plot is likely found in a piece of evidence in Krepper's German church personnel record.

Within his personnel file is a letter written on July 16, 1941.[8] This correspondence consists of a one-page autobiographical letter from Krepper to the Information Department (*Informationsabteilung*) of the German Foreign Ministry (the *Auswärtiges Amt*, or AA), which was the professional diplomatic corps of the Reich. Krepper stated to the Information Department that he was writing on the direction of the AO "of the NSDAP" about a personal matter. This is clear evidence that Krepper had been in contact with the AO, and had received direction from it. His reference to the NSDAP is an indication that Krepper saw his mission as having the blessing of the Nazi Party. The AO was most likely the point of connection between Krepper and Kappe, as Kappe's job was just that—to make contact with Germans returning from the United States.

In his letter, Krepper presented his "case" (*meinen Fall*). He gave a brief résumé of his background, including where he was born in Germany, who his parents were, and how he had been trained to work in the "foreign service" (*Auslandsdienst*) of the Lutheran Church at the Kropp Seminary. He then briefly detailed his 25 years of service in the United States, including the parishes he had served, as well as his education at Rutgers University (where he said he studied history, political science, economics, and pedagogy). In the same paragraph in which he presented his educational attainments, Krepper claimed that his job was made "impossible" by "Jewish influences." He cited the supposed point of contention: he belonged to the "Bund of the Friends of New Germany." Krepper was claiming that he was professionally harmed by "Jewish influences" in New Jersey. The implication is that he wanted to teach, as he claimed that it was "school authorities" who were under "Jewish influences" that made it "impossible" for him to work.

Krepper stated that during his holiday in Germany in the summer of 1935, he was employed at a parish church in Schleswig-Holstein, and that he was, as of the date of his letter (July 16, 1941), "permanently employed." Krepper detailed that he had received a call from the American embassy in Hamburg to return to the United States before September 4, "since on this day my passport expires." As he sailed from Lisbon, Portugal, on December 5, 1941, it is clear that the issues around his American passport and citizenship had already been resolved. On the list of United States citizens aboard the SS Excalibur who arrived in New York on December 16, 1941, was Carl Krepper, who, it was recorded, was naturalized as an American citizen at the General Court in Philadelphia in June 1922.[9]

Krepper wanted to "use this opportunity"—that is, his return to the United States—for a very specific purpose: "to serve my German countrymen and the majority of the American people." This service was very singular—"to stir up the false propaganda of a Jewish-plutocratic clique, through a presentation of the true conditions" prevailing in the Reich. As did Hitler and the members of the Nazi Party, Krepper believed that the majority of American citizens were longing to hear what he considered to be the "truth" of the insidious nature of "Jewish influences" within American society. Whatever Krepper meant by the "Jewish-plutocratic clique" in America is not spelled out in his letter. He assumed that the Information Department of the AA would know what he meant, and he was undoubtedly correct that they would understand such Nazi buzzwords and catchphrases.

Krepper then made a request in his presentation of his "case" that was quite unusual: "I would like this without a special order of a German Reich Office." He was asking permission to travel to the United States without official sanction from either the AA or the AO. He would, he said, assume the risk of such a trip himself. While he did not state this purpose in his letter to the AA, Krepper was actually traveling as an American citizen who would work as an agent on behalf of the *Abwehr*. As Kappe and the rest of the Nazi intelligence community knew, things were not easy for Bund members in the United States. With inner turmoil over leadership of the Bund, and the distrust of the Bund on the part of the majority of American citizens, it would not serve the *Abwehr's* interests for Krepper to relate directly back to the Fatherland with the usual AA or AO connections through the Bund. Krepper would have his contacts with Bundists in the United States as needed to facilitate his work as an agent of Nazi Germany (as the Kohler letter attests), but Kappe wanted Krepper to be free to operate without the constraints of the traditional Foreign Ministry or AO oversight. If Krepper was given permission to travel back to America without the official sanction of either *Auslands* ministry, he would possess a perfect cover for the work that Kappe intended for him: he would simply be a naturalized German-American citizen coming back to his adopted country.

"To execute my plan I need American currency," he stated, and he asked the AA for assistance in changing German Reichsmarks into U.S. dollars. Krepper arrived in New York in December 1941 with American cash as well as a great deal of money in foreign postage stamps. As strange as it may sound in the twenty-first century, postage stamps were, at times, used as a form of currency in the first half of the twentieth century, and they would be virtually untraceable as Krepper settled into his new life in New Jersey and New York.

Krepper's letter to the AA closed with the usual "complimentary closing" that was common in business and personal letters in Nazi Germany: "Heil Hitler." This "complimentary closing" was used regularly in correspondence within Germany from 1933 to the end of the Second World War, and four of the personal letters from various parties in Krepper's German personnel record end with this phrase.

When and how the necessary permissions for Krepper's trip to the United States were granted by the AA is not clear, but granted they were, and by December 1941 Carl Krepper had a mission in the United States, and he was ready to play his part in assisting the Reich.

A final note to the German church's assessment of Pastor Krepper's mission to the United States comes from another document in Krepper's German clergy record. After the Second World War ended, there was an assessment of the parish council of Krepper's congregation in Büdelsdorf.[10] The letter was sent to Dr. Wilhelm Halfmann,[11] the president of the provisional church government for the Schleswig-Holstein Lutheran Territorial Church (*Landeskirche*) at church headquarters in Kiel. The letter is a fascinating glimpse into what Krepper's church thought of his mission to the United States. This letter was dated November 26, 1945, just a little more than six months after the end of the war in Europe. It seems that the local parish council met on

November 24 and came to a unanimous decision regarding their pastor, Carl Krepper, who had been on leave from the church since the fall of 1941. The parish council stated that they knew the purpose of Pastor Krepper's trip to America—that he was busy doing propaganda work for the Nazi government (*Nazi-Regierung*). They considered their pastor a "conscript of the *Wehrmacht*" (the German armed forces).

This is a significant contemporary assessment of a man who was understood by his parish to simultaneously be a pastor and an agent of Nazi Germany. His parish council stated that they knew that Krepper was a member of the *Wehrmacht*. This is a fascinating statement on several levels. His parish did not compare Krepper to Bonhoeffer, who worked against Hitler through the *Abwehr*. Rather, unlike pastors such as Bonhoeffer and Niemöller, who suffered imprisonment, and in Bonhoeffer's case, death, for working against Hitler's Nazi policies, Krepper's parish in Büdelsdorf knew that their pastor actively supported Nazism and that he willingly came to the United States to work for the Nazi government. Furthermore, Krepper's parish council knew that he was not "conscripted" into the *Wehrmacht* as a chaplain; rather, he was "conscripted" to conduct propaganda for the Nazi government as an undercover operator. His congregation in Büdelsdorf therefore knew the bare bones of his clandestine mission. In short, Krepper's congregation knew that he was both a pastor and a spy.

The parish council stressed to President Halfmann that as they had been paying a pastor who had been absent from his parish for nearly four years, they were facing a very difficult financial burden. Even more to the point, in the aftermath of Germany's defeat in the war, Krepper's congregation made a bold statement: "It is intolerable that a pastor who has worked in such a manner for Nazism (*Nazitum*) would be left in his office." His congregation may not have known the full extent of Krepper's work with Kappe and the *Abwehr*, but they knew that his "conscription" by the *Wehrmacht* placed him in a unique position as a pastor who "worked" for Nazism. They did not believe such a pastor should continue in office.

Krepper's congregation appears to have been revolted by his service to the Reich. Church members saw an "intolerable" contradiction in Krepper's service as a pastor who simultaneously served the Nazi Reich in the manner that Krepper did. The war in Europe had ended with Germany's unconditional surrender on June 7, 1945. Nearly six months later, Krepper's parish council unanimously removed him from office and stopped paying his salary. They did not know that at that moment their pastor was in federal prison in the United States for being a Nazi agent. They had no idea where their pastor was, and what they seemed to care about most was to stop paying the salary of a man who had left the care of his flock to serve the Nazi regime.

Just when Krepper may have heard this news about the rescinding of his parish call is not known; neither is his reaction to his congregation's denunciation of his service to the Reich. What is clear is that after he was released from prison in 1951 at the age of 66, he first sought a clerical pension from the United Lutheran Church in America. He was denied it, as he had been transferred to the care of the church in Germany in 1937. He afterwards successfully petitioned the German Lutheran Church for a petition. Even though his congregation in Büdelsdorf had been declared vacant in 1945, he was granted a pension as a retired German pastor, and he received that German ecclesiastical pension until he died in 1972.

COMING BACK TO THE UNITED STATES VIA THE ABWEHR

When Carl Krepper returned to the United States, he returned to a country in which he had lived the majority of his adult life—from 1909 to 1935. He was ordained there, and prior to December 1935, he had served his entire ministry in North America. He had been married twice, had one son and became a stepfather to another. Yet he had been taught in seminary that the United States was part of the *Ausland*, the "foreign lands." He had lived in what the late German president Paul von Hindenburg had called the German "colony" of Newark, and there he had become a follower of the Nazi ideology and way of life. In the United States, Krepper learned Nazi values and ideals. He had nurtured and articulated a hatred of Jews, and through the Friends of New Germany and the German-American Business League, he had helped create and support a network that promoted pro-Nazi propaganda.

The *Abwehr* was headed by Admiral Wilhelm Canaris, who later supported the attempted assassination attempts on Hitler's life, and who was executed, along with Pastor Dietrich Bonhoeffer, at Flossenburg Concentration Camp on April 9, 1945. Lieutenant Walter Kappe specifically worked for *Abwehr* II, the branch of the German military intelligence that was charged with sabotage. This group specialized in covert sabotage operations, and was led by Colonel Erwin von Lahousen, who personally appointed Walter Kappe to head the *Abwehr* sabotage school. After the war, Colonel von Lahousen testified at the Nuremburg Trials to Canaris's resistance to Hitler.

Kappe had given Krepper codewords or passwords by which to recognize Kappe's agents and representatives.[12] Both of these passwords speak to Krepper's background as an immigrant. One was "Franz Daniel Pastorius" (from the illustrious seventeenth-century founder of the Germantown section of Philadelphia). As Krepper had served in Philadelphia from 1911 to 1924, he would have been familiar with, and proud of, Pastorius's life and work among the Pennsylvania Germans; moreover, the code word hearkens forward to the 1942 *Abwehr* sabotage plot, "Operation Pastorius." The second password was "Pastor Kaiser." It spoke to the era in which Krepper first came to the United States, when Germany had a kaiser and an empire, and to which Krepper was still loyal during World War I. It seems that these two passwords were given to Krepper before he left for the United States in December 1941. Apparently, "Pastor Kaiser" was Krepper's code to indicate to Kappe that Krepper had arrived safely. A third password, "Yorktown," was to be used by Krepper himself when contacted by German agents who sought Krepper's help and who addressed him with the password "Pastor Kaiser."[13]

Kappe sent Carl Krepper by something of a circuitous route, through Spain and on to Portugal, whence he caught a ship to New York. In October 1941, he had first been sent to Barcelona, Spain, where he was originally scheduled to board the ship.[14] While in Barcelona, Krepper met a German pastor, the Rev. Ernst Kloess (or Klöss), who agreed to forward mail between Krepper and his wife Bertha. Whether Pastor Kloess knew anything of Krepper's mission is unclear, but after discussing the matter with his pastoral colleague, Kloess agreed to act as a go-between for Carl and Bertha Krepper. Bertha, for her part, would forward messages on to Kappe from her husband. While in Barcelona, Krepper was able to purchase $1,650 in foreign postage stamps that he would use as a nontraceable international currency in the United States.

Due to restrictions on travel from Barcelona to the United States, Krepper had to proceed to Lisbon, Portugal, where he found passage on the American Export Lines ship the SS Excalibur, built in 1930 in Camden, New Jersey. The Excalibur sailed from Lisbon on December 5. While it was at sea, the Second World War came to the United States. Japan bombed Pearl Harbor on December 7, and the Third Reich declared war on the United States on December 11. The Excalibur arrived in New York on December 16, and so as Krepper walked onto American soil he was once again, as he had been during the First World

War, in a country at war with the Fatherland. The monumental difference was that as the United States was brought into the Second World War, Carl Krepper was an American citizen. As he disembarked from the Excalibur he was listed as a 57-year-old naturalized American citizen. His destination was "Clark Township, Rahway, New Jersey." He was, according to his passport, coming home. Returning to what he claimed on his passport and naturalization documents as his adopted country as it found itself at war with the Axis powers, he was on a mission for Nazi Germany sponsored by the *Abwehr*.

On January 8, 1942, within three-and-a-half weeks after Krepper walked off the SS Excalibur, the ship was requisitioned by the U.S. Navy. On May 1, 1942, the ship on which Nazi agent Carl Krepper had sailed was commissioned as a navy troop transport, the USS Joseph Hewes. In November 1942, the Joseph Hewes took part in Operation Torch, the invasion of North Africa, and successfully landed over a thousand U.S. troops and officers, together with supplies on the North African coast. Tragically, it was sunk off the coast of Morocco by a German U-Boat, the U-173, on November 11, 1942. In an irony of fate, the ship that had brought Krepper to America for his mission to work for Nazi Germany was sunk by a German submarine. Over 100 American military personnel died.

WATCH HIM: AN ALARM BELL SOUNDS

On March 6, 1942, FBI director J. Edgar Hoover sent a communication to the special agent in charge of the Newark, New Jersey, field office:

Dear Sir,
For your information I am transmitting herewith copies of an anonymous letter dated January 10, 1942 received at the Bureau in an envelope postmarked January 13, 1942 at New York, New York.

Very truly yours,
John Edgar Hoover
Director[15]

Attached to this internal FBI communication was the following handwritten anonymous letter (which had no punctuation and used a peculiar random capitalization of letters throughout):

Jan 10 1942

Dear Sir,

I would like to inform you about Pastor Carl Krepper he is an American Citizen he was in the United States for 32 years then went back to Germany was there the last 4 or five years you should watch him His wife went back to Germany last June and no respect for the United States witch [sic] fed and clothe her for 32 years She went to Germany to be with her husband now he is here look up his past and her's to [sic] and keep your eyes on him He is now staying with his wife's son This is his address E. A. Frey 5 Mountainview Road Clark Township Rahway, NJ

When this letter was received, the FBI had no idea why they should watch Pastor Carl Krepper, but as J. Edgar Hoover believed the letter was significant, it was maintained, and ended up being included later on in Krepper's FBI file. Krepper had only arrived back in the United States 25 days before this anonymous letter was sent. There was as yet nothing in the letter to merit a full-scale investigation of Carl Krepper. Whether it was written by a former parishioner who became suspicious of the sudden arrival of this pastor who had apparently forsaken his adopted country for Nazi Germany, or whether it was someone in the German-American community who overheard a conversation with or about him, we may never know. What is significant is that Krepper was put on the FBI's radar five whole months before the Pastorius saboteurs landed in America.

There appears to have been no immediate follow-up on the suggestion in the anonymous letter that Krepper be watched. After the Pastorius saboteurs were caught and Krepper's name and his stepson's name and address in Rahway were found in invisible ink on the handkerchiefs of the two group leaders of the saboteurs, the FBI quickly put two and two together. Starting on June 22, 1942, after they had used ammonia on the handkerchiefs carried by the *Abwehr*-trained saboteurs to bring out what was written on them, FBI agents discovered what they first believed was the name of a "Father Kregger." They soon learned that the name on the handkerchiefs was "Pastor Krepper," who was living at least part of the time with his stepson Eugene and Eugene's wife Hilda in Rahway, New Jersey. Hilda would later get into some difficulty for writing a letter from Krepper to Bertha Krepper after the federal government had ruled that private citizens could no longer correspond with Nazi Germany.

Five months after the anonymous letter to J. Edgar Hoover the Pastorius saboteurs landed on Long Island and in Florida, and Krepper came to the attention of the FBI as a Nazi agent and as a contact man for Nazi saboteurs and agents. As agents built their case around Krepper after the Pastorius sabotage plot, they discovered that in Carl Krepper they had on their hands a Nazi spy pastor, a man who had been placed in the United States by German military intelligence before the war even started.

CHAPTER SIX

Krepper and the Pastorius Plot

TO COMMIT SABOTAGE

Operation Pastorius was "the brainchild of Walter Kappe." It was the successor of Operation Drumbeat (*Paukenschlag*),[1] which began two weeks after Hitler declared war on the United States. Sailing out of Lorient in occupied France, Operation Drumbeat was a series of U-boat operations against American shipping that extended along the eastern seaboard of the United States. From the first U-boat attack on American merchant vessels in the Atlantic on December 23, 1941, through May 2, 1942, the German U-boats under the leadership of Reinhard Hardegen on his U-123 wreaked havoc among American shipping interests, and in the first months of 1942, his U-boat fleet sank over 100 Allied vessels (totaling more than 100,000 tons) off the East Coast of the United States. Nearly 40 U-boats participated in Drumbeat, sinking around 400 Allied ships.

Following upon the success of Operation Drumbeat, and with the blessing of Hitler himself, Walter Kappe and *Abwehr* II planned and launched Operation Pastorius. While the Führer had wanted terror attacks on the American mainland, the head of the *Abwehr*, Admiral Canaris, had been hesitant to conduct sabotage operations in the United States, as he was concerned over the effectiveness of such operations as opposed to their cost in terms of lives and the propaganda value for the enemy if they failed. Despite Canaris's initial hesitation, and because the Führer wanted such a strike on the American mainland, Kappe was given the green light to begin preparing for Pastorius. Kappe would be responsible to the highest levels of the Nazi leadership as he planned his two-pronged sabotage plot. Through his *Auslands-Organisation* dossiers on recently returned Germans who came back to the Fatherland from America, Kappe initially chose 12 recruits out of the thousands of possible candidates.[2] They were to be trained at the *Abwehr* II sabotage training center located at Quentz Lake, near Berlin. The eight men whom Kappe finally chose for Pastorius all had previous experience living and working in the United States or Canada. They had greater and lesser degrees of proficiency in the English language, but they all had a necessary familiarity with American society.

Their training at Quentz Lake began after they arrived on April 1, 1942. This *Abwehr* training facility was originally a Jewish-owned farm that had been confiscated by the Nazis.[3] *Abwehr* II restructured the original two-story farmhouse with 12 rooms into a dormitory for the saboteurs and the caretakers of the property, as well as living, reading, and dining rooms. The training facility also included another two-story building that housed a garage, a classroom, and a laboratory, and there was a working farm located on the property. The *Abwehr* built a gymnasium and a rifle and pistol range as well.

Kappe developed a regular weekly training regimen for the prospective saboteurs that ran from Mondays through Thursdays. Each day began at 7 a.m., and sometimes the training went into the evenings. On Fridays, Kappe met with the group leaders (George John Dasch and Edward Kerling) to go over details as the remaining men exercised or practiced another skill. The men had weekends off in Berlin.

The training of the recruits was multifaceted, and included bomb- and timer-making techniques from items that could be purchased at drug stores in the United States; undercover communications (including how to write with, and reveal, invisible ink—again, using items that were easily purchased at a local drug store); the concealment and proper use of TNT; hand-to-hand combat (including boxing and wrestling, as well as how to throw hand grenades and shoot pistols). They were also given instruction in American English, including American slang and the words to popular American songs such as "The Star Spangled Banner." Each day they were given time to read American magazines and newspapers to better acquaint themselves both with American English and with some of the latest American news and trends (even though these publications were several months old by the time they arrived at Quentz Lake). Because a focus of the planned sabotage effort was to disrupt war-related railroad transportation, the saboteurs were furthermore trained in the proper techniques of targeting railway tracks and bridges, using a section of railroad tracks installed at the facility for this very purpose. They were also given instructions on how best to blow up American factories and canals.

After a final test of their newly acquired skills at the Quentz Lake facility, the men were given two weeks off to say farewell to their families and loved ones, and then were taken by way of Paris to Lorient, the U-boat base used for Operation Drumbeat earlier in the year. From the German Navy's U-boat base in occupied France, Operation Pastorius was ready to be sprung on an unsuspecting nation.

The eight *Abwehr* men were broken up into two groups for their various missions. The first group came to America by way of U-202, landing at Amagansett, Long Island, on June 13, 1942. This group was headed by George John Dasch (who in 1927 had served in the U.S. Army Air Corps, and on June 22, 1939, had filed a petition for naturalization),[4] and included Richard Quirin, Heinrich Heinck, and Ernst Peter Burger (a naturalized American citizen who had served as a member of the Michigan National Guard, and who, when he returned to Germany in 1933, joined the *Sturmabteilung*, the SA storm troopers under Ernst Röhm, barely surviving the Night of the Long Knives to end up in a concentration camp for more than a year, until he was recruited by Kappe for Pastorius). They were to target the Aluminum Company of America plants in Tennessee, Illinois, and New York; the Cryolite Metals plant in Philadelphia; and the Ohio River locks between Pittsburgh and Louisville. The second group of saboteurs arrived on U-584, landing at Ponte Vedra, Florida, on June 17, 1942. This group was led by Edward John Kerling, and included Herbert Haupt (a naturalized American citizen), Werner Thiel, and Hermann Otto Neubauer. They were to target the Hell Gate Bridge in New York City; the Pennsylvania Railroad Terminal in Newark, New Jersey; the New York City water supply; and the Pennsylvania Railroad's Horseshoe Curve near Altoona, Pennsylvania. If successful, the *Abwehr*-trained agents would significantly assist the German war against the United States by slowing down production of goods needed for the American war effort, by disrupting transportation of civilians and military personnel, and by terrorizing American citizens. The destruction of these intended targets would not only have slowed the United States' participation in the war, the morale of the American populace and their enthusiasm for the war would have been negatively impacted as well. There was both a military and a propaganda component to Operation Pastorius. Walter Kappe and his *Abwehr* superiors, as well as Hitler himself, hoped that, if it was successful, this operation could help win the war.

PASTORIUS GOES AWRY

The Pastorius saboteurs were given $175,000 in cash to use on the mission, and detailed cover stories with false identities for each man. The two group leaders were given another tool that Kappe believed would help his agents achieve their missions: the names of contacts who could assist them in concrete ways in their work. These names were written on handkerchiefs in invisible ink made of pyrimidine (an ingredient found in laxatives). There were a few variations between the two sets of handkerchiefs, written by Dasch and Kerling, but the overall list of saboteurs' contacts included the following names: 1) "Maria Da Conceicao Lopez, Lisboa, Rua D. Carlos Mascarenhas 52" (this address was Rua Dom Carlos de Mascarenhas 52 Lisboa, Portugal, and was the location of one of Kappe's mail-drop locations in Portugal for communication between the saboteurs and *Abwehr* II); 2) "Pas Krepper c/o E. Frey, RFD 2, Box 40 F, Rahway" ("Pas Krepper" was the way Krepper's name was written on Kerling's handkerchief, while "Father Krepper" was written on Dasch's handkerchief—both with the rural free delivery postal address in Rahway of Krepper's stepson Eugene Frey); 3) "Walter Fröhling, 3643 N. Whipple St. Ch." (referring to Walter Otto Wilhelm Fröhling, a naturalized German-born American citizen and uncle of saboteur Herbert Haupt, who hid $9,500 in his home that Haupt had brought with him from Germany, an act that landed Fröhling and his wife Lucille in serious difficulty after the saboteurs were caught by the FBI; Fröhling was naturalized in 1931, lived at 3643 North Whipple Street, Chicago, and worked as a truck driver; he died in 1982); 4) "Ernest Dasch, 11 Pelham St., New London" (Ernst Dasch, George's younger brother, a German-born naturalized American citizen, who lived in Astoria, Queens, with his wife after becoming an American citizen in 1938; when Kappe had asked Dasch to provide a name and the address of a contact in the United States, he gave a false address for his brother, as he did not wish to involve him in the Pastorius plot)[5]; 5) "Helmut Leiner, 21-58 39 St., Astoria, Long Island" (Leiner was a German-born resident alien in the United States; he had joined the Nazi party in Germany and had come to the United

States with his parents and siblings in 1929 aboard the SS Bremen; he was a member of the German-American Bund, and a friend of Pastorius saboteur Edward Kerling, for whom he changed large-denomination bills into smaller ones, which landed him in serious trouble after the saboteurs were caught). On his handkerchief, Dasch then added the abbreviation and the code words to be used between the saboteurs and their contacts in the United States: "F. D. P. (Franz Daniel Pastorius)." The final name and address on Dasch's handkerchief was a repeat of the first listing, of Maria Lopez in Lisboa, Portugal (Dasch claimed that he added that name to "dupe the Nazi handlers into thinking that he was putting in more information than was necessary").[6]

The FBI recognized the variations in Krepper's name on the handkerchiefs of the two Pastorius group leaders:

Table 6.1 "handkerchiefs of the two Pastorius group leaders"[7]

Kerling's handkerchief:	Dasch's handkerchief:
Pas Krepper	Father Krepper
c/o E. Frey	c/o Gene Frey
RFD 2, Box 40F	RFD 2, Box 40F
Rahway	Rahway

The saboteurs tried to make contact with three of the names on these handkerchiefs: Carl Krepper, Walter Fröhling, and Helmut Leiner. They met with two of the three. Haupt met with Fröhling and his own parents in Chicago, and Kerling and Thiel contacted and met with Leiner in New York City. The only one they could not contact was the one man who actually could have helped them with safe lodgings that he maintained in Newark, New Jersey, and in New York City, and with obtaining forged documents. Through his son Ernst, Krepper had contact with a printer in New York, and thus he had access to a major resource that the saboteurs could have used to help in their mission. Among his other run-ins with the law, Ernst Krepper had been arrested for selling counterfeit sheet music. He and his father were followed by the FBI to a printing house, as they were under surveillance. The full potential of contacts such as these was not lost on the FBI as it investigated the dimensions of Kappe's plans for his agents in America.

Problems with the Pastorius plot began almost as soon as the saboteurs landed on the beaches of Long Island. As planned, the U-202 landed the first four *Abwehr*-trained agents ashore at Amagansett on the night of Saturday, June 13. Two rubber lifeboats, each manned by two German U-boat crewmen, brought Kappe's agents to the beach. As the U-202 lifeboats were ferrying the saboteurs ashore, the U-boat encountered its own difficulty, as the submarine found itself stranded on a sandbar for some time. Amazingly, partly because there was a great deal of fog on the beach that night, it was not discovered, and eventually the U-202 was able to escape and go back to sea.

Following Kappe's instructions, the men landed on American soil wearing German military uniforms, and then changed into their civilian clothing on the beach. Kappe's theory was that if the men were caught, they could claim that they landed as soldiers and not as spies, and so, according to Kappe, would not be executed. The men had brought explosives with them that had been provided by *Abwehr* II. According to the plan they buried the boxes of explosives, other supplies, and their uniforms on the beach, so that they could retrieve the ordnance when needed for the various targets on their terrorist mission.

Within minutes of their landing, their presence was discovered by the U.S. Coast Guard in the person of John Cullen, from the Amagansett Lifeboat Station.[8] Dasch tried to persuade Cullen that he and his fellow agents were fishermen stranded on their way from East Hampton to Montauk Point; Cullen tried to get him and the others to come back to the Coast Guard lifeboat station for the night. Dasch refused; he tried to bribe Cullen with cash, and then threatened his life. After Burger came on the scene, speaking German to Dasch, Cullen knew that he was in trouble, and he could easily have been overpowered by at least four suspicious German-speaking men. Dasch convinced Cullen that it was in his best interests to flee rather than be killed. Cullen raced back to his colleagues while the four saboteurs buried their explosives and uniforms. A major mistake on Dasch's part was that he left a number of incriminating pieces of evidence on the beach, including a pack of German cigarettes, a bottle of schnapps, and his clothing. The men were able to get off the beach before they were caught, but they knew that going back to retrieve their boxes of explosives would be difficult, if not impossible. They eventually made it by train to Jamaica, Queens, to begin touching base with their contacts in the United States and assessing their overall position.

Over the course of the next weeks, the U-584 landed the second group of saboteurs at Ponte Vedra, Florida, on June 17, 1942, and the saboteurs tried communicating with various contacts who could help make their part of the plan a success. Problems plagued both groups from the beginning. Kerling seemed more interested in attempting to reconcile his romantic life between his wife and his girlfriend, both of whom were living in the New York area. Nonetheless, on June 23, Kerling, along with his friend and Pastorius contact Helmut Leiner, traveled to Rahway, New Jersey, to contact a man who they were told by Walter Kappe could provide assistance to help Operation Pastorius—Pastor Carl Krepper.[9] What Kerling did not know was that when he and his men landed in Ponte Vedra, George Dasch had made his first contact with the FBI in New York City, and tried to betray Operation Pastorius.

By June 22, the day before Kerling and Leiner tried to connect with Carl Krepper, the FBI had started taking seriously what agents first believed were the ravings of a mad man. The New York office of the FBI did not initially believe Dasch's story of Nazi conspiracies and terrorist plots. Nonetheless, with Dasch's help, the FBI laboratory had recovered the invisible handwriting on Dasch's handkerchief. In particular, the bureau had recovered three names of interest in the evolving story of the sabotage plot—Helmut Leiner, Pastor Krepper, and Walter Fröhling.[10] Ernst Burger joined Dasch in betraying his comrades, and within three days of discovering the handwriting on the handkerchiefs and five days after the saboteurs' ill-fated trip to meet Carl Krepper, all eight of the saboteurs were in custody.

On June 25, three days before the last of the saboteurs were arrested, President Franklin D. Roosevelt issued Presidential Proclamation 2561, which established an extraordinary military tribunal to prosecute the eight Pastorius agents. Roosevelt, J. Edgar Hoover, and many other Americans favored the death penalty for the Pastorius operatives. A military tribunal was thought to be more likely to result in a penalty of death. Thus, Proclamation 2561 was very carefully worded to bypass language that could bring such trials into civilian courts. Roosevelt's proclamation was, furthermore, meant to serve as a warning against future sabotage efforts, and as a precedent for future espionage prosecutions. It stated:

> all enemies who have entered upon the territory of the United States as part of an invasion or predatory incursion, or who have entered in order to commit sabotage, espionage, or other hostile or warlike acts should be promptly tried in accordance with the laws of war.[11]

The Pastorius agents were placed in the District of Columbia jail during their trial. They were tried in Conference Room 5235, which had been reworked for the use of the military tribunal in the Department of Justice building. The trial began on Wednesday, July 8, 1942, presided over by seven U.S. Army generals: Major General Frank R. McCoy (president of the military commission), Major General Walter S. Grant, Major General Blanton Winship, Major General Lorenzo D. Gasser, Brigadier General Guy V. Henry, Brigadier General John T. Lewis, and Brigadier General John T. Kennedy. Prosecuting the government's case was U.S. Attorney General Francis Biddle. After a Supreme Court hearing that upheld the right of the military tribunal to prosecute the men, the court concluded on August 3, 1942. The Pastorius saboteurs were found guilty of conspiring to commit sabotage, and six were sentenced to death. On August 8, 1942, Kerling, Haupt, Neubauer, Thiel, Heinck, and Quirin were executed in the electric chair at the Washington, D.C., district jail. Because of their cooperation in helping to betray the terrorist plot, Dasch and Burger were spared the death penalty. Dasch was given 30 years in prison, and Burger was given life. President Harry S. Truman granted them executive clemency in 1948, and they were deported back to Germany.

Carl Krepper in 1912. (From the archives of the
German Evangelical Lutheran Friedens
Church, Philadelphia, PA. Courtesy of the
Lutheran Archives Center at Philadelphia, 7301
Germantown Avenue, Philadelphia, PA
19119-1794.)

Carl Krepper in 1917. (From the archives of the German Evangelical Lutheran Friedens Church, Philadelphia, PA. Courtesy of the Lutheran Archives Center at Philadelphia, 7301 Germantown Avenue, Philadelphia, PA 19119-1794.)

Carl Krepper in 1933. (From the archives of the First German Evangelical Lutheran St. John's Church, Newark, NJ. Found in the archives of Redeemer Lutheran Church, Irvington, NJ. Courtesy of the Lutheran Archives Center at Philadelphia, 7301 Germantown Avenue, Philadelphia, PA 19119-1794.)

Carl Krepper and St. John's, Newark Parish Council, 1933. Note: Krepper is holding the Hindenburg Bible. (From the archives of the First German Evangelical Lutheran St. John's Church, Newark, NJ. Found in the archives of Redeemer Lutheran Church, Irvington, NJ. Courtesy of the Lutheran Archives Center at Philadelphia, 7301 Germantown Avenue, Philadelphia, PA 19119-1794.)

Carl Krepper, "Nazi Spy Aide," 1944. (AP Wire
Photo, Associated Press license No.
LIC-00179661.)

Der
Ersten Deutschen Evangelisch-Lutherischen
Johanniskirche
in
Newark
aus Anlaß der Feier des 100 jährigen Bestehens
der Kolonie mit dem Wunsche gewidmet, daß,
eingedenk des Erbes der Väter, christliche Gesin-
nung und brüderliche Eintracht die Gemeinde
stets beseelen und leiten mögen!

Berlin, den 13. Oktober 1933.

v.H. Hindenburg

Hindenburg Bible. (From the archives of the First German Evangelical Lutheran St. John's Church, Newark, NJ. Found in the archives of Redeemer Lutheran Church, Irvington, NJ. Courtesy of the Lutheran Archives Center at Philadelphia, 7301 Germantown Avenue, Philadelphia, PA 19119-1794.)

20th Anniversary Service of Friedens Lutheran Church, Philadelphia, showing interior. (From the archives of the German Evangelical Lutheran Friedens Church, Philadelphia, PA. Courtesy of the Lutheran Archives Center at Philadelphia, 7301 Germantown Avenue, Philadelphia, PA 19119-1794.)

Exterior photo of Friedens Church, Philadelphia, where Carl Krepper met Bertha. (From the archives of the German Evangelical Lutheran Friedens Church, Philadelphia, PA. Courtesy of the Lutheran Archives Center at Philadelphia, 7301 Germantown Avenue, Philadelphia, PA 19119-1794.)

CHAPTER SEVEN

Spy vs. Counterspy

"A GOOD CONTACT AT ANY TIME"

As they realized the extent of Operation Pastorius and the potential threat that such a plot posed for an America that was still at war, the Federal Bureau of Investigation launched a nationwide investigation into the "Nazi spy aides." A June 22, 1942, memorandum from D. Milton ("Mickey") Ladd,[1] Assistant Director of the Domestic Intelligence Division of the FBI, to Assistant Director Edward A. Tamm[2] briefly detailed the hunt for the saboteur contacts in America:

> I called Assistant Donegan [Acting Special Agent of the New York office Thomas J. Donegan] of the New York [sic] at which time I gave him the following addresses which had been brought out by ammonia on the handkerchief. I told him that the first address was one at which Kerling is supposed to be able to be located:
>
> Helmut Leiner
> 21-58 either 93 or 39 Street
> Astoria, Long Island
>
> I told Mr. Donegan that I had been informed that there is no 93rd Street on Long Island so that it is very probably 39th Street.

Father Kregger or Krepper
c/o Gene Frey
RFD #2, Box 40 F
Rahway, New Jersey

I told Mr. Donegan that this address was given to them in Germany as a good contact at any time.

Walter Kroeling [sic; this should be Froehling]
3643 North Whipple
Chicago, Illinois

I advised Mr. Donegan that I had given Mr. Connelly all three of these addresses. I advised Mr. Donegan that there is supposed to have been a tobacco pouch in Berger's (sic) room in which were what would appear to be three loose matches. I told him that these were not matches but were used for the purpose of writing secret ink messages, that there is a compound of some kind in them and presumably the matches will not burn. I told him to be certain to check for the tobacco pouch and the matches. I told him also that Quirim [sic; this should be Quirin] was supposed to have had three of the same matches for writing messages and he should endeavor to obtain these and send them to us.

I told him to check the New Jersey and Long Island addresses in order to get the surveillance set up, that he should look into the possibilities both of technicals and mail covers.[3]

The Pastorius case was now officially entitled "George Dasch, et al., Sabotage," and as D. Milton Ladd's memorandum detailed, physical surveillance was put in place at both the New Jersey and Long Island locations of the three American Nazi contacts. Earl J. Connelly,[4] Assistant Director of Major Investigations in the Field, was charged with setting up this surveillance. It soon bore fruit, as two of the three Pastorius contacts in the United States were arrested. Walter Fröhling initially received a death sentence for "treason," which was eventually reduced to a term of five years in prison, while Helmut Leiner received 18 years for "trading with the enemy and concealing treason" (he was paroled in 1954).[5] The one Pastorius spy aide who could not initially be located was Carl Krepper. By June 24, the bureau had not yet located Krepper, but they had identified the "Pas Krepper" of the Pastorius handkerchiefs as Pastor Carl Emil Ludwig Krepper, Nazi spy aide and sometime Lutheran pastor in Williamstown, Philadelphia, Carteret, Rahway, and Newark.

Most of the modern historical accounts of Operation Pastorius have no detail about who Carl Krepper actually was, other than the bare bones of his being a Lutheran clergyman who had been living, it was assumed, in Rahway and Newark, New Jersey. Relying merely on the Pastorius handkerchiefs, modern scholarship has variously called him "Father Emil Krepper," "Pastor Krepper," or "Pas Krepper."[6] The FBI would learn a great deal about this man and his life as a pastor and as a spy over the next several years.

From George Dasch, the FBI had learned that Krepper's name had been given to the leaders of the Pastorius operatives back in Germany by Walter Kappe, who dubbed Krepper "a good contact at any time." Kappe clearly believed that Krepper could both materially and logistically support the saboteurs as they went about their work. Krepper's was the only name on the list of American contacts for the Pastorius agents that was so annotated. The other two American contacts on the Pastorius handkerchiefs were family or friends of the saboteurs. It doesn't appear that Krepper personally knew any of the Pastorius saboteurs. Nonetheless, Kappe knew that Krepper had a wide variety of contacts with "Bundists" in and around the greater New York area from his time working with the Friends of New Germany and with the German-American Business League. So it was that Kappe trusted that Krepper had the connections and the contacts to help the saboteurs achieve their goals. He was a "good contact" who could aid the saboteurs in very concrete ways. It was also assumed that Krepper could be contacted at just about any time through his stepson Eugene Frey in Rahway.

Through a confidential informant, the Newark field office of the FBI was able to trace a good bit of Krepper's story in the United States.[7] Before the last Pastorius operative was apprehended, the bureau knew where Krepper had served in churches, and that he had been involved in local politics in Carteret, serving as an assistant tax collector. Furthermore, they were aware that Krepper had made at least one trip "of unknown duration" to Germany, and that he had received his theological education at the Kropp Seminary in Germany. From this informant, the bureau learned that Krepper had received his bachelor's degree from Rutgers University with honors, and as of 1932, he was working towards his master of arts degree (at that time master of theology graduates of the New Brunswick Seminary were given master of arts degree standing). More significantly, the FBI learned that Carl Krepper was "considered intellectual," and that "it is reported that he is strongly impressed with National Socialism." The confidential informant provided information on Eugene Frey and his work experience, as well as Krepper's son Ernst. The report also detailed the initial surveillance at Frey's residence as the bureau searched for the final Pastorius Nazi spy aide.

Whoever the confidential informant was, this individual knew a great deal about the extended Krepper family, and was able to provide the FBI with significant background details of Krepper's life and career. It is fascinating that this informant did not mention that Krepper had served his last congregation in the United States in Newark, New Jersey. Nonetheless, this person also was able to confirm a very important piece of contextual evidence for the bureau, that Krepper was "strongly impressed with National Socialism." The confidential informant seems to have been aware of Krepper's work with the Friends of New Germany and with the German-American Business League. This was an important piece of the puzzle for the FBI. As agents delved into the background stories of who the Nazi spy aides really were, it was discovered that names and addresses of Krepper and Walter Fröhling had been "given . . . by Lieutenant Kappe, who is in charge of the Training School in Berlin."[8] The information provided by the confidential informant connected the dots, so to speak, for the investigators who were discovering the extent of the American side of Operation Pastorius. They would learn that Carl Krepper had also been given the same password from Kappe for the Pastorius plot—Franz Daniel Pastorius—which Krepper used as a code in communications and in face-to-face contacts with supposed Nazi agents in the United States. Prior to the arrest of the last Pastorius agent, with the information received from its confidential informant, the FBI was beginning to understand the level of Nazi support for such terrorist operations in the United States. What the bureau needed next was to set up surveillance to discover the whereabouts of the final Pastorius contact.

Thus it was that the scope of the FBI's investigations into American support for the Nazi terrorists was extended into Clark Township, Rahway, New Jersey. On June 24, 1942, J. Edgar Hoover wrote a "personal and confidential" memorandum to Francis Biddle, the U.S. attorney general.[9] Within weeks of Hoover's memorandum, Biddle would serve as the prosecutor of the Pastorius saboteurs at their trial in Washington, D.C. Hoover informed Biddle that "some of the subjects under investigation are in contact with Eugene A. Frey, 5 Mountain View Road, Clark Township, Rahway, New Jersey." He "urgently recommended" that Biddle authorize technical surveillance on Frey. This was approved, and the FBI began its hunt for Carl Krepper.

As the FBI began their surveillance to help them locate Krepper, they simultaneously drew together all they had in their files about this man who was identified as both "strongly impressed with National Socialism" and a contact for the Pastorius saboteurs. On June 25, 1942, Special Agent Duane L. Traynor, who worked directly under Assistant Director D. Milton Ladd, drew up a list of 19 individuals who were connected to the Pastorius sabotage plot.[10] Carl Krepper was listed as number 13 on this list, ahead of saboteurs Hermann Neubauer (number 15), Richard Quirin (number 18), and Werner Thiel (number 19). Traynor was the agent who had received George Dasch's initial phone call and conducted the detailed interviews with him concerning the terrorist plot. For each of the 19 individuals on Traynor's list he provided a summary of what the bureau had in their files.

The memorandum on "Carl Krepper, alias Father Krepper"[11] that was attached to Traynor's list offered a little more detail than had been included in the memorandum of the previous day. Included in the June 25 summary was the fact that Krepper's name and address in the United States were written in "secret ink" on the handkerchief carried by George Dasch, "leader of Group No. 1 of the German sabotage agents who landed at Amagansett, Long Island, New York, from a German submarine on June 13, 1942." This summary included information on Krepper from his World War I record, indicating his strong pro-German sentiment when he served his Philadelphia congregation, as well as biographical information on his birth, his education, and the churches that he served, including the fact that he also served a church in Newark, New Jersey.

The FBI was working quickly. The June 25 summary connected the January 10, 1942, anonymous note that had been addressed to Hoover suggested that the then recently arrived Krepper should be watched. While the FBI summary indicated that "[n]o description of Carl Krepper is available," the bureau already knew, likely through George Dasch, whom Traynor had interviewed in great detail, that Krepper and Kappe had met again while the former was living in Germany. One more important piece of information came in on June 26: "Krepper reported to now be smooth shaven and without mustache."[12] This information would be helpful as the bureau searched for Carl Krepper, as most of the available photographs of Krepper showed him with the Hitler-style "toothbrush" mustache that he sported in the 1930s. There are a number of extant photographs that portray Krepper through his pastoral career in the United States, from shortly after his ordination in 1910 to 1933 (for the 100th anniversary of St. John's, Newark). All the surviving photographs of Krepper with the exception of the portrait taken around the time of his ordination show him with a mustache of one type or another (Friedens Church in Philadelphia had its pastor's portrait taken for the church's 20th anniversary in 1917, and in that photograph Krepper sported a full-lipped "chevron" mustache; all other portraits show Krepper with the "toothbrush" mustache). The information that Krepper had shaved off his mustache would help the agents assigned to watch for him. Through some good hard detective work, along with a dose of luck, the various pieces of the puzzle of Krepper's identity were beginning to fit into place. The bureau needed to tighten the net around this Nazi spy aide who was a "good contact at any time" as quickly as possible, before he communicated with others involved in the Pastorius plot.

KAPPE VS. HOOVER

As was the case with the larger Pastorius investigation, J. Edgar Hoover was personally involved with overseeing aspects of the hunt for Carl Krepper. He sent memoranda and he received an incredible amount of reports from special agents and other FBI staff as they searched for and investigated the man whose name was given to the Pastorius operatives as a contact person in New Jersey. In terms of the FBI investigation, Krepper was seen as an essential part of the larger Pastorius plot. A June 30, 1942, memorandum to D. Milton Ladd from R. P. Kramer noted that

> Krepper is "hot" because the two leaders of the two groups of Germans, DASCH and KERLING, had specific instructions that if they wanted advice here in the United States or wanted to get anything back over to Germany to contact Krepper and they could get anything they wanted from him. The entire group was not given Krepper as a contact, only the two leaders of the groups.[13]

As the FBI discovered, the mastermind of Pastorius was Walter Kappe, the head of the *Abwehr* sabotage school near Berlin. During their interrogations of the Pastorius leaders, the bureau found that George Dasch and Edward Kerling had been given Krepper's name by Kappe himself. Krepper was to serve as an advisor to the saboteurs within the United States. He was said to be able to produce false birth certificates and other papers to help the saboteurs maintain their assumed identities as they went about their undercover work. Krepper had funds, and he had safe lodgings in Newark, New Jersey, and in New York City. Through his Bund contacts, Krepper would also be able to provide a variety of resources to the Pastorius operatives. They "could get anything they wanted from him." Equally important for the saboteurs, Krepper could "get anything back over to Germany." He had in place his mail drop in Barcelona, Pastor Ernst Kloess, who, through Bertha Krepper, would forward messages between Krepper and Kappe.

In an April 13, 1942, letter to her husband, Bertha Krepper had written from Germany about a variety of news items, and had informed her husband that "Pastor Kaiser is also expecting mail."[14] Walter Kappe was expecting mail from Carl Krepper. This was an extremely important piece of information for the bureau. This letter had come from Germany by way of Spain, and it was a clear statement indicating that Walter Kappe was expecting communication from Krepper that he was in place in the United States. Bertha Krepper knew that she had to pass on this word from "Pastor Kaiser," to whom Krepper was accountable. It is likely no coincidence that Bertha's letter was dated two months to the day from the landing of the first group of saboteurs on Long Island. "Pastor Kaiser," aka Walter Kappe, was anxious that his plant in the United States, the man who could get the saboteurs "anything they wanted," Carl Krepper, was in place for Operation Pastorius. ("Pastor Kaiser" was Kappe's code name, and it was also the password to be used by those whom he sent to Krepper in the United States.)

As the investigation of Carl Krepper expanded over the next two and a half years, it became almost a matter of principle for J. Edgar Hoover to break this case and bring Carl Krepper to justice. The ongoing Pastorius investigation became the case of the top American spy-buster, J. Edgar Hoover, trying to outfox one of Germany's top spy-makers, Walter Kappe. From the saboteurs themselves, Hoover and his colleagues at the FBI had learned that Krepper was deeply involved in the Pastorius case, and that he was an agent who had been sent and was being handled by Walter Kappe in Germany. Assistant Director Earl J. Connelly was speaking for Hoover and the rest of the bureau when he stated in October 1942, "Krepper . . . we definitely know, of course, is an espionage agent."[15]

Hoover had no doubt that Kappe had sent Krepper to the United States for the purpose of assisting the Pastorius operatives and other

Nazi agents. In a July 22, 1942, "Memorandum for the Attorney General," Hoover stated unequivocally that "undoubtedly Krepper must have been sent over to this country by [Walter Kappe] to aid not only the saboteurs in this case but others since he was the only contact directly furnished by [Walter Kappe to the] saboteurs."[16] If they did not catch Krepper, Hoover was worried that he could assist other Nazi agents who might be able to slip into the United States.

A SERIOUS BLUNDER

On July 1, it became clear that the FBI's investigation of Carl Krepper had the potential to be seriously hampered, not from a lack of evidence, but from an intergovernmental conflict over jurisdiction. Special Agent Percy E. Foxworth[17] authored a memorandum to the FBI director and to the special agent in charge in Newark about a potentially serious problem with the ongoing investigation of Carl Krepper. The Immigration and Naturalization Service had previously conducted the "denaturalization program" that identified and proceeded to cancel the United States citizenship of naturalized citizens whose loyalty to the United States was in question. In particular, this program was aimed at pro-Nazi members of the German-American Bund, such as Krepper's colleague from the Friends of New Germany, Dr. Francis Just. Jurisdiction over this denaturalization process was handed over to the attorney general, who worked with the FBI to examine such cases because of the bureau's greater investigative abilities.

It turned out that a mere nine days before the first Pastorius saboteurs landed in the United States, the Special Inspections Division of the Immigration and Naturalization Service questioned Carl Krepper. Krepper had just fought a multiyear battle with his German church colleagues to be granted permission to be permanently employed within the Reich as an American citizen that went all the way up to the Reich minister of church affairs. Now, after winning that battle, Krepper was back in the United States, and ironically, the American government was considering revoking his citizenship. The Immigration and Naturalization Service was alerted to Krepper's "Nazi sympathies" by correspondence from Germany that showed where his true allegiance lay.

When he was interviewed on June 4 by the Special Inspections Division, Krepper showed proof of his American citizenship. Upon further questioning, Krepper also stated that he was a Lutheran minister, but at present had no church. He was, he said, "passing his time in the stamp business," and was presently living at 425 West 57th Street in New York City. He told the agents from the Immigration and Naturalization Service that he was employed by the Schoenbach Stamp Exchange. The agents also apparently interviewed Hilda Frey, Eugene's wife, in Rahway, New Jersey. She told the agents that Krepper considered her home as his permanent address but only resided there on weekends. Otherwise, she said, Krepper lived at 689 Prospect Street (in reality, 689 Mt. Prospect Avenue), Newark, care of Bertha Keller. With many of the Pastorius "spy aides" still on the loose, the New York and Newark field offices were shocked that an investigation with major implications for national security might be in jeopardy because of an intergovernmental blunder by an agency that, in their minds, had clearly overstepped its bounds.

Special Agent Foxworth of the New York field office discovered that the Immigration and Naturalization Service was actually considering canceling Krepper's American citizenship. This would have meant that Krepper would be interred prior to deportation back to Germany. Such an action would have effectively ended the FBI search for the man Kappe had sent as a contact for Nazi agents, and for any network of Axis spies with whom Krepper may have been in contact. Foxworth alerted the New Jersey Office and J. Edgar Hoover to the potential disaster to their investigation.

> Inquiry is presently being made to ascertain the full extent of the investigation conducted by the Special Inspections Division of the Immigration and Naturalization inasmuch as it clearly appears that they have encroached upon the jurisdiction of the Bureau in connection with this matter.[18]

The next day, when he heard about what had happened to his investigation, J. Edgar Hoover blew his stack. This was not just a matter of one governmental body trespassing into the realm of another. It was a matter of national security, as the whole Pastorius spy ring could evaporate in one fell swoop. First, Hoover sent off a memorandum to E. A. Tamm and D. M. Ladd:

> I do want to know why the Immigration and Naturalization Service was making an investigation of Father Carl Krepper. Please see that I get this information because it is noted that they initiated this on June 4 and it is entirely probable that their investigation

has prevented our apprehending him in connection with the Dasch case. I would like to know exactly for what reason they were making inquiry about Krepper.[19]

Hoover was clearly shocked that the Krepper connection to Pastorius could be so easily lost. He wanted answers from his agents, who were undoubtedly as mystified as Hoover was about the turn of events.

In another memorandum to Duane L. Traynor, Hoover speculated that the FBI's difficulty in locating Krepper might have been due to Krepper's being spooked by the questions of the Immigration and Naturalization agents. Krepper would have been aware of the difficulties his friend Francis Just had endured from these agents, and the real fear that they would cancel his citizenship. Hoover suggested that "it is entirely possible that he (Krepper) is refraining away from his usual habits" because of the Immigration and Naturalization agents.

Hoover then went to Attorney General Francis Biddle with his "great concern."[20] Hoover told Biddle that he believed that the leadership of the Immigration and Naturalization Service were deliberately disobeying a directive from the attorney general that the FBI would be solely charged with conducting denaturalization investigations of "individuals of possible subversive and pro-Axis tendencies." Hoover then detailed the point at issue and how Krepper's correspondence brought him to the attention of the Immigration and Naturalization Service agents in the first place. Nonetheless, Hoover argued that the very fact that agents from the Immigration and Naturalization Service investigated such a case at all demonstrated, in his eyes, that they were contravening a direct order from the attorney general. Hoover argued, "The instructions which you issued relative to the Federal Bureau of Investigation conducting denaturalization investigations in cases where pro-Axis sympathies were exhibited were issued in order to avoid just such a blunder as this."

Hoover claimed that this "blunder" could have adverse consequences on the larger Pastorius case, and in particular, on its investigation of Krepper. Such cross purposes from another federal agency

can only cause Krepper to become extremely apprehensive and cause him either to cease his activities . . . or to cover them up with even greater care, possibly ruining all opportunities for the Federal Bureau of Investigation to properly track him down and bring him to justice. . . .

Hoover went on to explain his theory that Krepper was not simply sent over to aid the Pastorius saboteurs, but also other Nazi agents who were coming or might come into the United States for similar terroristic purposes. Hoover argued that the Immigration and Naturalization Service agents "should be prohibited from any further bungling" in such matters, as they pertain solely to the purview of the FBI. This was a great deal more than a case of interdepartmental rivalry.

Nonetheless, despite Hoover's worst fears, on July 3, two days after his agents discovered the potentially disastrous consequences of what they saw as the interference of the Immigration and Naturalization Service, they finally spotted Krepper. He was seen entering the home of Bertha Keller at 689 Mount Prospect Street, Newark. The bureau was to discover that Bertha Keller, otherwise known as Bertha Keller Scott, was a divorcee whose entire German-American family was quite active in the German-American Bund.[21] She also was believed to be "infatuated" with Carl Krepper.[22] Bertha Keller was said to regularly attend meetings of the Bund at various locations in New Jersey, including Montgomery Park, Irvington, Union Park in Springfield, and Schwabenhalle in Newark. She "frequently attended Camp Nordland," the Bund-sponsored camp in Andover, New Jersey. Keller's father was "very pro-Nazi and frequently compared the photographs of Roosevelt and Hitler and remarked how weak President Roosevelt looked in comparison to Hitler." In trying to establish the connection between Krepper and Keller, the bureau learned that while Krepper was pastor in Carteret in 1930, Keller had used him as a job reference for a position at Prudential Life Insurance Company in Newark. Bertha Keller was born in Philadelphia, and was three months older than Krepper's son Ernst. Friedens Church in Philadelphia, Krepper's second congregation in the United States, was likely the original link between Pastor Krepper and the Keller family.

Full-time surveillance was made by the Newark field office to ensure that agents would not lose Krepper now that they had found him. Considering the purpose of his mission in America, and what Kappe hoped he could do to assist his Pastorius operatives in the war against the United States, it is ironic that Hoover's agents followed Krepper to his stepson's home in Rahway for an Independence Day celebration.

CHAPTER EIGHT

Trailing a Spy

THE SURVEILLANCE BEGINS: THE LITTLE OLD LADY FROM RAHWAY

For a man who was sent on a secret mission by the head of German military intelligence to be a covert contact for saboteurs and spies, Krepper somehow managed to draw a good deal of attention to himself. For whatever reason, and unbeknownst to him, Krepper ended up on the radar of several rather loud whistle-blowers. In addition to the January 10, 1942, anonymous letter that was sent from New York to J. Edgar Hoover that encouraged the bureau to "watch him," a second anonymous note was sent to the "FBI, Washington, D.C." This letter was mailed on July 10, 1942, from Rahway, New Jersey. The letter was sent "from the Little Old Lady." Similar in content and style to the first anonymous letter, it was also written without proper punctuation in rambling handwriting. The two letters seem to have been written by the same hand. Both were dated two days after the letters were postmarked. Like the first anonymous note, the second letter urged the bureau to "watch" Carl Krepper:

Rahway, NJ

July 12/42

My dear Gov.,

Please watch a certain pastor of Clark Township of Rahway his name
is Mr. Krepper he used to preach in Rahway a few years ago. He went
back to Germany didn't like it here made his wife go back with him
about 1 year ago he came back here but left his wife over there he gave
up his preaching and is now supposed to be working in NY which
sounds fishy to a number of we people. . . . Please look into this

Enough said

From the Little Old Lady.[1]

The "Little Old Lady" from Rahway had no idea that the bureau was
indeed already watching Pastor Carl Krepper. The remainder of the
anonymous note called on the bureau to watch a German-American
woman named "Anna Kretzhaum," a member of a German social club
in Rahway, who, according to the "Little Old Lady," "says the Japs are
just as good as we Americans."

There are, without a doubt, a number of curious features to this
anonymous letter to the Federal Bureau of Investigation. First of all, the
letter was addressed to "My dear Gov." It is not clear if this is an inac-
curate reference to J. Edgar Hoover's title and position at the FBI, or if it
is a general reference to the American "government," which should be
on guard against Krepper and his cohorts. Second, the letter would
appear to be from someone who knew Krepper in Rahway. While he
was serving his two-point parish, Krepper was not as deeply connected
with the Rahway community as he was with Carteret, for the simple fact
that he lived in Carteret. He was involved in Carteret at a number of
different levels, and in ways that he could not be in Rahway. Nonetheless,
the author of the anonymous letter made no effort to hide the fact that
the correspondence was sent from Rahway, and that the "Little Old
Lady" knew Krepper used "to preach" in the town. Even more, the
author of the anonymous note knew something about Krepper's personal life, where he was "officially" living in 1942 (in Clark Township,
Rahway), and that his wife was still in Germany while he came back to
the United States on his own, as well as his cover story (that he was
working in New York City). This "Little Old Lady" knew a significant
amount about Krepper. She may have written her note with a genuine

concern for the national security of the United States, or she may have just been a crank from Rahway with a grudge against a former pastor who had served in that community. Nonetheless, whatever her motivation was for contacting the FBI, the instincts of the "Little Old Lady" from Rahway were very much on target—Krepper was indeed someone who needed watching, and Hoover and the FBI knew it.

As the Washington headquarters of the bureau was busy bringing together all the information available on Carl Krepper, the FBI's Newark field office was quite busy as well. Six FBI agents were tasked with conducting surveillance on Krepper and his known associates as part of the ongoing Pastorius investigation.[2] The same day that Traynor compiled the summary on Krepper, Special Agent Ralph Batch of the Newark division had done a good bit of legwork in New Jersey. He had discovered that Krepper's stepson Eugene Frey worked with a German-American immigrant named Louis Jenewein. Jenewein was Frey's neighbor on Mountain View Road, Clark Township, Rahway, New Jersey, and the two were in business together with two gasoline stations that were directly across the street from each other on Route 1 in Linden, New Jersey. Actually, Frey worked for Jenewein, and he and his wife Sophie were personal friends of Carl and Bertha Krepper.[3]

Special Agent Batch found that there were five telephones located in the gas stations in question; two numbers were listed and three were unlisted. Special Agent in Charge R. P. Kramer reported to Assistant Director Ladd that Batch believed "this presented a good opportunity for espionage work."[4] It was believed that this rather large collection of telephones, and especially the unlisted telephone numbers, could be utilized by German spies for either the passing on of secrets or the receiving of clandestine messages. Furthermore, as they brought together background material on Jenewein and Frey, it was discovered, according to their sources, that the two were "one hundred percent Nazi and state that Hitler will win the war."[5]

A day before Hermann Neubauer (the last Pastorius saboteur who was on the run) was apprehended, J. Edgar Hoover sent a memorandum to Attorney General Francis Biddle requesting permission for surveillance of Alvis Louis Jenewein.[6] Hoover believed that this surveillance of Jenewein could assist in the "effort to locate the subjects under investigation and to ascertain their activities." Hoover was particularly concerned here about locating and discovering the activities of Carl Krepper, who, as the saboteurs had been told back in Germany, was "a good contact at any time." In his memorandum to the attorney general, Hoover stated that "it is deemed most important that a technical surveillance be established concerning Mr. Jenewein." This requested surveillance was granted, and immediately the FBI learned some significant details that could have possibly shed light on the Krepper investigation. As the bureau looked into Jenewein's background, agents found that he had claimed to be "one of the first members of the Nazi Party," and that he had "boasted of being well acquainted with ranking Nazis in Germany, such as Hitler, Goering, Himmler, and Fritz Todt" (a German civil engineer who built the autobahn and served as Reich minister of armaments and ammunition).[7] If this were true, that Jenewein was as deeply connected with the Nazi leadership in Germany as he claimed to be, he could have been a useful resource person for the saboteurs and for other Nazi agents in New Jersey. As the FBI soon learned, Jenewein actually knew Carl Krepper, who both was in the United States and, through his mail drop in Spain, had means to communicate with the Pastorius spy-master, Walter Kappe. Because Jenewein's service stations were located near the Linden oil refineries, there was concern that if he was indeed associated with Krepper, these locations could provide a springboard for sabotage of the refineries.

The agents assigned to the Krepper case were especially interested in a report that Jenewein possessed a "radio short wave receiver and convertible transmission set" in his 1942 Lincoln Zephyr. The bureau speculated that if this was the case, this may have been another avenue by which Krepper was able to send communications back and forth to Germany. The radio lead proved to be a blind alley, and despite his pro-Nazi credentials and his association with Carl Krepper, the FBI investigators decided that Jenewein and Krepper were not working together.[8]

INVESTIGATING THE MAN WHO EMPLOYED A SPY

The bureau also spent a great deal of effort investigating Krepper's employer at the Schoenbach Stamp Exchange in New York. Four months before the Pastorius saboteurs landed on Long Island, the FBI's New York field office took a long hard look at Alvin Schoenbach, who had come to the United States from Germany in 1938. He was a German Jew who had come to the United States and set up a stamp business out of his apartment on West 57th Street in Manhattan. Schoenbach was known to be "anti-Hitler."[9] Nonetheless, in March 1941, Schoenbach came to the attention of the U.S. Secret Service and the New York Police Department, as well as the FBI, because of the fact that he received packages of foreign stamps from Europe through Lisbon, Portugal, and South American countries. The bureau was interested that Schoenbach apparently encouraged his European purchases to be sent to the United States via Lisbon by American air travelers in order that they would not be held up by the British censors in Bermuda (as part of British intelligence during World War II, censors would open and read mail traveling back and forth across the Atlantic; it could take censors in Bermuda up to two weeks to examine mail traveling to the United States).

In November 1941, the New York Police Department investigated Schoenbach and found that there was nothing on him in their files to indicate that he was either "criminal or subversive," and they found nothing suspicious in his business dealings. His case was closed in February 1942. Nonetheless, Schoenbach came back onto the FBI radar in June 1942 because he had hired Carl Krepper to work for him in the business of buying and selling foreign postage stamps.

Krepper had come to the United States with foreign stamps that he had purchased prior to his departure from Europe. Foreign postage stamps could be easily exchanged for cash, and Krepper would therefore not have had to declare those funds when he entered the United States in December 1941 on his secret mission from Walter Kappe. It was indeed a strange twist in the Krepper investigation when the FBI discovered that an "anti-Hitler" Jewish refugee from Nazi Germany had hired a man to work for him who turned out to be a pro-Hitler Nazi agent who was deeply embroiled in Operation Pastorius. While Krepper had no idea when he went to work for him that Schoenbach had been investigated by the Secret Service, the FBI, and the New York Police Department, Krepper brought more trouble to Schoenbach by accepting a job offer from him. For Krepper's part, it was certainly a good cover to be working for a Jewish stamp dealer. Krepper believed that he would be virtually beyond suspicion with such an employer. By working for a Jewish refugee from Nazi Germany, Krepper hoped that no one would suspect that he was an agent sent by the head of the *Abwehr* sabotage school as a contact person for Nazi agents in America.

It does not appear that Schoenbach knew anything of Krepper's work with the Friends of New Germany or with the German-American Business League (DAWA), and he certainly knew nothing of Krepper's mission from Walter Kappe to assist "Bundists persecuted by Jews" in the United States. A mere seven years before he went to work for Schoenbach, as a leader and organizer of the DAWA right across the river from Manhattan in the mid-1930s, Krepper would have supported a boycott of Jewish-owned businesses such as the Schoenbach Stamp Exchange. Furthermore, according to his own statements, Krepper had come to the United States to work against the "Plutocratic Jewish cliques" that Krepper claimed were running American society. Working at the "anti-Hitler" Schoenbach Stamp Exchange was a brilliant move on Krepper's part. It was a perfect cover for a man who was in reality a Nazi spy aide.

In time, the FBI was able to discover that Schoenbach's "connection with Krepper has not been found to be based on anything other than the stamp business." The bureau would learn that Krepper was referred to Schoenbach by a Jewish stamp dealer in Lisbon, Portugal, "who gave Krepper a quantity of stamps to deliver to Schoenbach."[10] Schoenbach was selling stamps from Nazi Germany and the lands occupied by the Nazis, and had individuals like Krepper transport them to the United States.

Because of the fact that Krepper worked for him, for many months Schoenbach would be thoroughly investigated and, as he traveled on his various business trips throughout the United States in order to purchase stamps, he was trailed by agents of the FBI. Thus it was that on June 30, 1942, J. Edgar Hoover sent a "Personal and Confidential Memorandum" to Attorney General Francis Biddle requesting "technical surveillance" on Alvin Schoenbach:

> In connection with an investigation presently being conducted by this Bureau concerning Nazi sabotage activities in the United States, relative to which you have been previously advised, it has been ascertained that some of the subjects under investigation are in contact with Alvin Schoenbach, 425 West 57th Street, New York, New York. In order that the whereabouts of these subjects may be ascertained and in order that their activities may be closely followed, I urgently recommend that you authorize the establishment of a technical surveillance to cover Alvin Schoenbach. . . .[11]

For Schoenbach, it was a case of guilt by association, for while Hoover argued for surveillance of the Stamp Exchange owner in order to determine Krepper's whereabouts and gauge his activities with other foreign agents, the agents trailing Schoenbach believed that his journeys around the country could provide opportunities to pass on Krepper's communications with enemy agents. As they followed him from hotels, bars, and restaurants over nearly five months, it eventually became apparent that Schoenbach was what he claimed to be, a legitimate stamp dealer. In a November 5, 1942, report to Hoover, the New York field office noted, "It is not believed by NY Office that Schoenbach is involved in any espionage or sabotage activities with Krepper and therefore a physical surveillance of Schoenbach . . . does not appear warranted."[12] The bureau would continue to keep tabs on Schoenbach for some time. He changed his name to Alvin James Fairbrook, and in 1945 he testified at Krepper's federal trial.

Over the next two years, the FBI conducted background checks and surveillance on a number of Krepper's contacts. As agents sought to learn more about Krepper's role as a Nazi agent in the United States, they would pursue a wide variety of leads and check on many aspects of Krepper's cover story.

A CLERICAL INTERLUDE

A strange twist in the Krepper case came early in the FBI's investigation after agents followed up on a comment from Krepper's stepson's wife, Hilda Frey, to the effect that Krepper "had been named pastor of a church in New York." The bureau was curious about this development, but the church "name and location (were) not given, and no other information (is) available to substantiate this."[13] This lead had come from a confidential source, and as the FBI was trying to track Krepper, the suggestion was given that the New York field office "attempt to verify this among German Lutheran circles."

Special Agent Robert H. Hodgin contacted the Reverend Dr. Ralph H. Long, the assistant secretary of the National Lutheran Council in New York.[14] Hodgin did not mention Krepper by name, but he asked Pastor Long to provide a list of recent pastoral "appointments" to Lutheran congregations in the New York area. Long told the agent that there were no new appointments of which he was aware. In an effort to assist this inquiry, Long then telephoned Reverend Dr. Samuel G. Trexler, the president of the United Lutheran Synod of New York. Trexler also confirmed that there had been no recent pastoral calls to congregations issued in the New York area. The following day, Special Agent Hodgin received a surprise phone call from Long and was told that Dr. Trexler "had some information which might have some bearing on the previous day's inquiry." Hodgin contacted Trexler, who "advised that several months ago Carl Krepper had approached him and attempted to obtain a position in a New York Lutheran Church."

President Trexler stated unequivocally that he had refused Krepper's request for a new congregation. Of course, Krepper was no longer an

American Lutheran pastor. He had been removed from the roster of the United Lutheran Church in America and transferred to the clerical roster of the Lutheran Church in Germany. That alone would have been sufficient grounds to refuse a new American appointment to Krepper. Of course, there were German Lutheran pastors who came to the United States in the years leading up to World War II who were welcomed with open arms. Pastor Krepper's replacement at St. John's Church in Newark, Pastor Heinz Kugler, was one of them. The fact that he had been transferred to the clerical roster of the German church was not, in principle, what precluded Trexler from allowing Krepper to serve another American congregation. Trexler stated quite clearly to Agent Hodgin the real reason he refused to consider Krepper for a position in a congregation in New York:

> he would not consider appointing Krepper under any circumstances because he believed that Krepper was pro-German in sentiment and that the Church would not be benefited by the services of such a man.

Trexler knew that the United States was then at war with Germany. While there were many Lutherans of German descent and origin in the greater New York area, Trexler also knew Carl Krepper's reputation. As the president who had installed him in his last American congregation, Trexler knew why Krepper had left his church in Newark. Krepper had gone to serve within the German Reich he had so publicly admired from afar. Trexler would also likely have been aware of Krepper's outspoken support of National Socialism within his congregation and within the larger Newark community. Dr. Trexler understood that the placement of a man such as Krepper so soon after Germany had declared war on the United States would have hurt the name and reputation of the Lutheran Church in the New York area, as well as the spiritual health of any congregation he would have been called to serve. Trexler was not the only American Lutheran pastor to remember the troubles that the American Lutheran Church had had with some of the Kropp Seminary graduates in the Great War. During World War I, some German-American pastors were accused of praying for German victory, and trying to sow the seeds of racial disharmony in the United States to dampen American resolve in the war. Though loyal American clergy had checked the pro-German propaganda of such pastors during the First World War, Trexler did not want to see such accusations leveled at the Lutheran

Church again. Under no circumstances would he offer Krepper another Lutheran congregation to serve.

While he was still officially the pastor of his church back in Germany, Krepper had sought to secure a Lutheran parish in New York City as his cover while in the United States. This was news to the FBI. In that role as pastor of a congregation, Krepper would certainly have been easier to track down when the saboteurs arrived in New York City. It would have been a strange twist to Krepper's role in the Pastorius plot if his plans to become the pastor of another American Lutheran Church succeeded. It, too, would have been an excellent cover, as he could justify going out to meet with, and facilitate logistics for, the saboteurs, while claiming that he was going out on pastoral visits, for example.

If his plan had succeeded, Krepper would have been pastor of two congregations at the same time, and he would have collected salaries from both churches. Even more, such a move, if it had succeeded, might have made things easier for the Pastorius operatives. Instead of traveling to New Jersey and searching for Krepper in a private dwelling, as they were forced to do, finding him in his church office would have been quite a bit easier for the Pastorius agents.

What the FBI did not know then, and what agents did not learn over the next two years as they investigated the case that soon became known as "Carl Emil Ludwig Krepper, with alias, et al.; Sabotage," was that Krepper's congregation in Germany considered him to be a "conscript" of the *Wehrmacht*, and that his parish in Germany knew that the purpose of his journey to the United States was to serve "the Nazi regime." Reflecting on what this curious clerical interlude could have meant to the Krepper case, the FBI had no way of knowing these things.

As it was, Trexler refused to consider Krepper for another parish, and Krepper fell back on the job at hand, in the stamp business. That, too, was a good cover; because he worked for a German Jewish refugee with an outspoken hatred of Hitler, no one would suspect that Krepper himself was a Nazi agent—until the FBI discovered his name as a contact on the handkerchiefs of the Pastorius saboteurs.

FAMILY, FRIENDS, AND GIRLFRIENDS

Many people who met Krepper or observed him during his time in the United States as an operative for Walter Kappe said that he generally avoided the company of others. He did not have many friends, and it was observed that "Krepper always seemed to shun other people, never speaks unless spoken to, usually leaves the house if company arrives, and appears to have nothing to do with anyone in the neighborhood."[15]

Nonetheless, as Krepper went about his work of establishing himself back in the United States, he used a variety of resources, including family members, friends, and even several girlfriends. He used his stepson Eugene and his wife Hilda to lend him both credibility and a permanent contact location. The name and address of Eugene Frey had been given to the leaders of the two groups of Pastorius agents when they were still in Germany, and after his return to the United States Krepper often came to visit his stepson and his family on weekends at that address.

After his arrival in the United States in December 1941, Carl Krepper also reconnected with his son Ernst (Ernest or Ernie, as he was variously called by his family). Born Ernst Wilhelm Krepper on October 10, 1913, in Philadelphia, he was baptized by his father at Friedens Church. Ernst Krepper had health problems when he was quite young, suffering from spinal meningitis, which left him with poor vision and hearing problems that deteriorated with age. Ernst's parents divorced before he was 10 years old. He suffered from a complete loss of hearing by 1935, just before his 22nd birthday.

In addition to his health troubles, Ernst also had a number of serious run-ins with the law over the years. As they trailed Carl Krepper and his son during their investigation, the FBI soon discovered just who Ernst Krepper was. They found that he had used multiple aliases, and that he had been arrested at least five times for a variety of crimes ranging from burglary to rape, violation of copyright laws, and unlawful possession of slugs (counterfeit coins used for illegal purchases in vending machines, coin-operated washing machines, dryers, slot machines, and pay phones). He had served time at Rikers Island in New York and the Annandale Reformatory in New Jersey, as well as a county jail in New Jersey.[16] Ernst Krepper's aliases included "Ernest Krepler, Martin Nash, and Martin Weiss."

From his first incarceration, when he was 15 years old (for burglary), Ernst Krepper had walked down what his father the pastor might have called a wide, winding road of perdition. Ernst Krepper's last arrest before his father's return to the United States, on March 27, 1941, was for the possession and distribution of slugs. While it may sound odd to modern ears, the production and use of counterfeit slugs was a nationwide epidemic in the early 1940s, and cost American businesses 5 million dollars a year in lost profits.[17] State and federal laws were passed that tried to curb the use of slugs. Slugs cost less than the coins they replicated (for example, a quarter slug to be used in a quarter coin slot may have cost ten to fifteen cents, and so on). People would buy slugs in bulk to save money in coin-operated devices (like at the old Horn and Hardart establishments). Ernst Krepper was arrested in a combined operation of the U.S. Secret Service and the New York Police Department for distributing slugs in the greater New York area. It was subsequently discovered that Ernst was distributing the slugs for a company called the De Vere Novelty Company, which was located in Dayton, Ohio, and was the largest manufacturer of counterfeit slugs in the United States. Ernst Krepper pled guilty to this charge and was sentenced on April 10, 1941, to five months at Riker's Island. Ernst's arrest on the streets of New York in 1941 actually had a national impact on the illegal traffic in slugs. As Ernst Krepper's FBI report puts it, "The principals in this . . . organization (the De Vere Novelty Company, Dayton, Ohio) were also arrested."

The arrest of Ernst Krepper in April 1941 and the subsequent arrest of the executives at the De Vere Novelty Company exemplified a growing federal effort to stamp out the illegal use of slugs in vending machines across the country. Besides the major negative impact on the American economy, as millions of dollars were stolen from American businesses, there was also a growing war-related need for aluminum that was being adversely affected by the illegal slug industry. In April 1944, President Roosevelt signed a law that made it a federal crime to make or sell slugs. Those found guilty could be fined $3,000 and be imprisoned for up a year.[18] The arrest of Ernst Krepper in 1941 played a minor, yet not insignificant, role in this history.

Ernst Krepper was released from Riker's Island just about three months before his father returned to the United States on an *Abwehr*-supported mission that within three years would land his father in federal prison for 10 years.

As they trailed Krepper and his son over the next months, the FBI agents trailing them witnessed a few real father and son moments, as the two ate together, walked New York together (with and without female accompaniment), and as they sat on park benches, communicating by writing on a pad of paper.

One aspect of Ernst's criminal past seems to have intersected with his father's criminal intent as a Nazi spy aide. Several of Ernst's various scams revolved around the printing business. First, Ernst Krepper claimed to be the publisher of a magazine called *Family Life*, which apparently never appeared in print.[19] Ernst used a Manhattan mailing address, 1472 Broadway, for his magazine. Second, when he was arrested for the slug scam, Ernst was known to the bureau as a peddler of sheet music. His principal business appeared to be selling counterfeit song sheets to popular music in the vicinity of Washington Irving High School, located in the Gramercy Park section of downtown Manhattan. His arrest on August 5, 1938, was for copyright infringement. He had been selling bootleg song sheets and was sentenced to six months at the workhouse (his sentence was eventually suspended).

On Tuesday, July 7, Carl and Ernst Krepper were followed by a number of special agents from the New York field office, C. L. Green, C. E. Airhart, C. A. Bass, and S. H. Moore, Jr. After dining at the Horn and Hardart Restaurant at 57th Street and Eighth Avenue, father and son "visited the Crown Card and Paper Company" on West 24th Street. Later that day, after Carl and Ernst Krepper went their separate ways, Ernst

> secured a package of song sheets entitled "Broadway Song Hits" from a group of men on 14th Street and then spent the balance of the evening selling these song sheets on 86th Street and later at various points in the Times Square section of the New York City.[20]

Ernst was clearly still making his living by selling counterfeit song sheets of popular music. While the source of these song sheets was not known, the special agents did not take the time to trace the "group of men" from whom Ernst acquired the song sheets in question. These men were not even peripheral to the Nazi spy aide investigation. Agents took note of the fact, though, that Ernst Krepper had access to printers as well as distributors of counterfeit materials. From the leaders of the two Pastorius sabotage groups, the bureau had learned that Walter Kappe in Germany had said that Krepper was able to assist them in the printing of false documents. Dasch and Kerling were informed that Krepper could provide "assistance such as obtaining birth certificates and identification papers."[21] Through his son's contacts, it would seem, Carl Krepper may indeed have had an ability to secure counterfeit documents for the saboteurs and other enemy agents with whom he came in contact.

The very next day, July 8, father and son met again at the Horn and Hardart Restaurant for breakfast, and from thence they visited an odd assortment of businesses, including a printing company, a paper company, a machine corporation, and a manufacturing company. After Ernst and Carl Krepper split up for the day, Carl meandered around downtown New York until he ended up at Walker Square. He sat on a park bench until three o'clock, when an unknown man arrived for what was clearly a prearranged meeting. The strange man was carrying a 10-by 12-inch manila envelope from which he withdrew a slip of paper. Krepper removed a slip of paper from his briefcase, and the two men exchanged papers.

Krepper and the stranger then parted company, with Krepper returning to Bertha Keller's home in Newark. After visiting an office building on West 42nd Street in Manhattan for nearly an hour and a half, the stranger took the Hudson Tubes to Newark, ending up at 42 Camp Street in Newark. Inside that building was Carl Krepper, who had been followed by agents from the Newark field office. A bit of legwork uncovered the fact that 42 Camp Street was owned by a woman who would loom large in Krepper's life for some years to come, Marianne Mayer. Mayer was born in Germany on November 4, 1892, and was the widow of Karl Mayer. She was naturalized in New York on April 11, 1939. The FBI found that she had recently come to Newark from West 78th Street in Manhattan, and rented a one-family dwelling with 13 rooms and two bathrooms.[22] She would go on to own a series of rooming houses in Newark, expanding from 42 Camp Street to properties extending from 66 to 74 James Street, Newark, all of which were run through Mayer's Hopestead House, Inc., management company (which operated out of 42 Camp Street).

The Newark field office of the bureau would know Marianne Mayer as Carl Krepper's girlfriend and lover. They would regularly travel to Washington Rock State Park in Watchung, New Jersey, for romantic walks. After he was released from prison, she would even travel to Germany to fight for his German church pension.[23] Marianne Mayer was, however, just one of Carl Krepper's several girlfriends in the greater New York area.

On July 9, Krepper once again met his son Ernst in New York, at the Schoenbach Stamp Exchange. At 4 p.m., Krepper walked to Central Park alone. At 4:30 p.m., he met another German-American widow named Margaret Diehl, with whom he proceeded to the Yorkville section of Manhattan where they ate dinner at the Café Geiger, a well-known German restaurant. After dinner, the couple walked to a house on East 84th Street. According to the FBI report, "they entered and did not leave the premises again that evening." The agents trailing Krepper found that the apartment occupied that night by Margaret Diehl and Carl Krepper was actually rented under the name of Diehl's sister and brother-in-law, Martin and Leni Kropp. Over the next months, Krepper would spend a good deal of time in the company of the woman whom the FBI's New York field office called Krepper's "lady friend."[24] In a September 5, 1942, "Memorandum for the Director," it was noted that Krepper

> spends considerable time with Margaret Diehl, characterized by the New York Office as a girl friend of Krepper, who resides with a brother at 612 East 84th Street, New York City. . . . Krepper has been observed to stay overnight on numerous occasions at Diehl's apartment.[25]

Krepper would frequently travel with Margaret Diehl and the Kropp family over the next few years to a farm in Sandisfield, Massachusetts. Agents of the Federal Bureau of Investigation routinely followed them back and forth between New York and Massachusetts.

Margaret P. Diehl was born Margaret Pauline Grebenstein on February 15, 1889, in Germany. Her parents were Herman and Pauline Behrend Grebenstein. Her husband died in Germany in 1933, and she came to America in 1934. She worked as a seamstress for the Jane Engel Co. of New York City, retiring in 1957. After her retirement, she moved back with her sister and brother-in-law, Martin and Helene (Leni) Kropp, in Sandisfield, Massachusetts, in the Berkshires. She died on December 26, 1977.

Martin Kropp was born in Germany in 1901. He trained as a dentist, and after he emigrated Kropp became a naturalized citizen on April 20, 1940. He and his family spent many weekends and holidays at a farm in Sandisfield. Upon his retirement, Kropp and his wife retired to Sandisfield. Martin Kropp died in the same town on April 19, 1967, at age 65. Krepper appears to have developed a real friendship with this German-American dentist and his wife, and after his release from prison, Krepper eventually ended up moving to Sandisfield to join his friends in retirement.

During their investigation, the FBI soon discovered that the Reverend Carl Krepper was something of a lothario. In addition to Margaret Diehl, Krepper also was romantically involved with Bertha Keller and Marianne Mayer. As the FBI traced his whereabouts, they learned that Krepper's "work" with the Schoenbach Stamp Exchange and his clandestine meetings with unknown individuals often revolved around his days and nights spent in the company of these three assorted widowed "girlfriends." Assistant Director D. Milton Ladd wrote in a memorandum to Hoover:

It is interesting to note that the Newark Office in commenting on the fact that while Krepper was out with Mrs. Mayer, he left her and proceeded to the home of Bertha Scott and thereafter returned to Mrs. Mayer's house, that there is a strong indication that both women are infatuated with Krepper.[26]

Within two months, the bureau had learned a great deal about Krepper and his known associates, who could help him in different ways in his work and his cover as a Nazi spy aide. Between the New York and Newark offices, they learned that through his son, Carl Krepper did indeed have contacts that could help with the printing of false identity papers, as the leaders of the two Pastorius sabotage groups, Dasch and Kerling, had been told. They also learned that through one of Krepper's girlfriends, Marianne Mayer, Krepper had access to lodgings that the saboteurs could have used as they went about their deadly work. Along with these known associates of family, friends, and girlfriends, Krepper had dealings with other known German agents as well. These dealings with enemy agents brought further scrutiny from the FBI, and would soon cause Krepper great worry.

CHAPTER NINE

The Reluctant Spy

CARL KREPPER, "ESPIONAGE AGENT"

Walter Kappe had placed a great deal of confidence in Carl Krepper's abilities as an enemy agent. Kappe had told the Pastorius saboteurs that Krepper was an agent who could get any necessary supplies that they might need for their terroristic attacks on the United States. If they needed messages transmitted back and forth between the United States and Germany, Krepper was the man for the job. Nonetheless, for all that Walter Kappe built him up to be, Carl Krepper was a somewhat reluctant enemy agent. He had, of course, planted himself within the greater New York community, with a base of operations in both Newark and New York. He had set up arrangements to assist fellow German agents if they followed the established protocol and met him with the proper passwords, "Franz Daniel Pastorius" or "Pastor Kaiser." Krepper had been vetted for his pro-Nazi bona fides when he was in Germany, and his journey to the United States in December 1942 was approved by the German Foreign Ministry. His mission to the United States was conducted at the behest of Walter Kappe and the *Abwehr*, and so it was that Assistant FBI Director Earl J. Connelley summed up the feeling of J. Edgar Hoover and the bureau as a whole when he said: "Krepper . . . we definitely know, of course, is an espionage agent."[1]

Even though he had been sent to the United States before war was declared, Krepper handled the outbreak of hostilities between Germany and the United States with what could be described as a calm resolve. He did what was expected of him, and he registered for the draft on April 26, 1942.[2] Krepper also did what Kappe expected him to do. At his trial he would claim that after war was declared he considered his deal with Kappe null and void. Nonetheless, when he sent the Operation Pastorius saboteurs to the United States in June 1942, Walter Kappe clearly believed that in Krepper he had a man in place who was "a good contact at any time." Krepper had shown a willingness and a resolve to work for the interests of the Third Reich in the United States at a time of war between the two countries.

During the summer of 1942, Krepper did indeed meet with some strange and shady characters. Among those was a known German courier named Ernst or Ernest Lack, who transported messages between the United States and Canada. Ernst Lack was born on February 25, 1905, in Bueckeburg, Germany. Like Carl Krepper, Lack lived in Altona, Germany, prior to his departure for the United States from Hamburg aboard the SS Milwaukee. Arriving in the United States on September 16, 1929, Lack filed his declaration of intention to become a United States citizen on May 3, 1933. On his November 9, 1939, petition for naturalization, Lack listed his occupation as a salesperson, and he was then living at 158 East 22nd Street, New York. Over the years he would work variously as a driver for a bakery and as a cabinetmaker. Lack was, furthermore, a trained airplane pilot. He died in November 1975.

Early into the FBI's investigation of Krepper it was noted by Special Agent C. L. Green that "Krepper also has been seen with Ernest Lack, known to have been a 'go between' in mail between German courier and Emil Zaech, a known German espionage agent in Canada."[3]

When he met with Krepper, Lack was already known to the bureau. He had been implicated as a lower-level accomplice in the famous prewar espionage investigation called the "Rumrich Case," in which the American-born and German-educated Günther Gustav Rumrich (a deserter from the U.S. Army) attempted to acquire 50 American passport applications at the passport office in New York City. This raised some serious questions on the part of the Department of State, which then informed the FBI. After an FBI investigation, 18 members of what was called "the Rumrich spy ring" were indicted on June 24, 1938. Rumrich and his cohorts were charged with plotting to steal defense secrets regarding American military defenses along the Eastern seaboard. The secrets thus discovered were to be sent on to Germany by way of couriers who used counterfeit passports, as well as merchant seamen traveling back to Germany. Rumrich admitted to being recruited by German military intelligence, and he, along with Dr. Ignatz T. Griebl, a former clinical assistant at Harlem Hospital and former head of the Friends of New Germany, and three others were questioned by the FBI. Griebl fled back to Germany, while Rumrich and the three others were put on trial in October 1938. Rumrich and the others were found guilty of espionage and sentenced to prison for terms from two to six years.[4]

Ernst Lack was interviewed by agents of the bureau's New York field office on January 17 and 18, 1940, regarding another related German espionage investigation. During this interview, Lack admitted to receiving messages from one of the principal couriers in the Rumrich case, a German seaman named Hebert Jaenichen. Without denying any criminal culpability, Lack admitted to forwarding and receiving messages for this German courier at his home address in New York.[5]

On July 10, 1942, Ernst Lack reappeared on the FBI radar, this time, as a driver for Carl Krepper and Margaret Diehl. That day, he picked up Krepper and Diehl from her apartment on East 84th Street, and he drove the couple to an address on 142nd Street in the Bronx. To the agents trailing Krepper, who observed his meeting with Lack and then followed the two men to the address in the Bronx, it was apparent that Krepper and Lack were "well acquainted."[6] Serious hackles were being raised among the FBI agents on the Krepper case. The bureau now knew that in addition to his mail drop in Barcelona through Pastor Kloess, Krepper was familiar with a man who had experience transmitting messages to and from Nazi Germany.

On July 13, 1942, while the Pastorius trial was being conducted in Washington, D.C., and as the agents charged with following Krepper and his known associates went about their work, the bureau announced that it had also brought in 14 individuals who were charged with supporting the Pastorius operatives after they landed in the United States. These were largely family members and friends of the saboteurs who were charged with treason and conspiracy to commit espionage and sabotage, as well as a felony charge of aiding and abetting sabotage.[7] Among those for whom the bureau was searching was Walter Kappe. In Krepper's FBI file, it is recorded that on July 13, the same day J. Edgar Hoover announced the arrest of the 14 men and women who supported the saboteurs, the bureau was trying to gather information on Walter Kappe. On July 25, the bureau announced a nationwide manhunt for Kappe, and agents would soon begin a fruitless search for him in the United States (since he was in Germany).[8] There was some concern that, as he had intimated to the Pastorius saboteurs, Kappe would not only send another sabotage group to the United States, but he himself also planned to come over to supervise agents of the Reich in the United States. Even though Kappe remained in Germany and never returned to the United States, wanted posters of Kappe were posted all over the country.

Despite the questioning he received from Immigration and Naturalization prior to the arrival of Pastorius agents, in many ways, Krepper was behaving like a spy. As FBI agents followed him around on his journeys between New York and Newark, and occasionally up to Sandisfield, Massachusetts, they were convinced that he was engaged in espionage activities on behalf of the Third Reich. Nonetheless, as July 1942 came to a close, Krepper would have known that not only did nearly everyone in the country now know who his handler was—he also would have known that things were looking grim for the Pastorius saboteurs. His handler was still in Germany, but Krepper believed that his cover remained secure. There were other German agents in the United States for whom he would keep watch; and so he did, until December 1944, when he was arrested by agents of the FBI.

THE EXECUTION OF THE SABOTEURS

It is not clear how Carl Krepper responded to the execution of the Pastorius saboteurs on August 8. There is a fascinating document in Carl Krepper's FBI file from Duane L. Traynor that dates from August 7, the day before the saboteurs were put to death in the electric chair.[9] It is a letter to Colonel Kenneth Royall at the Pentagon. Royall was the presidentially appointed counsel for the Pastorius saboteurs. President Roosevelt had personally assigned him to be the defense counsel for the eight *Abwehr*-trained agents. After the trial concluded, and prior to the execution of the saboteurs, Royall apparently inquired after the names of the agents who assisted him in his work of defending the German agents before the military commission. Presumably Royall wanted to thank them for their assistance. Traynor listed the agents as follows: Clyde Tolson, Assistant to the Director; D. M. Ladd, Assistant Director; E. J. Connelley, Assistant Director; W. R. Glavin, Assistant Director; and T. J. Donegan, Special Agent in Charge. Traynor told Royall that all of the FBI staff listed were located at the Washington, D.C., headquarters of the bureau, with the exception of Donegan, who was at the FBI headquarters in New York. With the exception of Glavin, these individuals would play one role or another in the Krepper investigation.

Leading up to the execution of the Pastorius agents, on August 5 through 7, Krepper traveled between two of his girlfriends, Margaret Diehl and Marianne Mayer.[10] On August 5, he left Margaret Diehl at her apartment and took the IRT and the Hudson Tubes down to lower Manhattan, and from there the train to Newark. He ended up at one of Marianne Mayer's rooming houses, 68 James Street, Newark. It would be while he was staying at this address that Krepper would be arrested in December 1944. On August 7, Krepper traveled back into Manhattan to Margaret Diehl's apartment, where he remained until the morning of August 8, when Krepper traveled in the company of Margaret Diehl, Martin Kropp, and another German-American named Henry Lecher, to Sandsifield, Massachusetts. No activity on the part of Krepper or the Kropps was noticed by the agents on either the afternoon of August 8 or just about all day on August 9. As the Pastorius saboteurs were executed, Krepper was far away, seemingly removed from the action, and he remained indoors as the country digested the news. Krepper remained in Sandisfield with the Kropps until the evening of August 9, when all except Margaret Diehl returned to New York. They arrived back to the Kropp/Diehl apartment around 11:30 p.m. Very early the following morning, August 10, Krepper dropped a letter in a mailbox at the corner of 84th Street and Third Avenue. He then traveled to Newark, to the rooming house of Marianne Mayer at 68 James Street. The FBI found that the letter that Krepper mailed in New York was addressed to the "United States Attorney, Southern District of New York," and it consisted of an "alien travel permit" (a travel permit was required of "enemy aliens" at the time if they traveled from one state to another). The alien travel permit that Krepper mailed to the attorney general's office was for Margaret Diehl, and according to the legal requirements then in force, it stated that she had traveled to Sandisfield, Massachusetts, and intended to remain there for two weeks.

On August 12, four days after the six saboteurs were executed, an FBI report was filed with information on the Krepper investigation that was gleaned from interviews with the one leader of the sabotage group who was not executed, George John Dasch. "Dasch was informed . . . that Krepper, a Lutheran pastor, was 'all right.'" Dasch had been told by Kappe back in Germany that Krepper was "an individual who would render assistance to them in the United States." Quite significantly, Dasch told the federal investigators that when Krepper had "returned to the United States . . . he was in possession of the password 'Franz Daniel Pastorius' which had been furnished to the saboteurs." This was the same password written out on George Dasch's handkerchief as the code to be used between Krepper and the other German assets in America.[11] The two surviving Pastorius saboteurs would greatly assist in apprehending the last of the Nazi spy aides. Dasch's testimony would help the bureau in its investigation of Carl Krepper, and Ernst Peter Burger's testimony at Krepper's trial would assist in securing a conviction.

CONTINUING DEVELOPMENTS: A MAJOR DECISION AND SOME ROMANTIC CONFUSION

On August 20, 1942, J. Edgar Hoover reported on an investigation of postal deliveries to the Frey home in Rahway, New Jersey. After Eugene Frey's name and address were discovered on the Pastorius handkerchiefs, Hoover had the Office of Censorship conduct a survey of "back traffic" to see if Frey had received anything out of the ordinary in the mail. It was noted that a unique package was received at the Frey home in Rahway, New Jersey. It had been mailed from Lisbon, Portugal, and it arrived at the Frey home on September 12, 1941. A copy of the original two-page Office of Censorship report is contained in Krepper's files. The package came from a certain "J. A. De Souza, Rua De Commercio 24, Lisbon, Portugal." Federal agents had no idea who "J. A. De Souza" was, but they found that the package contained "a list of pictures by famous artists." The artists in the list included Velasquez, Tiepolo, Vermeyen, Greco, Goya, Titian, and Moro. In and of itself, there seemed to be nothing terribly unusual in this listing of painters and paintings. Hoover noted that the mailing came around the time that Krepper left Germany for the United States by way of Portugal (actually, the package had been mailed from Portugal several months before Krepper's arrival in the United States). Hoover speculated that this "material received from Portugal may contain secret messages."[12] What was significant for the bureau was that the address on the mailing came from Lisbon to "Mr. Eugene Frey, R.F.D. H2, Box 40 F, Rahway, NJ, USA," the same address that was given to Pastorius saboteurs in June 1942. The mailing from Lisbon to the Frey home in 1941 was likely a feint meant to test the waters for other mailings to Krepper via the route that had been established by Kappe.

On August 20, the same day that J. Edgar Hoover speculated on the mailing to Eugene Frey, and as the government was preparing for the trials of the "associates" of the saboteurs who had been taken into custody on July 13, Assistant Director D. Milton Ladd sent a significant report to Assistant to the Director Edward A. Tamm. The report was about the trial of one of the Pastorius "associates," Helmut Leiner. Leiner was a friend of saboteur Edward Kerling, who was living in Astoria, Queens. He was one of the three American Nazi spy aides listed on one of the Pastorius handkerchiefs. On August 20, Ladd informed Tamm about an important decision in the trial of the Pastorius "associates" that was set to begin on October 26, 1942. The bureau would not bring the handkerchief with Leiner's name and address as evidence at Leiner's trial. They would use Ernst Peter Burger's testimony about Kerling being an enemy of the United States, and then would simply show that Leiner aided and abetted Kerling. More to the point, they wanted to keep the evidence of the names on the Pastorius handkerchief to use against Carl Krepper:

> It was further pointed out that to introduce the handkerchief in evidence would disclose the Bureau's investigation of Carl Krepper and therefore was not desirable. Mr. Donegan was told that in view of this the summary report in this case for the trial of the associates should make no reference to this handkerchief.[13]

It was a major decision to not use the Pastorius handkerchief in the trial of Helmut Leiner, and it would have major consequences for Krepper. First of all, it bought the FBI time in its investigation. As agents built the case against Krepper, they already had their major piece of evidence. J. Edgar Hoover was looking for Krepper to lead the bureau to a major German spy ring. If the name on the handkerchief were made public in the Leiner trial, Krepper could have fled or gone underground, or he could have been alerted to the threat of being trailed by the FBI, and the possibility of discovering a larger Nazi spy ring would have been lost for good. When the handkerchief was displayed as evidence during Krepper's federal trial in Newark in 1945, this major decision on the FBI's part sealed the deal for his conviction. Along with everyone else in the courtroom, Krepper was able to see his name and his stepson's address appear as the invisible ink was brought out by the ammonia. His name was displayed as clear as day, and he would be forever linked with the failed Operation Pastorius.

The remainder of the month of August looked at first to be rather uneventful, as agents trailed Krepper while he spent a week at the Kropp farm in the Berkshires with girlfriend Margaret Diehl. He returned alone to New York on August 23.[14]

Three days later, things looked to be heating up a bit in the Krepper case. At noon on August 26, Krepper received a telephone call in Newark that got the bureau's attention. It appeared as if someone was "attempting to contact subject."[15] The bureau and Krepper himself seemed to take it that this phone call was a possible contact from a German agent. It was noted that that same afternoon, "Subject left Newark . . . and went to New York City."

Whatever happened in New York that day, it was not recorded in Krepper's FBI file. On August 28, Krepper ended up back at Marianne Mayer's home at 68 James Street, where he remained for the whole day.

As the agents following Krepper noted, while he did not put a whole lot of effort into his work life, Krepper's love life seemed to be flourishing. Throughout the summer of 1942, Krepper went from one girlfriend to another, and he made every effort to keep them apart. Diehl was his only female companion in Manhattan, but in Newark Krepper had two girlfriends, Bertha Keller and Marianne Mayer. Towards the end of July, agents witnessed a bizarre incident. On July 23, Krepper walked in Newark with Marianne Mayer. He was with one girlfriend in a city where he had another. At one point in their travels, Krepper and Mayer

> separated and Krepper continued to 658 Mt. Prospect Avenue, which is the address of Bertha Keller Scott. . . . Krepper remained at this address for only a few minutes and then rejoined Mrs. Mayer and returned to 42 Camp Street. It was assumed that Krepper did not permit Mrs. Mayer to accompany him to the home of Mrs. Scott, as there is a strong indication that both women are infatuated with him.[16]

Being in the company of a woman seemed as if it were part of Krepper's cover, whether he was in New York or in Newark. All three of Krepper's girlfriends were widows, and they all three were somewhat established in their own ways. Bertha Keller had a job with the Prudential Insurance Company. Marianne Mayer owned and operated rooming houses in Newark. Margaret Diehl lived with her sister and brother-in-law. All three women had come to the United States from Germany, and all three were proud of their German heritage. To one degree or another, all three women also supported the German Reich. There does not appear to be any indication that Marianne Mayer or Margaret Diehl knew that Krepper was married and had a wife back in Germany. Bertha Keller not only knew that Krepper was married, but she also knew the extended Krepper family, including Bertha Krepper, and Carl's son Ernst. In a March 9, 1942, letter to Hilda Frey and Carl Krepper, Bertha Krepper thanked Bertha Keller for her notes to her in Germany.[17] How much these three women knew about Krepper's past or about his intended mission in the United States is not known. The FBI investigated all three of Krepper's girlfriends to discover their known associates, their extended families, and their work history or lack thereof. There is no indication in Krepper's FBI file that would substantiate a belief that they willingly supported his work as an agent of the Third Reich. The one girlfriend out of the three who stood by Krepper after he was arrested was Marianne Mayer. After Krepper's release from prison, she both petitioned the United Lutheran Church in America on Krepper's behalf for a church pension, and when that was denied, she traveled to Germany to do the same there.

Towards the end of August, as they were spending so much time on the Krepper case, a decision was made between the New York and Newark field offices to change the name of the case in which Carl Krepper was now the major subject. The New York field office asserted that there was confusion in its filing system because Carl Krepper was now, after the execution of the Pastorius saboteurs, the principal subject under investigation. At the instigation of Special Agent E. F. Emrich, the New York field office officially requested permission to change the subject heading of the investigation to "Carl Krepper." On August 28, Duane L. Traynor noted,

> that the Krepper angle of this case should be carried under the title of George John Dasch was confusing to the files system of the New York Office. I told him that it would not make any difference to us whether they carried it as a separate case or carried it in the Dasch case, provided there was some assurance that the reports and communications would get directly to the Sabotage Section. I told him that from now on the title of the Krepper angle should be carried as Carl Krepper, Alvin Schoenbach, Eugene Frey, et al., Sabotage, and that he should notify the Newark Office of this change.[18]

On August 29, the day after the Krepper case was given its new name, Assistant Director P. E. Foxworth sent a "confidential" letter to J. Edgar Hoover requesting something that would eventually help bring the

Krepper case to a successful conclusion. Agents needed to get closer to Krepper, and the bureau envisioned that its own agents could pose as German agents. It was hoped that by having a base of operations right in the building where Krepper had his official place of business, they could learn more about the network of German agents in the United States, and about the full nature of Krepper's own mission under Walter Kappe, together with Krepper's role in Operation Pastorius. An apartment in Manhattan could effectively be used by FBI agents both as a "listening post" and for a base of operations as they posed as Nazi spies to meet with Krepper. While the FBI speculated on using the apartment for an operation in which its agents would pose as German agents in order to trap Krepper and/or Schoenbach (which they eventually did in Krepper's case elsewhere), it only used this particular apartment as a listening post to eavesdrop on conversations between Krepper and Schoenbach. Assistant Director Foxworth wrote to Hoover:

Dear Sir:

For use in the above investigation the New York Office desires to secure Apartment 5-G, 425 West 57th Street, New York City. The rental for this apartment will be seventy-five dollars ($75.00) per month. Authority for this rental is requested.

Very truly yours,

P. E. Foxworth

Assistant Director[19]

This was the apartment building where Alvin Schoenbach had his apartment/stamp business, and where Krepper was a regular visitor. Renting an apartment in the same building was something of a daring move, but from there agents would be in the middle of things, so to speak, and they could have easy access to either Krepper or Schoenbach if need be.

J. Edgar Hoover also thought this was a good idea, and he responded in the affirmative.

The New York field office was tasked with setting up this apartment:

Dear Sir:

Reference is made to your letter dated August 29, 1942, requesting authority to rent an apartment at 425 West 57th Street, New York

City, at a rental of $75 per month. Authority to rent this apartment is hereby granted.

Very truly yours,

John Edgar Hoover

Director[20]

This development would greatly assist the bureau over the next two years as it set up clandestine meetings between Carl Krepper and FBI agents who posed as German spies.

TO SPY OR NOT TO SPY, THAT IS THE QUESTION

As the FBI agents were setting up the apartment in Manhattan for use in the surveillance of Krepper that had been approved by J. Edgar Hoover, the next bombshell in the Krepper case came on October 7, when Krepper received a strange phone call while he was at Alvin Schoenbach's apartment in New York. This phone call was overheard by agents of the FBI, who were conducting a "mechanical surveillance" on the Schoenbach home in the hope of just such an eventuality. The phone call for Krepper came in at 11:55 a.m., and the caller, described as having a "pronounced Brooklyn type accent with several possible traces of German speaking characteristics,"[21] asked to speak with Carl Krepper. The English-language conversation that ensued provided the first real connection, beyond the Pastorius handkerchief and the testimony of Pastorius operatives Dasch and Burger, between Krepper and other German agents in the United States. The conversation was almost comical in its brevity. Neither man wanted to say too much over the phone for fear that they were being overheard by federal agents, which, of course, they were.

The unknown man started off by asking for "Mr. Krepper."[22] When he confirmed that it was Krepper on the phone, the man then said: "I have something to tell you." Krepper asked the man his name: "Yes, who is it?" The man replied: "Well, I . . . know . . . I don't want to tell my name over the wire. See? Could you meet me?" Krepper responded, "You want to talk to me?" The man answered, "Yes, that's right." Krepper pressed the unknown individual, "Who are you?" The man was clearly worried about FBI eavesdropping, and he replied, "Well, I don't want to talk over the phone to you." Krepper was clearly on his guard. "I'm not interested in that," he responded. "Can you write, please?" The man was thrown off by Krepper's intransigence. "Hello?" he asked. Krepper was insistent: "Can you write?" The man seemed bewildered. He responded, "Can I write to you?" "Yes," Krepper said. "Send me a letter?" The man continued, trying to get his point across, "Yea, well, that's why I want to talk to you." Seemingly taken aback by the man's insistence, Krepper muttered "Umm. . . ." The FBI agents who overheard the conversation said that Krepper said this "under his breath—wondering."

The unknown man was sure that all would fit in place when he and Krepper met: "When you see me you'll know who I am." There was then a pause in the conversation. Krepper then seemed to realize that he needed to ensure that he was indeed speaking with another German agent. He pointedly asked, "What's your first name?" Again, there was a pause in the conversation.

As Assistant Director D. Milton Ladd reflected on this very pregnant question, he was asking for the password given him by Walter Kappe back in Germany: "Krepper, after attempting to obtain the identity of the unknown individual, asked the question, 'What's your first name' which might indicate that he was endeavoring to have this individual use part of the password 'Franz Daniel Pastorius.'"[23]

As the phone conversation between Krepper and the caller continued, the man made it clear that he knew that their phone conversation might have been tapped. He also made it clear that he knew what the stakes were and that he was not going to play by Krepper's rules. "Listen," he said, "I don't want to talk on the telephone, it is for your benefit too you know and if I talk on the telephone everybody knows what I'm talking about." The unknown caller was more concerned about FBI surveillance than was Krepper, who did not seem as if he wanted to commit to even meeting this stranger who knew his name and one of his contact numbers. He replied with a noncommittal "Ya. . . ." The agents listening in believed that Krepper was "still wondering." The man wanted to press his point: "You understand?" Krepper finally admitted the wisdom of the caller's concern. "I understand it, yes," Krepper said. "So, can you meet me?" the man asked. Krepper replied, "Where then?" The man gave Krepper a definite street: "You go down to 42nd Street." Krepper confirmed, "42nd Street?" "Yea," the man said, "there's a theater down there, the Selwyn Theater. . . . S-E-L-W-Y-N. . . . It's between 8th Ave. and Broadway. Can you be down there?" Krepper agreed, "All right." "I meet you," the man said, "in a half hour there?" "No," Krepper replied, "I couldn't be in a half hour there." The man pressed Krepper, "Can you meet there tomorrow?" "Tomorrow?" Krepper asked.

("[A]lmost to himself," the FBI agents listening in later reflected.) "I . . . my . . . how's one o'clock?" Krepper inquired. "One o'clock?" the man asked. "Alright," he said, "one o'clock. I see you there." "Where is it?" Krepper asked. "42nd Street," the caller repeated, "Selwyn Theater, S-E-L-W-Y-N, that's between 8th Ave. and Broadway, New York, you understand?" Krepper confirmed that he did, "Ya, sure." "You go down there," the man said, "buy a ticket and you go inside, I see you inside right by the door because I don't want nobody see me talking to you." "Alright," Krepper said. As a final confirmation, the unknown caller confirmed the time: "One o'clock."

The bureau's New York field office overheard the entire conversation and created a transcript of it for future reference that is contained in Krepper's FBI file. As agents reviewed the phone call, "the New York Office points out that it was obvious that Krepper was not only greatly surprised but sounded frightened upon receipt of this call." The surprised and frightened Krepper had confirmed a meeting with an unknown individual, likely a fellow German operative, on October 8, 1942. What had frightened Krepper so about this conversation was the reality that the man on the other end of the line was clearly a German agent. He had recognized that the phones had likely been tapped by the FBI, and he had shown knowledge of the fact that there was indeed a protocol for his meeting with Krepper. Even though he did not use the "Franz Daniel Pastorius" password as Kappe had insisted, the caller obviously knew that such a code existed. He just did not want to speak it over the phone where it could be overheard by listening ears. The caller had wanted to meet Krepper that day, a mere half hour later. Krepper's surprise was evident in his insistence on changing the date of the meeting to the following day. For his part, Krepper did what he had been trained to do. He had tried to use the established protocol, asking for the caller's first name. He had tried to get the caller to use Kappe's password. This contact did not proceed as Krepper had expected such a conversation would go. He clearly needed to collect his thoughts.

Assistant Director Earl J. Connelley wrote a memorandum about the phone call for Hoover. "The conversation," Connelley reported, "indicates rather definitely it was an agent making contact with Krepper."[24] Even though he was "surprised" and "frightened" by the phone call, Krepper had agreed to meet the caller the next day. There was a definite time and a definite place for the meeting. The agreed-upon date, October 8, would be a "make or break" day for Carl Krepper.

The enemy agent wanted to meet Krepper in a very well-known and popular venue, not a run-down, out-of-the-way spot. The Selwyn Theater, where the meeting between Krepper and the German agent was to take place, was built in 1918. It is located at 229 West 42nd Street, and was built by New York architect George Keister, who also built the Apollo Theater, the Bronx Opera House, the Belasco Theatre (originally the Stuyvesant), as well as the First Baptist Church at 79th and Broadway. Whatever Krepper knew or did not know about the Selwyn Theatre, he was to meet a man there on October 8 who might actually put his skills and contacts to use.

Now that the bureau had a definite contact for Krepper, agents planned accordingly. They had agents in place within and outside the Selwyn Theatre from 12:15 p.m. to 2:30 p.m., in position to observe suspicious characters inside the lobby of the theatre, as well as directly outside and across the street.[25] Assistant Director D. Milton Ladd detailed what happened next, that "the New York Office immediately, after the receipt of this information, arranged for an appropriate coverage of the meeting."[26] What the bureau found was that after his phone call from what appeared to be a German agent, Krepper left Schoenbach's home and went to visit his "lady friend, Margaret Diehl." He stayed there until that evening when he went back to Newark to Marianne Mayer's rooming house, "with whom he resides." After spending the afternoon and night with two of his girlfriends, the next day Krepper left 68 James Street at 12:22 p.m. The agents who were in place to follow Krepper to the meeting noted that Krepper "acted suspiciously and that he looked around on several occasions as though to determine if he was being followed."[27] Rather than taking a bus into New York for the arranged meeting at the Selwyn Theatre that was to begin in 50 minutes, Krepper instead simply walked around the block and went back into Marianne Mayer's rooming house. He did not travel into New York City at all that day. Rather than meeting his caller from the previous day, Carl Krepper decided to go on a "date" with Marianne Mayer. Incredible as it seemed to the agents following him, at 1:15 p.m. on October 8, Krepper and Mayer left 68 James Street and traveled by bus along Route 29 to Plainfield, New Jersey. Arriving around 2:15 p.m., the couple "walked around town rather aimlessly and then proceeded into the country along a country road to a local point of interest known as 'Washington Rock,' a rather high elevation, presumably sightseeing."[28]

There, at Washington Rock State Park in Watchung, New Jersey, Krepper and Mayer took in the sights in what is one of the oldest state parks in New Jersey. It is a scenic lookout that marks the spot where General George Washington spotted the British troops under General William Howe and was thus able to cut off their retreat near Westfield, New Jersey, during the American Revolution. As they walked back to Plainfield, the couple was seen "engaged in a little love making along the road." The agents following the couple were confident that Krepper and Mayer were unaware of their presence, "as the activities between the two, he and Marianne Mayer, were such that they would not have engaged in these actions probably if they believed they had been surveilled."

Around 5:15 p.m. they made it back to Plainfield for dinner. They walked a little more than three miles to Dunellen, New Jersey, where they boarded a bus back to Newark. They arrived back at 68 James Street around 7:30 p.m.

Krepper had missed his opportunity to meet the caller from the previous day at the Selwyn Theatre, as they had agreed. Instead of doing what he had promised Walter Kappe he would do for the Fatherland, he had engaged in a "little love making" with one of his girlfriends. Krepper may have thought he was following protocol by not making contact with someone who did not immediately use the established password. He might have let the surprise and fear he felt the day before get the better of him. Whatever his reasoning, for at least that day, Krepper had been a reluctant spy.

Despite the missed opportunity on October 8, the FBI hoped that it could recoup its losses in the future. The bureau speculated that the "possible agent" who had contacted Krepper on October 7 "will again contact him in the near future," and hoped that Krepper "will keep the contact in question."[29] Agents believed that their "best possibilities in this case" would be if the caller called Krepper again, and Krepper actually met with him.

Regardless of this setback, the bureau did not let any grass grow under its feet. On October 9, the day after Krepper's erstwhile meeting with what agents believed to be a German agent, Assistant Director P. E. Foxworth informed Hoover of a plan to use the recording of the conversation between Krepper and the unknown caller of October 7. Foxworth suggested that they allow Ernst Peter Burger to listen to the recording to see if he recognized the voice of the speaker from his sabotage training in Germany. If it was another *Abwehr*-trained agent, they would therefore be able to identify the man for whom they were searching.

Foxworth and his colleagues feared that the man who had contacted Krepper was another German agent or saboteur who was at large in the country, and who was trying to do what Dasch and Burger and the rest of the saboteurs could not do—that is, make actual contact with Carl Krepper. If the agent could actually meet with Krepper, he could have lodgings and other resources that might facilitate his work. Thus it was that on October 10, Assistant Director Foxworth forwarded the recording of the conversation between Krepper and the unknown caller to FBI headquarters so that Ernst Peter Burger could listen and hopefully identify the voice of the unknown man.[30] In a November 27, 1942, report, Special Agent Charles L. Green of the New York field office speculated that "Billy Braubender, with aliases Billy Smith, and Billy Dempsey, has been considered a possible suspect as the person to meet Krepper."[31] Like the other Pastorius saboteurs, Braubender had lived in the United States, working as a middleweight prizefighter and a trainer.[32] When he left Kappe's training school at Quentz Lake, he told the other saboteurs that he would "see you boys over there," indicating that he would be coming over for another sabotage mission later in 1942. Special Agent Green laid out what the FBI knew about this Billy or Bill Braubender:

> [I]t is known [he] attended a sabotage school in Germany and was scheduled to lead a third group to this country, not arriving with the other two groups because of the fact that two men were let out of the school and one was physically incapacitated. Information available indicates that possibly Braubender was scheduled to come to the United States in September or October of this year as leader of the third group.[33]

The bureau set up surveillance at two hotels in Manhattan: the Dixie Hotel at West 42nd Street, nearly adjacent to the Selwyn Theatre, and the Pennsylvania Hotel, part of the Statler Corporation, for whom Billy Braubender had previously worked as a bellhop. The surveillances did not bear fruit, and Braubender was not found.

As it turned out, both Burger and Dasch listened to the recording, but neither was able to identify the voice of Krepper's unknown caller.[34] Whether or not the man who called Krepper on October 7 was Braubender has never been ascertained.

As a last word on the recording the FBI made of Krepper and the unknown individual on October 7, 1942, there is in Krepper's FBI file an office memorandum dated March 12, 1946.[35] The memorandum is to Louis B. Nichols, Assistant Director of the Administrative Division, from R. F. Cartwright. Cartwright believed that since the recording was played for two people (Burger and Dasch), neither of whom could identify the voice of the "unknown individual," "it appears that this record is of no value to the Bureau." Cartwright concluded that as "this enclosure is occupying valuable space in the Records Section, it is requested that this file be reviewed by the Security Division for an expression as to the disposition of this material. It is recommended that this enclosure be destroyed here at the Seat of Government." While the recording is gone, the transcript of the conversation survives. It serves as a brief glimpse into what could have led to a major break in the Krepper case—a glimpse into the work of a spy who was at best hesitant, and at worst disinclined to follow his orders from Germany. With the destruction of the recording of the conversation between Carl Krepper and his unknown caller, the question of the enemy agent's identity will probably never be definitively answered.

CHAPTER TEN

Bring Him In: Plans to Catch a "Nazi Spy Aide"

PROS AND CONS

On the 19th and 20th of October, there was serious discussion among Thomas J. Donegan, D. Milton Ladd, Duane L. Traynor, and Earl J. Connelley about discontinuing the surveillance on Krepper and simply bringing him in for questioning. The suggestion came from Special Agent in Charge Donegan of the New York office. Traynor admitted that Donegan made a fair point:

> He stated that a number of Agents have been tied up on this matter for some time and nothing productive has been developed with the exception of the one anonymous telephone call which turned out unsuccessfully insofar as a contact was concerned.[1]

While he believed that Krepper's suggestion that the unknown man write to him might actually bear fruit, Traynor suggested that Donegan's analysis be accepted and they pick up Krepper, "since he apparently is very apprehensive of the possible surveillance."

For a number of months in the latter half of 1942, the leaders of the bureau's investigation of Carl Krepper weighed the pros and cons of bringing him in. A month later, Assistant Director Foxworth advised that the bureau should seriously consider having Krepper questioned:

> It is believed that if Krepper was brought in and vigorously questioned as to his activities, associates, etc., both in this country and in Germany, it is likely that definite information of value will be developed as a result of such an interview. It is also felt that if Krepper is confronted with the definite information which we have concerning the part he was to play in the activities of the eight saboteurs he would undoubtedly find himself in a position where he could not do anything else but cooperate with us as to any future activities he might plan, and thus his activities could be closely supervised by us.[2]

Foxworth argued that Krepper undoubtedly "has considerable information regarding individuals who might have come to this country prior to the eight individuals who were apprehended by the Bureau." That Krepper had knowledge of other agents who came to the United States prior to Operation Pastorius is not as hokey a supposition as it might first appear. After all, at least part of Krepper's value to Walter Kappe was his Bundist contacts from his days with the Friends of New Germany. He had ministered solely to German-American congregations between 1910 and 1935, and he organized the Essex County branch of the German-American Business League. In his own words, he proudly flew the swastika flag in his church and used the uniformed Order Service men at his church services. It was far from inconceivable that when he was recruited by Kappe, Krepper would have been given other contacts from the Reich who were already here prior to his arrival in December 1941. Foxworth also speculated on the real possibility, at which Pastorius operatives Dasch and Burger had hinted, that there might be a third group of saboteurs coming to the United States at a later date. Foxworth posited that Krepper "may possibly have information as to the other individuals who might come to this country in the future."

Assistant Director Foxworth also recognized that the Krepper investigation was unlikely to bear fruit if it continued on its current path. "It is," Foxworth argued, "believed that we are more likely to develop such information through a vigorous interview. . . ."[3] Because of the Pastorius handkerchief alone, there was no doubt at all in the minds of the FBI leadership that Krepper was a German agent. Nonetheless, speculation concerning the merits of simply bringing Krepper in and sweating him into a confession continued to the end of the year. On December 5,

1942, Assistant Director Earl J. Connelley ruminated on the challenges of bringing Krepper in:

> Krepper undoubtedly is very definitely pro-Nazi in his sympathies and might be a difficult individual to influence as a cooperator with the Bureau. On the other hand, it is realized that he probably feels that he is in a rather serious position as a result of the execution of certain of the eight saboteurs. We as yet have no definite information that Krepper is aware of the fact that he was to be made a contact for these eight saboteurs. He may, of course, have been advised of this in some manner by Germany.[4]

These internal reflections are fascinating on a number of levels. First, the bureau understood that despite all its agents' technical and physical surveillance of Krepper, he still might have received communications from Nazi Germany without their knowledge. Second, Connelley recognized the difficulty of breaking or turning an individual who passionately held onto his or her ideologies and beliefs, as twisted as they might have been. A passionate Nazi was a hard nut to crack. Third, Connelley speculated that Krepper may not have known about his name appearing on the Pastorius handkerchiefs. That seems unlikely, since at his trial he admitted to coming to the United States with a very specific mission from Walter Kappe that brought him into contact with the three things that the saboteurs would have needed to survive and carry out their terrorist mission: Bundists who supported the German war effort, safe houses in which to lodge the conspirators away from inquiring eyes and ears, and printing presses with which to produce false identity papers. Fourth, Connelley, like J. Edgar Hoover himself, was not afraid to use the trump card of the Pastorius executions as a tool to bring Krepper to heel and to "encourage" him to divulge more information on German operatives in the United States.

Connelley had a very specific plan regarding how the FBI could bring Krepper in and sway him to see the light of the FBI's reason—a "vigorous interrogation of Krepper":

> It is believed that possibly if this individual were brought in on the early morning of some day without the knowledge of anyone else, that we might be able to get this information from him sufficient to require him to cooperate thereafter with us in disclosing other persons operating in the United States, if he is familiar with any such persons.[5]

Connelley had also thought through what might happen if Krepper refused to cooperate after he was brought in. He speculated that the bureau might need to bring in the Freys and the Schoenbachs, as well as Krepper's assorted girlfriends, and question them as well.

It is not surprising that J. Edgar Hoover himself got involved in the discussion around the pros and cons of bringing Krepper in. Hoover was in favor of "vigorously and thoroughly" interviewing Krepper. But even more, the top spy-breaker in America had other things in mind for Carl Krepper: "It is also desired that consideration be given to attempting to make arrangements for Krepper to serve as a double agent, dependent upon the cooperation obtained from him."[6] Carl Krepper as a "double agent" was a fascinating concept for Hoover and the bureau to consider. After all, Krepper was still an American citizen. He still had family in his adopted country. Nothing was detailed, though, in J. Edgar Hoover's reflections on the effort or the encouragement that would be necessary to try and get Krepper to willingly serve as a double agent for the United States against the Reich. As Connelley had previously speculated, Krepper was likely a difficult individual to try and turn.

FURTIVE GLANCES

Apparently, there was good reason to wonder about Krepper's response to being brought in by the bureau. Among the records contained within Krepper's FBI file is a report of two serious blunders that had taken place just several days apart in September 1942. Very similar in origin and in effect to what had happened with the Immigration and Naturalization Service questioning of Krepper earlier in 1942, these blunders on the part of two separate but friendly services had likely made it impossible to turn Krepper into a double agent.

As it was treated in a November 27, 1942, report by Special Agent Charles L. Green, in September, Krepper had experienced two incidents that would likely have hurt the bureau's chances of winning Krepper over. The first revolved around a New York Police Department patrolman named Frederick Schuchman.[7] A few minutes before four on the afternoon of September 22, Krepper left Schoenbach's apartment on his way back to 68 James Street in Newark. A portion of his route took Krepper to the 57th Street Eighth Avenue subway station, where he walked under the tunnel. Apparently, Officer Schuchman was also in the tunnel when his perceptive eyes observed Krepper being trailed by two men whom he took to be thieves. In reality, they were FBI special agents (Stanley D. Baskin and L. Vernon Ewing). Up to that point, Krepper had no idea that he was being followed. For their part, the FBI agents trailing Krepper on September 22 had no idea that an off-duty police officer had noticed them. Neither did they have any idea that the officer had informed Krepper about their presence. All the agents knew was that Krepper disappeared from under the tunnel into a corner of Central Park. It looked to the agents as if he may have gone into the bar of the Central Park Hotel. But all that Special Agents Baskin and Ewing knew was that Krepper had disappeared.

They would later learn that, after he burst into the nearly empty hotel bar, Krepper ran through the establishment in a frightened manner saying, "Two men are following me!" Krepper apparently escaped out a side door before Special Agent Baskin followed him into the bar. The agent was then greeted by the only bar patrons with a question of whether or not he was following someone. Special Agent Baskin feigned knowledge of the incident, whereupon a bar patron then stated that a "'large man' had just hurried through a bar," saying that he was being followed. Baskin then left the bar to regroup with his colleague outside.

The next day, September 23, Krepper was overheard telling Schoenbach that he had been followed by two men the day before, but that he had given them the slip. A few days later, on September 25, Special Agents Baskin and Ewing were standing on the corner of 10th Avenue and 57th Street, when the now off-duty patrolman approached Baskin and identified "himself by a shield as a patrolman assigned to the 18th Precinct of the New York Police Department."[8] The officer asked Baskin if he was "following or waiting for a person on that street." Baskin said no. Schuchman then told Baskin that he had been observed on September 22, 1942, with another man (whom the officer did not know was Special Agent Ewing). The patrolman then stated that it was clear that the two men, Baskin and Ewing, were following a third man. Schuchman then contacted Krepper, who identified himself as "Reverend Carl Krepper." Krepper thereupon told the officer that he was a stamp dealer, and gave as his address the Schoenbach Stamp Exchange. The officer stated that Krepper "did not know why he was being followed as he had not done anything and was in possession of nothing of value." When he heard Krepper speak, the officer said that he recognized that the man before him was German, "and at that time he realized and feared that he had probably 'blown up' some case." The officer believed that he "had gained Krepper's confidence and might be of assistance in any investigation being conducted." He then took Krepper up

on an invitation to visit his "office" at the Schoenbach apartment, which
he did. Krepper was not there. Later that day, Special Agent Baskin went
to the 18th Precinct on West 54th Street to verify that Schuchman was
who he said he was. On September 28, Baskin went back to the station
to "advise Schuchman of his identity. . . . Schuchman was requested not
to contact Reverend Krepper again either on the street or at his residence." The officer was advised to treat their discussion "in strictest confidence." The officer promised he would do so, but he "claimed this
action [was] taken by him to prevent possible robbery."

Even more would transpire to compound Krepper's paranoia and
fuel his worries that he was being watched. Several days after what the
FBI called the "Schuchman incident," Krepper and Schoenbach were
brought in and questioned by an Inspector of the Foreign Funds Control
Division of the United States Treasury, established in November 1941.
An Inspector Gershin had visited Alvin Schoenbach's on October 1,
1942. The inspector was interested in "stamps issued by Germany or
by German occupied countries since their occupation and since
the United States has been at war with Germany."[9] Schoenbach told
Gershin that stamps of that sort were provided to him by "Reverend
Krepper." Gershin called both Krepper and Schoenbach into his office
on October 2. Krepper was asked about his background, his recent residence in Germany, and the purchase of the German stamps he brought
into the United States in December 1942. Krepper claimed to have
bought the stamps "from some Jewish person in Lisbon," and stated that
this Portuguese Jewish stamp merchant had also given him the name
and address of Schoenbach as a resource to assist in selling the stamps.
As the selling of such stamps was illegal in the United States at that time,
the Foreign Funds Control Division Inspector required Schoenbach
and Krepper to produce an inventory of Krepper's stamps, as well as a
detailed list of all foreign and domestic sales conducted by them.

The bureau learned that the questioning of Schoenbach and Krepper
was part of a larger investigation that had to do with the "importation and
sale of stamps issued in Axis and Axis controlled countries which is in
violation of the foreign funds control regulations."[10] While what the two
men were doing was illegal, Krepper and Schoenbach were apparently
small fry in a much bigger kettle of fish in which the Treasury Department
was interested. Therefore, after Special Agent Green informed Inspector
Gershin that there was an ongoing investigation of Krepper that revolved
around national security issues, Gershin agreed to put the Treasury
Department investigation of Krepper and Schoenbach in abeyance.

The combination of these two experiences, with Patrolman Schuchman and Inspector Gershin, caused Krepper a great deal of worry. Agents saw that he continuously turned around when outdoors, and at least on one occasion, he even had Marianne Mayer turn around for him to look for someone following him when he entered a subway station.[11] Between a New York police officer and a Foreign Funds Control Division inspector doing their jobs, Carl Krepper, German espionage agent, was feeling that the walls were closing in upon him. Little did he know the full extent of the federal case that was being built against him, or the sheer volume of resources that had gone into pursuing him.

Things would come to a head at 3 p.m. on October 7, 1942, when, after the phone call from the unknown German man insisting on a meeting at the Selwyn Theatre, Krepper would have something of a nervous breakdown. "Krepper . . . walked the entire distance to 162 East 84th Street, entering Central Park at Columbus Circle and leaving the park at 79th Street and Fifth Avenue." This meandering journey through New York's Central Park was clearly a direct result of the two unconnected blunders that were out of the control of the bureau but that nonetheless conspired to get in the way of the FBI's investigation. Special Agent Green reported:

> It was noted by reporting agent who was conducting the surveillance on that date that Krepper's actions were somewhat peculiar as if he may have been intoxicated or ill. Walking through the park, Krepper stopped on three occasions and sat on park benches for considerable periods of time. He appeared to be worried and was continually drawing very hard on the pipe he was smoking. When he walked, his gait was unsteady at times and on more than one occasion after leaving the park, he stumbled and almost fell down. He was continually casting furtive glances around throughout the time he was walking to 162 East 84 Street. . . .[12]

After the phone call from the unknown man on October 7, Krepper was seen to be almost falling apart, psychologically and emotionally. In addition, circumstances out of the control of the FBI had made Carl Krepper suspicious to the point of paranoia. His suspicions would have been well founded if he had only known the extent of the FBI apparatus in place to catch him in the act of espionage. Over the next several days, as he recovered from his episode in Central Park, Krepper would find comfort in the arms of several women. As he went between the homes of Margaret Diehl and Marianne Mayer, Krepper would take a pass on the meeting at the Selwyn Theatre and regroup.

A CHANGE OF SCENERY

A significant change came for Krepper on January 5, 1943. After the events of late September and early October, Krepper sought new employment on the New Jersey side of the Hudson River. On January 25, under the name of "Charles Krepper," the sometime employee of the Schoenbach Stamp Exchange was hired by H. Braverman and Company, Certified Public Accountants, as a junior accountant.[13] Instead of traveling into Manhattan each day, Krepper had less than two miles to commute to the Newark office of H. Braverman and Company, located at 1060 Broad Street in Newark, New Jersey. The bureau knew that the company was "principally engaged as municipal accountants," and that it also audited the books for a ceramic company in Keasbey, New Jersey (located between Edison and Perth Amboy). Harry Braverman had built up a strong and reliable business in New Jersey, having worked for the New Jersey State Attorney General, and serving as the chief examiner for the department of banking and insurance of the state of New Jersey. He was, furthermore, well respected by the U.S. Treasury Department in Washington, D.C.

During Krepper's trial, Braverman testified that Krepper had worked on municipal audits in a number of different communities in northern New Jersey, including Newark, Perth Amboy, Bound Brook, Manville, Englewood, Plainfield, Clifton, Bayonne, and West New York.[14]

Just two days after "Charles Krepper" was employed by Harry Braverman, the FBI approached Krepper's employer and asked him to provide the Newark field office "with complete information concerning Krepper's activities." Braverman willingly agreed to this request.[15] On February 11, 1943, just 17 days after commencing his employment at H. Braverman and Company, Charles Emil Ludwig Krepper signed his application for a Social Security number. The irony was likely not lost on Krepper, who had reluctantly registered for the draft as a non-naturalized alien in the First World War, and who had come to the United States on a mission to provide support to men planning to help overthrow American freedom. As he registered to become part of the Social Security system, Krepper was infiltrating himself deeper into American society. He was doing what those around him were doing. Whether or not he was planning on a future in the United States, when Charles Krepper, aka Carl

Krepper, received his Social Security number, he had tapped into a system that would leave a permanent record of his existence in America.

As he started his new job, Krepper also made a significant move that had the potential to bring him into a different sphere of influence and respectability that could further his cover in the United States. Working for H. Braverman and Company, Krepper could have access to a whole new range of municipal and business contacts. He did not know that the FBI had other plans for him.

While Charles Krepper sought to achieve a level of respectability within American society as an accountant, J. Edgar Hoover knew many of the secrets that Carl Krepper hoped would remain hidden during his time in the United States. When Krepper started working for Harry Braverman, Hoover and the bureau delved deep into Krepper's financial dealings going back to his arrival in the United States on December 16, 1941. Hoover scrutinized the information from the report of the Foreign Funds Control Section that detailed Krepper's stamp collection, brought with him from Europe. In his declaration to U.S. customs officials, he had said that his stamps from Axis countries were his own private collection, and were not for sale. On March 24, 1943, Hoover wanted the New York field office to investigate the possibility of prosecuting Krepper for a violation of U.S. customs laws by misrepresenting the nature of his stamp collection.[16] Stamps could be and were used as a form of underground currency, often unreported, and in the early 1940s, stamps from Axis countries and countries conquered by the Axis powers were highly collectable in certain circles. Krepper's stamps were basically an unreported asset. J. Edgar Hoover wanted to leverage his knowledge of Krepper's violation of the customs laws in the FBI's, and thereby the United States', favor.

Krepper would work for H. Braverman and Company from January 5 until July 30, 1943, and then again from October 18, 1943 to February 9, 1944. At that point, Krepper worked as a "chief steward," and then as a bookkeeper at the Downtown Club in Newark. It was 10 months later, while working as the chief steward of a club, that he was arrested at the home of his girlfriend in Newark. In the long term, Krepper's change of scenery brought him closer to the federal penitentiary in Lewisburg, Pennsylvania.

WHO IS PASTOR KAISER?

On February 19, 1943, the special agent in charge of the Newark field office, S. K. McKee, penned a "Personal and Confidential Letter to the

Director." The letter to Hoover offered McKee's reflections on another piece of mail that Krepper had received from Europe, written in German and dated October 19, 1942. The envelope was curiously addressed to "Sr. Don Carlos Krepper, c/o Eugene Frey, R.F.D. #2, Box 40 F, Rahway, N.J." The return address was "A. Kloess, C. Moya 2 Barcelona."[17] The letter, it turned out, was from Krepper's wife Bertha, and it was mailed through Pastor Kloess in Barcelona, Spain. It was one of a number of letters that made it through the Office of Censorship to Krepper from his wife. There were two things about this particular letter that stirred up the interest of the special agent in charge in Newark. The first thing was the mention of "Drasda." No one knew who or what "Drasda" was, and why Bertha would be receiving money from that source. McKee believed that Krepper needed to be "thoroughly interrogated" to discover why his wife was in the habit of receiving money from that person or agency. The second item of interest in Bertha's letter was her statement that "I have not heard from Pastor Kaiser for a long time."

There were a number of reference to "Pastor Kaiser" in Bertha's other correspondence to her husband. In a letter that she wrote on December 14, 1941, she said that she had sent her husband's "greetings to P. Kaiser."[18] She detailed for her husband how she entertained this "Pastor":

P. Kaiser was with us on Sunday evening December 12, and remained with us 3 hours, I refreshed him with nice buttercakes, good coffee and cookies as also a glass of wine, I assume that it pleased him very much, for he invited me, in case I sometime come to Stuttgart, to visit and become acquainted with his family, he told me that a man whom he knows well, spoke to you in Barcelona and that you appeared very nervous. I hope that this has changed. Well the Dice fell on the 11th of December. What will become of you, I ask myself and many others. . . . Since I am speaking of Kiel, it occurs to me that I spoke to P. Kaiser in regard to permission for a vacation. He said that everything was in order.

This letter from Bertha Krepper was written on December 18, 1941, from Büdelsdorf-Rendsburg. The reference to the three-hour visit with "Pastor Kaiser" is fascinating. This individual was treated to cake, cookies, coffee, and wine as an honored guest. He in turn was able to tell Bertha a bit about her husband and invite her to visit with his family in Stuttgart, and somehow he was able to grant permission for vacations. The "Pastor" was a very unusual character, to say the least. The hospitality shown to him by the wife of a fellow pastor would be not at all unusual, and Bertha's letters to her husband are otherwise filled with references to visits from various neighboring clergymen and their families. There was something different about the way Bertha always wrote to Pastor Krepper about "Pastor Kaiser." In time, the FBI would learn who this "Pastor" was and what he knew—and how, in the midst of a multifronted war, he could make things like vacations happen.

The mentioning of the dice falling on December 11 is an obvious reference to Adolf Hitler's declaration of war on the United States. The visit of "Pastor Kaiser" to Bertha Krepper came a week to the day after Germany declared war on the United States, and Bertha and "Pastor Kaiser" both knew that with the declaration of war, things would change for Carl Krepper. The long visit, the invitations to visit family, and the promises of vacations stand out. For all her homey discussion of cakes and cookies in her letter, Bertha obviously understood that there were many things that had changed, for Germany and for her husband and herself, and "Pastor Kaiser" was in some way trying to assure and comfort her at a very difficult time. He was also clearly a man who could get things done. When this letter was analyzed by the FBI laboratory in Washington, D.C., at first no one picked up on the unusual nature of these references to "Pastor Kaiser." As Bertha's letters continued to make curious references to this otherwise unknown man, some at the bureau, not the least of which being Special Agent in Charge McKee, became very suspicious.

"Krepper should also be closely questioned," McKee suggested, "regarding the identity of both 'Drasda' and 'Pastor Kaiser' and the connection of these individuals with the Krepper family."[19] It would come out later in 1944, when an undercover agent posing as a German saboteur had gained Krepper's confidence, that "Pastor Kaiser" was none other than Walter Kappe, the head of the *Abwehr* sabotage school that had sent eight men to try and wreak terror upon the United States. The bureau would also learn that the correct counter-password to "Pastor Kaiser" was "Yorktown." As they reread the correspondence between Carl and Bertha Krepper in the coming months, they recognized that Bertha Krepper was also a part of the whole plan.

McKee, along with a number of other men at the bureau, suggested Krepper's "detention" and a "thorough interrogation" of him if he proved uncooperative. There would be serious debate over the next months about how and when to bring Krepper in. Many agents wanted, as soon as possible, to lock up this man who they were sure was an enemy agent, a spy, who was living large, and who had the gall to register for a Social Security number in the country that he was working against. The arguments about how best to proceed with the eventual arrest and trial of Carl Krepper were long and detailed. Through those discussions a plan began to emerge.

SOME POSSIBILITIES

Many ideas were tossed around about how to best proceed with the Krepper case at the FBI headquarters and at the New York and Newark field offices. There were moments where Krepper seemed blissfully unaware of his surroundings, and then there were moments when he acted with real fear and paranoia. In order to exploit his knowledge as well as to stop him from supporting any future spies, everyone in the bureau needed to be on the same page. In the meantime, there were plenty of ideas floating around.

As early as December 4, 1942, the suggestion was made by the New York office that one of its agents call Krepper up on the telephone and pretend to be a saboteur.[20] This, it was hoped, would encourage Krepper to use the password "Franz Daniel Pastorius." Special Agent in Charge Foxworth contacted J. Edgar Hoover and made just this suggestion. He even had an agent in mind who had an "excellent" command of German, Peter Hoehl. Agent Hoehl would, Foxworth argued, "make contact in such (a) manner as will appear as genuine as possible." The bureau wanted Krepper to be caught in the act, so to speak, using the password that Kappe had given to him and to the Pastorius saboteurs. Foxworth believed this plan to be so good that he suggested that unless the New York office heard otherwise, they would go ahead with this proposal. At the bottom of this page in Krepper's file it is noted in handwriting that Foxworth had "[c]alled Donegan and [was] told to hold up on this until Mr. Connelley replies to our request regarding picking Krepper up." This note was scrawled on the page in question on December 18, 1942. Foxworth's plan was, without a doubt, a good one. But as the chain of command had to add its input, it was decided to put this plan on hold until other minds had evaluated the bureau's next step.

On December 5, 1942, Earl J. Connelley added his own reflections. While Connelley suspected that Krepper might be a "difficult individual to influence"[21] during questioning, he also believed that if he were brought in early in the morning, unbeknownst to anyone else, being aware, he might be made to cooperate in disclosing names of other

German operatives in the United States. If he refused to cooperate, Connelley suggested that there might be a need to also bring in the Freys and Schoenbachs, as well as Krepper's various girlfriends, and see if they could provide any information which could be used against him.[22]

Special Agent Duane L. Traynor also chimed in on this discussion on December 7, 1942. Traynor spoke on the phone with Assistant Director Earl J. Connelley about New York's suggestion to pick up and question Krepper, as well as the suggestion to use a German-speaking agent to call Krepper up and "see if some admissions of value might be obtained from him."[23]

According to Traynor, Connelley did not believe that this action could hurt anything in terms of the Krepper investigation. "We would have nothing to lose," Connelley said. A "skillful Agent might draw Krepper out" and encourage Krepper to introduce the bureau's agent as a "German saboteur to other German sabotage or espionage agents who Krepper knows about." Traynor believed that the bureau could flip Krepper and turn him into a double agent. Connelley commented that such an endeavor could be a "gamble," which, if it did not work, would entail putting Krepper into a tighter surveillance, as he would be a flight risk or give the bureau the "double-cross."

Traynor put forth Special Agent Peter Hoehl as the one who might do the talking on the telephone to Krepper. Connelley said that while he knew Hoehl, he did not believe that Hoehl "is the Agent for this particular assignment." Connelley went so far as to say that "Hoehl is probably not heavy enough to handle this thing skillfully."

As March 1943 rolled around, E. E. Conroy, Special Agent in Charge, New York, sent a report to J. Edgar Hoover detailing what he saw as possible future directions for the Krepper case.[24] As the top agent on the spot in New York City, Conroy thought through three possibilities for the bureau to consider. The first possibility was to actually physically pick Krepper up and "vigorously question him." The best case scenario for this possibility would be that Krepper would "break down and admit his connections with the saboteurs." Conroy reflected on whether this was a realistic goal. There was the possibility that, on the one hand, while Krepper's name was given to the saboteurs by Kappe, on the other hand, Krepper may not have known to whom his name was given or when he could expect to be contacted. "This is borne out," Conroy suggested, "by the fact that Krepper left Germany during October 1941 at a time when the Sabotage School of Quenz Lake was still only in formative stages and its membership not known." Dasch had confirmed to the bureau that the German Foreign Office had held up the opening of the school until just before it was scheduled to open in April 1942.

Another thing to consider if they simply picked Krepper up was the fact that, as Conroy saw it, "Krepper is possessed of plenty of nerve and clever enough."[25] For that matter, Conroy argued, when the sabotage plot made newspaper headlines in June 1942, the name of Krepper's handler, Walter Kappe, "was prominently mentioned." Conroy presumed that, while Krepper did not know for sure if the Pastorius saboteurs were expected to make contact with him, because Kappe had worked with Krepper in Germany, in time the saboteurs would have tried to make contact. The fact that the eight *Abwehr*-trained saboteurs were caught and six were executed would naturally have made Krepper more apprehensive and "cautious in his actions." He would, so Conroy suggested, do everything in his power not to be connected to Kappe.

The second possibility that Conroy suggested was that they could conduct a search of the Mayer home at 68 James Street when Mayer and Krepper were out. They might then be able to take a good look at the briefcase "that Krepper habitually carried with him." Just about every morning he carried it with him when he left whatever girlfriend's home he was visiting, and he would bring it home at night. Neighbors described him as always carrying what they described as a "bulging briefcase." Krepper was even known throughout the neighborhood around 68 James Street as "The Man with the Satchel."[26] He had not carried the briefcase since he stated working for H. Braverman and Company. He would begin carrying the bag again in February 1944, when he started work at the Downtown Club in Newark. The bureau wanted very much to get their hands on Krepper's briefcase that he had previously carried with him everywhere. Conroy believed that they could concoct a very plausible reason for searching the Mayer home. Nonetheless, on the flip side of that possibility was the likelihood that Krepper would not keep his valuable papers simply sitting in his case so that anyone and everyone could look at them any time he was not home. Conroy asserted that finding any papers associated with Kappe, the saboteurs, or other German agents in America, if Krepper had them, would not be easy.

The third possibility came from the Newark field office, which wanted to place an FBI agent in Marianne Mayer's boarding house, as long as there was a room to rent at that address: "Such a move, if successful, will in all probability result in obtaining more information regarding Krepper and his activities, Mrs. Mayer and others, than the Bureau has previously obtained through surveillances." These moves all had their own benefits and risks, and all had a chance of either success or failure. Conroy's reflections were added to the pile of suggestions that agents were formulating on a regular basis.

As the FBI finalized its plans to bring Krepper in, it used a combination of ideas put forth by their experts at the FBI headquarters in Washington and in the field. As the plan evolved, agents would use a combination of ideas and possibilities, making contact with Krepper by telephone, with several undercover agents posing as saboteurs, and they would bring him in and interrogate him. As they brought all their various resources and methods into play, the FBI would bring down and bring in Carl Krepper, "Nazi spy aide" and "German agent."

CHAPTER ELEVEN

The Arrest of a Nazi Agent

IT STARTED WITH A DROP-IN AND A LETTER

The bureau wanted to set up a situation for Krepper to meet with FBI men posing as German agents and catch him in the act, so to speak, as he laid out the extent of the Reich's clandestine network within the United States. That was the hope, at least. An important piece of the puzzle of the Krepper case was the appropriate use of approved passwords. George John Dasch had told the FBI that the reason he wrote it on the handkerchief was because that was the established password that Walter Kappe had given them in Germany, and that was the password they were to use when they met with Pastor Carl Krepper. Through the letters that Bertha Krepper sent to her husband, the bureau now knew that there was another password, "Pastor Kaiser." Which one would work, and with whom, the federal agents did not fully know. Their goal was to use those passwords and set up a multipronged sting operation that would enable them to catch Krepper in his role as a Nazi spy aide.

By March 11, 1944, the FBI had its assets in place to do this. On that date, an FBI agent posing as "Otto Kasten," a "Nazi saboteur," dropped by 68 James Street in Newark.[1] He met Marianne Mayer at the door and asked her if she were "Mrs. Krepper."[2] Krepper would later "reproach" "Otto Kasten" for both coming to his rooming house and for presuming that Marianne Mayer was Mrs. Krepper. "Otto Kasten" then met Krepper and used the Operation Pastorius password "Franz Daniel Pastorius." Krepper, the bureau reported, "refused to acknowledge" the password,[3] but agents believed that Krepper accepted the fact that "Otto Kasten" was who he claimed to be, a German agent.

The next stage of the FBI's operation took place on March 14, 1944, when "Kasten" sent a letter to "Pastor Krepper" at 68 James Street, Newark. The letter asked Krepper to meet "Kasten" at the corner of 109th Street and Columbus Avenue in Manhattan at 7:30 p.m. on March 16. Significantly, "Kasten" signed the letter with the second password, "Pastor Kaiser."

Now that the bait was set, the New York and Newark field offices hoped that Krepper would bite. If the second password worked, Krepper would arrive at 7:30 p.m., and "Kasten" would be in. If not, the bureau would have to come up with something fast and hope that Krepper would not be alerted to the fact that he was the subject of an FBI sting operation.

The meeting place was deliberately chosen, and provided easy access from public transportation. The location of the meet was set one block south of Morningside Park and the Cathedral of St. John the Divine in uptown Manhattan. Two blocks east was the northern end of Central Park, and two blocks northwest was Columbia University. This neighborhood epitomized the hustle and bustle of 1940s New York. It was near cultural and religious landmarks in the heart of the largest city in the United States. The meeting place between "Kasten" and Krepper was also a half mile south of Union Theological Seminary, where five years earlier, fellow German Lutheran pastor Dietrich Bonhoeffer had come for a second journey to the United States. The night that Krepper was to meet "Kasten," Pastor Bonhoeffer was imprisoned at Tegel Prison in Germany for his resistance to Hitler. It is an irony of history that both Bonhoeffer and Krepper were recruits of the *Abwehr*—Bonhoeffer worked under, and in league with, those members of the *Abwehr* who supported the overthrow of Hitler; Krepper worked for Walter Kappe as a loyal supporter of Hitler.

As the agents set up the apartments for this meeting, they knew that Walter Kappe had intended for the Pastorius saboteurs to hit two significant targets in Manhattan, the New York water supply and the Hell Gate Bridge. If the real saboteurs had met Carl Krepper in 1942, the agents recognized that New York could have been a very different place than it was on March 16, 1944.

In anticipation of the meeting, the bureau had rented several apartments at 969 Columbus Avenue, New York, one on the third floor and another on the fourth. In the apartment on the fourth floor, which was to be the meeting place between Krepper and the supposed German agent, they planted hidden microphones so that any conversation could be recorded. Listening in on the third floor were Special Agents George R. Fowler and Ludwig W. Oberdorf.

To the bureau's great relief, Krepper took the bait, and when he left 68 James Street, Newark, FBI agents followed him into Manhattan and uptown to the corner of 109th Street and Columbus Avenue. There, at 7:30 p.m., "Otto Kasten" was waiting for him. Krepper followed "Kasten" to the apartment at 969 Columbus Avenue, and on up to the fourth floor, where the two engaged in a two-hour long conversation. From Krepper's perspective, it had taken three long and somewhat difficult years to make this connection, and he knew what he had to do with an agent who had given the correct password.

With Agents Fowler and Oberdorf listening in on earphones, Krepper admitted that "Pastor Kaiser" was the correct password, and that the counter-password from Krepper was to be "Yorktown." Krepper then "admitted that he knew that 'Otto Kasten' was from Walter Kappe and that he would not have met 'Kasten' if 'Kasten' had not given the password 'Pastor Kaiser.'"[4] Krepper told the man he thought was a German spy that he himself had come up with the password "Pastor Kaiser," as it would not be unusual for a Lutheran pastor to refer to another pastor in conversation or in correspondence. Of course, the agents listening in on this conversation knew that it had almost worked. It took them years to realize who "Pastor Kaiser" really was. If it had not been for a few curious things in Bertha Krepper's letters where she mentioned that "Pastor Kaiser" was able to accomplish certain things that a pastor would not necessarily be doing, and one too many times that "Pastor Kaiser" was said to be expecting mail or sending greetings, no one would have been the wiser. Krepper said he knew that anyone using that password "must have come from Walter Kappe since only he and Walter Kappe knew this 'password.'" After two hours, Krepper returned to Newark. The agents who listened in to this conversation had heard what they needed to hear. Krepper had admitted to being in the United States at the behest of Walter Kappe and the *Abwehr*. He admitted to, and explained, the passwords that the bureau knew were so important to the Pastorius case and that could provide insight into understanding German espionage efforts elsewhere.

In the course of this meeting, "Kasten" told Krepper that he would need a passport, as he wanted to find work in a war plant. He told Krepper that there was one plant in particular that "he wanted to get into so he could put machinery out of order by putting sand into the equipment."[5] It seems that the factory "Kasten" had in mind was a factory that manufactured airplane bombsights.[6] Curiously, Krepper responded to this by saying that "Germany already had enough sights for thirty-thousand bombers," and, "Kasten" continued, "he (Krepper) wondered why they weren't bombing New York."

After two hours, Krepper traveled back to 68 James Street in Newark, undoubtedly both excited and a bit nervous. He would be excited to finally be doing what Kappe sent him to do; he would also be nervous that after nearly three years he was being activated.

It had taken a drop in to 68 James Street and a letter mailed to that address, but the FBI's plan was working. Krepper was talking.

HIS HEART WAS IN GERMANY

"Otto Kasten" and Krepper met again on March 22 back at the apartment that the bureau was renting at 969 Columbus Avenue. At this meeting, Krepper told "Kasten" that "he had four or five boarding houses that he could go back to, in case someone came to him to be hidden."[7] The only ones who came, Krepper said, were "those eight men who had been caught on the beaches, six of whom had been electrocuted." He had specific rooms available for a year, Krepper told "Kasten," but no one else came.

When questions about sabotage arose, Krepper had some very definite opinions that he shared with the prospective saboteur. He said that at the present time "it would be foolish to try any sabotage in the United States." Speaking of himself, Krepper said that as "a student of psychology he felt sabotage would arouse public opinion against Germany and hurts that country's chance to reach an agreement with America to end the war."[8]

Speaking about his arrangements with Walter Kappe, Krepper said that he had "signed an agreement in Germany not to tell anyone why he was in this country," and that he felt he was here "for the duration." He admitted that he had signed his agreement with Kappe in Berlin in September 1941. When he signed on to come to America he was given 1,000 Reichsmarks, as well as his passage to the United States.

Like the Pastorius agents who knew him as "Pas Krepper," Krepper would expect that any operative who came to him with the password

"Pastor Kaiser" knew that he was a pastor. With the ice broken, during this March 22 meeting Krepper told "Kasten" a bit about himself. He told his newfound compatriot about being pastor of his church in Germany, even while in the United States, and that his wife was receiving his yearly salary of 6,000 Reichsmarks a year. Deducted from that was the salary of his assistant pastor, who served in Krepper's place. Krepper told "Kasten" that even though he was an American citizen, "his heart was in Germany."[9]

"Otto Kasten" remained in contact with Krepper over the next several months. Then, on July 10, 1944, "Kasten" introduced Krepper to a man named "Willy Rudolph." He was introduced as another German saboteur. When Krepper met this new "German agent" at the apartment at 969 Columbus Avenue, he did not know that "Willy Rudolph" was another FBI special agent named Ludwig W. Oberdorf, one of the agents who had listened in on Krepper's first conversation at 969 Columbus Avenue. Krepper repeated the same basic information to "Rudolph" that he had told to "Kasten," that he "had a written agreement to put men up sent from Germany."[10] Krepper told "Rudolph" that he had "three rooms available and expected visitors," but they were caught and "electrified," referring to the Pastorius saboteurs. Krepper referred to the Pastorius operatives as "men from Kappe."

Krepper advised the younger "German agents" that it would be "foolish" to try and commit sabotage against the United States at that moment. The agents reported that Krepper "said they should wait."[11] "Kasten" then told Krepper that they were really not interested in sabotage any more, but were looking to "find a house where they could set up a radio transmitter to send to Germany information about defense plants in the United States."[12] The "German agents" then gave Krepper a list of houses that they thought would be suitable for them, and Krepper agreed to "look them over."

Over the course of six months, Krepper had been meeting with men he believed were agents sent from Germany by Walter Kappe. They had the correct password, and they seemed like they meant business. Unlike the October 7, 1942, phone call that had set Krepper nervously running through Central Park, Krepper went out of his way to meet with the agents and assist them as he could. He had admitted to a range of things that answered a number of questions on the bureau's part. Now that they had followed the suggestions that had been put forward by the top minds at the FBI, calling on Krepper, sending a letter to him with what turned out to be the proper password, and then meeting him in the guise of German agents, the next suggestion was to bring Krepper in. This they did on September 29, 1944.

PULLED IN: THE BEGINNING OF THE END

After getting what they could from him in the apartment at 969 Columbus Avenue, the Newark field office was charged with interviewing Krepper. Accordingly, Krepper was brought in from 68 James Street to the Newark field office on September 29, 1944. There he was interviewed and questioned about a variety of topics. It was hoped that this would scare him into opening up further about his work and what he knew about other operatives in the United States. According to one of the FBI reports, Krepper was

> questioned about his activities in Germany prior to coming to the United States in December, 1941. Krepper said that he wanted to come to the United States to retain his citizenship. He further stated that he wanted to get out of Germany $2,500 in American money which he had taken there in 1935, 1937, and 1938, and in order to get his money out of Germany, he had to be identified by Lieutenant Walter Kappe, who at the time was said to be in the Propaganda Ministry in Berlin, Germany.[13]

This was a line that he repeated publicly time and time again. Krepper then told the bureau his other line—that in order to get his money, he agreed to do two things for Kappe in the United States:

> first, to tell people in the United States that Germany was not responsible for the war and to paint the picture as favorably as possible for the German people; second, to furnish a hide-out for the German-American Bund members who were allegedly being "persecuted" in the United States at that time.

Under interrogation, Krepper also confirmed that Kappe and he had devised the password "Pastor Kaiser" and it's response, "Yorktown." When "Pastor Kaiser" appeared in letters, it referred to Walter Kappe. As he had told the "German agents" in New York, so he told the FBI, that the name "Pastor Kaiser" would not draw suspicion as it would refer to just "another pastor." Krepper denied all culpability or wrongdoing. His conscience was clear, except for one thing, he said. He told the agents at the Newark field office that "[t]he only mistake he had made was in not coming to the FBI to tell them about his meetings with 'Otto Kasten.'" Over six months Krepper had unwittingly told the bureau a great deal. Now it was time to end Krepper's "mission." A federal grand jury in Newark indicted Krepper on a number of charges: violating the United States censorship laws, the Foreign Agents' Registration Act, and the Trading with the Enemy Act, as well as conspiracy to commit sabotage.

"EX-PASTOR SEIZED AS NAZI SPY AIDE"

The axe fell for Carl Krepper on the morning of Wednesday, December 20, 1944. Just as he was preparing to leave for his day's work at the Downtown Club, as the United States was in the midst of what would be the deadliest battle of World War II, the Battle of the Bulge, special agents from the FBI entered 68 James Street and took Krepper away. As the German Reich launched what they called "the Ardennes Offensive," Krepper, 60 years old, an American citizen whose heart was in Germany, was taken into custody by federal agents. It was discovered that in his 12- by 16-foot apartment on the parlor floor Krepper had a daybed, a couch, a wardrobe, a desk, and "a three-foot shelf of romantic German novels."[14] He was arraigned before the U.S. commissioner, William J. Bartholomew, in Newark, New Jersey.[15] The assistant United States attorney, Vincent Hull, appeared before Judge Thomas F. Meaney.[16] Krepper's bail was set at 30,000 dollars, and in lieu of bail he was taken away to the Hudson County Jail in Jersey City. During the Battle of the Bulge, 100,000 German soldiers were killed, wounded, or taken prisoner. American forces saw 81,000 killed, wounded, or taken prisoner. It was a desperate battle that raged on from December 16, 1944, to January 16, 1945, and victory could have won the war in Europe for either side. When he was arrested on December 20, some of the bloodiest fighting of the entire war was taking place, and Americans had no idea if they would win the battle or the war. In the midst of this national turmoil, Carl Krepper's arrest was an important statement as the United States tracked and caught an agent of the Third Reich in the heart of America. Krepper would have been shocked to see the level of attention his arrest elicited throughout the world. The arrest of the Lutheran pastor turned Nazi agent made headlines in America and around the globe. The arrest of an enemy agent in Newark made the front page of the *Newark Evening News* on the very day of Krepper's arrest: "Nab Ex-Pastor as Nazi Agent: Invisible Ink Address on U-Boat Saboteur on Long Island Is Clew [sic]." The *New York Times* front-page story on December 21 said it all: "Ex-Pastor Seized as Nazi Spy Aide: Conspiracy to Help 8 Saboteurs of June, 1942, Is Charged in Newark Indictments." In Carteret, New Jersey, the arrest of one of the town's former pastors made the front page of the *Carteret News* on Friday, December 22, 1944, just two days after his arrest: "Indicted Nazi Is Known Here: 'Contact' for Saboteurs Once Local Minister and Tax Employe [sic]." Headlines such as these appeared in newspapers in just about every state in the Union. Even the *Canberra Times* in Australia covered the story on its front page on December 22: "German Cleric Indicted for Sabotage." Photos of the clean-shaven Krepper were printed in newspapers all over the world. He apparently tried to cover his face when photographers first tried to take his photo, but upon being urged to uncover his face, he stood full-faced and glared stoically into the cameras.

Krepper's arrest touched a raw nerve in war-weary America. As our soldiers were bleeding and dying in Europe and in the Pacific, we had in our midst a naturalized American citizen who took sides against his adopted country at a time of war. J. Edgar Hoover got out in front of the media coverage: "The arrest of the sixty-year-old naturalized American citizen of German birth followed two years of intensive inquiry by the Federal Bureau of Investigation, Director J. Edgar Hoover revealed."[17] Among the information provided by the bureau on December 20 was the fact that Krepper's name and address were found on the saboteur handkerchiefs, as well as the password that broke open the case, "Pastor Kaiser," and the response, "Yorktown." The identity of Walter Kappe, and Bertha's letters with information on Kappe were all presented to the press, as well as details such as the fact that Krepper was the "Old Man with Satchel" to his neighbors. Before the end of December, most of America would have read something about the Reverend Carl Emil Ludwig Krepper and his role in the war in the United States.[18]

Specifically, the charges against Krepper were as follows:

1. Krepper was to establish himself here as a United States citizen in order to provide lodging and other facilities for German secret agents sent to this country.
2. He was to communicate with Kappe and his wife, Bertha Krepper, in Germany, keeping them apprised of his whereabouts and availability.
3. Kappe, or Bertha Krepper, or certain other co-conspirators not named in the indictment, would come to this country for the purpose of committing sabotage and would be given assistance and refuge by Krepper.[19]

If Krepper were found guilty and sentenced to the maximum, he could have received 32 years in prison and a 30,000-dollar fine.

NAZI SPY TRIALS

On December 29, 1944, Krepper stood before federal judge Thomas F. Meaney and plead "not guilty." He also told the judge that he had no funds to pay for an attorney. The judge appointed a former president of the American Bar Association and future New Jersey State chief justice, Arthur T. Vanderbilt, as Krepper's counsel. Judge Meaney set Krepper's trial for February 13, 1945.[20] On January 10, 1945, Krepper was "again indicted for violation of the Censorship Laws [the letters back and forth to Germany via Spain using a password], trading with the enemy [his Axis stamp collection, which, at least in part, helped fund his mission in America], and conspiracy to violate the Censorship Laws and to commit sabotage [through his admissions to "Kasten" and "Rudolph," as well as the all-important Pastorius handkerchief].[21] His January 10 indictment included the addition of co-conspirators, the eight saboteurs, Lieutenant Walter Kappe, and Krepper's wife, Bertha.

The selection of the jury commenced on Tuesday, February 13, and within 20 minutes, seven men and five women were chosen, with one man and one woman as alternates.[22] Prosecuting Krepper was Assistant United States Attorney Vincent Hull, and George R. Sommer replaced Vanderbilt on Krepper's defense. In opening arguments, Hull announced that he would call a "score" of witnesses, including Pastorius saboteur Ernst Peter Burger, who testified on the first day of the trial about his own background and his dealings with Walter Kappe.

The second day of the trial brought testimony from bureau agents who told the court how they found Krepper's name and address on the handkerchiefs that were discovered on Pastorius saboteurs Dasch and Kerling when they were captured. The highlight of the second day of the trial had FBI laboratory chemist Joseph W. McGee called to the stand. He brought out the Pastorius handkerchiefs, and in a dramatic demonstration that made headlines around the country, he revealed Pastor Krepper's name on each of them.[23] Bringing out a small table and an enamel tray into which he dipped the handkerchiefs, McGee showed how the names and addresses of the Pastorius saboteur contacts were written in visible ink. Before the eyes of the jurors, who one by one filed past the little wooden table, they beheld the name and address of the last American Nazi spy aide who was on the run: "Pas Krepper, c/o

E. Frey, RFD No. 2, Rahway." Typical of the press coverage was the *New York Times* headline that read "Secret Printing on Saboteur's Handkerchief Restored at Krepper Spy Trial in Jersey" (February 15, 1945). Vincent Hull then read for the record Krepper's signed statement from his September 29, 1944, questioning by the FBI in Newark. In his own words, the jury heard Krepper admit that in 1941 he had entered into an agreement with Lieutenant Walter Kappe, head of the German spy school near Berlin, to come to America to "do propaganda work for Germany in the United States and provide funds and haven for Bundists who were persecuted by Jews."[24]

The jury heard in Krepper's own words that Walter Kappe had arranged for Krepper's trip to America in 1941, and that he was to conduct propaganda on behalf of the German Reich. The FBI chemist demonstrated how both Pastorius handkerchiefs had Krepper's name and address written on them in invisible ink. In addition to Krepper's own statement, Krepper's words to "Otto Kasten" were read into evidence as well. Krepper insisted that he had "tried to dissuade the German from carrying out his proposed activities," but the fact that Krepper had told the supposed agents to "wait" was understood by the prosecution as a clear indication that he had been sent here for more than propaganda. Another piece of evidence that was brought forward by the prosecution were the letters he had received from his mail drop in Spain. Besides mail that was sent to him in care of his stepson, Eugene Frey, in Rahway, Krepper also received mail from Spain (that had been sent from Germany) through an old parishioner of his in Rahway named Anthony Boresch. Boresch and Krepper's stepdaughter-in-law, Hilda Frey, testified to the arrival of these letters to Krepper from Spain. Introduced into evidence as well was a letter that Krepper had dictated to Hilda Frey that was ultimately sent on through Spain to Germany after war was declared. Such communications violated federal law and were considered to be communications with the enemy. Two of the letters received at the Boresch home were apparently self-addressed in Krepper's own hand, and they too were introduced into evidence. The references in the various letters to "Pastor Kaiser," aka Walter Kappe, were brought out and highlighted. The jury took note of what were considered to be such illegal communications with the enemy at a time of war.

Krepper's life in America as a pastor was laid out for the jury. The jury heard about Krepper's trips back and forth to Germany before the war, as well as his anti-Semitic rantings about wanting to help "Bundists persecuted by Jews." Thirty-four government witnesses were called, including 15 FBI agents, in addition to Nazi saboteur Ernst Peter Burger.[25] In all, it was a pretty impressive case against the former American clergyman turned Nazi spy aide.

Several interesting developments came out in Krepper's testimony on the stand.[26] Krepper denied that he had become a member of the Nazi Party, or that he had to do so to remain in office as a pastor in Germany. Vincent Hull asked Krepper "[w]hy Pastor Niemöller was arrested in Germany." This is a reference to the Confessing Church pastor, Martin Niemöller, who at that moment was imprisoned at Dachau for his resistance to Hitler. Krepper replied, "Because he said the German people were bestowing upon Hitler the honors that only belong to God." Even though he was an ordained pastor and still technically pastor of a church back in Germany, Krepper also admitted to rarely attending church in the United States since his arrival in December 1941. "Christ did not say we had to," Krepper stated. "It says so here in my Bible. . . . Will you permit me to read it?" he asked. Judge Meaney "said he did not question Krepper's knowledge of the Bible."

The defense finally rested on February 21, 1945. The trial only lasted six days. It only took the jury an hour and 20 minutes to return a verdict of guilty. Krepper was said to have received the guilty verdict "without emotion." Judge Meaney remanded Krepper back to the Hudson County Jail in Jersey City in lieu of his 30,000-dollar bail. March 16 was set as the date of Krepper's sentencing. He could have received two years in prison, with a 10,000-dollar fine. It was noted that Krepper would also go on trial facing three further indictments on charges of violating the Foreign Agent Registration and censorship statutes.

On March 14, 1945, Krepper was tried once again at the federal courthouse in Newark on indictments for violating the Trading with the Enemy Act and censorship laws; these involved the sending of a coded message to Germany after the formal declaration of war. Five witnesses were called by the prosecution, including Hilda Frey, who testified that her stepfather-in-law dictated a letter to her to her mother-in-law, Bertha Krepper, on December 19, 1941. In that letter Krepper asked her to write that he had arrived in the United States, and to give "greetings to Pastor Kaiser."[27] No witnesses were called for the defense. By mid-afternoon on March 14, the case went to the jury, and 40 minutes later, Krepper once again heard the verdict of guilty as charged. As the *Newark Evening News* headline put it, Krepper was "[c]onvicted for the second time in three weeks" (March 15, 1945).[28] The *New York Times* headline read "Krepper Guilty as Spy: Former Lutheran Minister Convicted after One-Day Trial" (March 15, 1945). Krepper was facing a maximum of 20 additional years behind bars plus a fine of 20,000 dollars. Krepper was once again remanded to the Hudson County Jail to await sentencing.

On March 23, 1945, Krepper was sentenced at the United States District Court in Newark. As anticipated, he received the maximum sentences:

> [T]wo years on the conspiracy indictment and ten years on each of
> the two counts of the censorship indictment. . . . The court ordered
> the two ten-year sentences to run concurrently and the two-year
> sentences to run consecutively with the ten-year sentences, mak-
> ing a total sentence for Krepper of 12 years.[29]

Like his arrest, Krepper's sentencing also made headlines. By then, U.S. troops had won the Battle of the Bulge, and the war in Europe was continuing to turn in favor of the Allied forces. Krepper went to serve his term at Lewisburg Federal Penitentiary in Pennsylvania. At Lewisburg were other German-Americans convicted of espionage and of being aides to spies, including the wrongfully convicted Lutheran pastor Kurt Molzahn. Like Krepper, Molzahn was a Kropp Seminary graduate who was accused of assisting a Nazi spy ring. Molzahn was eventually released and pardoned by President Eisenhower.[30]

Despite the overwhelming amount of evidence against him, Krepper's attorney George R. Sommer worked tirelessly in attempting to secure an appeal for Krepper's conviction. In November 1946, Krepper would seek an appeal from the U.S. Circuit Court of Appeals in Philadelphia. The court ordered Krepper's release while he awaited the outcome of his appeal, but he could not raise the 25,000-dollar bail, and so he remained in prison.[31] George S. Pearse, for Sommer, argued for an appeal based on five perceived "errors" that they held were found in Judge Thomas Meaney's handling of Krepper's case. They held that the district court "erred" in allowing Krepper to be charged with a violation of the "First War Power Acts, 1941" in regard to the letter that Krepper sent to his wife Bertha (dictated to Hilda Frey) in December 1941. The federal charge against Krepper was that the letter was sent after the "First War Powers Act, 1941" (December 18, 1941) was made the law of the land. While Krepper denied this, the government had argued that, according to Hilda Frey's testimony, this letter was indeed sent after the law was put in to effect. By writing to his wife care of "Reverend Kloess, Barcelona," and by using a coded password ("Pastor Kaiser"), Krepper violated federal law. Pearse argued that because Krepper wrote the letter to his wife, who was a United States citizen, there was "no proof to support the allegations of either Count of the indictment." Pearse claimed that Krepper's motion to Judge Meaney to "direct a verdict" was denied improperly, as, Krepper claimed, there was no proof of the charges against him. The district court also erred, Pearse claimed, because, Krepper "could not be guilty of the offense charged" (that is, the "Trading with the Enemy Act") because the law did not go into effect until the day after the letter was written. The district court erred further, Pearse stated, by not dismissing the first count, and by not including "certain phraseology" from the grand jury indictment of December 15, 1944. Pearse's arguments were not convincing, and on December 11, 1946, the Third Circuit Court of Appeals ruled against Krepper's appeal:

> We, therefore, conclude that the defendant-appellant (Krepper) had a fair, just, impartial trial, and no cause for reversal has been found to exist in the record, and in view of our rulings in connection with the assignments of error, judgment of the court below is affirmed.[32]

Sommer then appealed Krepper's conviction to the U.S. Supreme Court. Krepper's appeal to the Supreme Court was presented by Sommer in *Carl Emil Ludwig Krepper v. United States of America*.[33] Krepper's petition was filed in February 1947 (during the Supreme Court's October term in 1946). Sommer asserted that when the Third Circuit Court of Appeals in Philadelphia expressed its opinion and denied Krepper's appeal in December 1946, it had expressed an opinion that was in conflict with previous decisions of both the United States Supreme Court and with other circuit courts around the country. Sommer's argument was that the district court that convicted Krepper had improperly struck what Judge Meaney had called "excessive verbiage" from Krepper's grand jury indictment of December 15, 1944. Sommer claimed that by so doing, Judge Meaney had incorrectly altered the indictment for which Krepper was eventually convicted. By allowing the district court's decision to stand, Sommer argued, the Third Circuit Court of Appeals, along with the original District Court that convicted Krepper, had erred. Sommer once again argued that the Trading with the Enemy Act was not in effect when Krepper wrote his letter to Bertha Krepper, and that there was no proof that the letter was written after the law was put into effect. He also questioned whether or not Bertha Krepper could be reasonably considered to be an enemy of the United States or an ally of an enemy according to the law. The government argued that, according to Krepper's own testimony to the FBI on September 29, 1944, Krepper told his wife that the code or password "Pastor Kaiser" was meant to indicate Walter Kappe, and that his letters to Bertha were to be a conduit for messages between Krepper and Kappe. By sending these letters back and forth via Reverend Kloess in Barcelona, Krepper was violating federal law. On March 2, 1947, the Supreme Court refused to review Krepper's conviction.[34]

Sommer continued to press for the dismissal of Krepper's indictments, and in 1947, he went back to the federal district court in Newark, where he successfully argued for the dismissal of three of the charges against Krepper. The dismissal of the charges was approved by U.S. Attorney General Tom C. Clark. The three dismissed charges actually were for things that Krepper admitted to doing when he was questioned by the FBI and in the recordings of conversations between himself and "Otto Kasten" in the apartment on Columbus Avenue in 1944: 1) that he was a German agent; 2) that he attempted to send messages to enemies of the United States in Germany and Spain; and 3) that he conspired with his wife Bertha and with "Walter Kappe, German spy teacher, against the security of the United States."[35] On July 1, 1947, the dismissal of these charges were filed in federal court. Nonetheless, despite this small victory, Krepper remained in Lewisburg on the other charges. In October 1948, George Sommer once again unsuccessfully argued before the Third Circuit Court of Appeals in Philadelphia for an appeal of Krepper's conviction for violating the censorship and trading with the enemy laws. A final attempt was made to go back to the U.S. district court in Newark in 1949, where Sommer once again argued before Judge Thomas Meaney that the "current war hysteria" as well as Krepper's original German birth led the prosecution to an illegal conviction. The repetition of Sommer's arguments did not convince the judge who originally convicted him in 1945, and therefore the motion for a new hearing was denied on November 7, 1949.

Krepper would remain in prison until February 3, 1951, when he was paroled.[36] After his release from prison, Krepper tried to rehabilitate himself, eventually residing in Sandisfield, Massachusetts, where he died on June 21, 1972. Prior to and after his release from prison, through friends in the United States and in Germany, he tried to recast himself as a victim of war-related hysteria.

CHAPTER TWELVE

"God and the Reich Were Closely Identified in His Mind"

THE PASTOR KREPPER DEFENSE COMMITTEE

Even prior to his release on parole from Lewisburg in 1951, Carl Krepper had friends who sought to rehabilitate his name. With the war over and the Marshall Plan (officially known as the European Recovery Program) rebuilding war-torn Europe, there were some who claimed that, like Pastor Kurt Molzahn, Krepper was the victim of anti-German war-related hysteria. As he had run out of legal options around November 1949, efforts were being made to secure a presidential pardon for Krepper by what became known as the "Pastor Krepper Defense Committee (PKDC)."[1] Within the United Lutheran Church in America (ULCA), the Committee on German Interests sought to strengthen pastoral ministry within German-American Lutheran congregations. Fellow Kropp Seminary graduates involved with this committee worked with several German-American laypersons to secure Krepper's release and a full pardon. It is not known if the members of this committee knew the full extent of the FBI's investigation of Krepper, or what was contained in his German church personnel record—that Krepper bragged about flying the swastika flag in church and that he indeed had a secret mission to come to the United States in December 1941.

A spokesman for the PKDC was Alfred Fetz, a naturalized German-American from Detroit, Michigan, who had known Krepper in Newark. He tried to secure the support of the United Lutheran Church in America for the work of the committee. In December 1949, Alfred Fetz sent a "vehement appeal" to ULCA president Dr. Franklin Clark Fry on behalf of Pastor Krepper.[2] Dr. Fry replied to Fetz on January 19, 1950, stating, "[A]lthough I am devoted to even-handed justice, I am in unable to be an effective advocate for him [Pastor Krepper] or to even to judge his innocence for myself." Dr. Fry encouraged Fetz to work through Pastor John Teutsch, a German-American pastor involved with the Committee on German Interests, and pastor of St. Peter's German-Saxon Evangelical Lutheran Church in Detroit, Michigan (*Deutch-Sächsich Ev. Lutherische St. Petrus Kirche*). Pastor Teutsch expressed the hope of the PKDC that the ULCA as a whole would be "oriented in the matter of Pastor Krepper and do protest against his mistrial."[3] According to Pastor Teutsch, the PKDC did not expect that the ULCA would "unroll a new lawsuit in the matter," but that there would be a "protest by the church." The PKDC hoped to use the pressure of the leadership of the American Lutheran Church to secure Krepper's pardon and to rehabilitate his name.

Other pastors interested in the work of Krepper's "defense committee" were the Rev. Heinrich A. Kropp, President of the German Seamen's Mission in New York, and the Rev. Fritz O. Evers, who had first greeted Pastor Krepper at his church in Englewood, New Jersey, upon his arrival in the United States in 1909. Among the lay participants in the PKDC was none other than Marianne Mayer.[4] At the same time she was working with the PKDC, she also traveled to Germany to make a formal request for Krepper's German church pension. On June 11, 1951, Mayer was granted a power of attorney for Krepper that was witnessed by the consul general of the Federal Republic of Germany. According to Bishop Wilhelm Halfmann, who had oversight of Krepper's congregation in Germany, Mayer came to him on September 24, 1951.[5] "Mrs. Mayer," Halfmann wrote, "knew a lot about the whole Krepper affair and among his friends she seems to be the one who has the courage to stand up for him." Mayer told Bishop Halfmann that Krepper was released on parole, "which may correspond to something of our release under police supervision." She told the Bishop that Krepper was "penniless and is sustained by friends." Bishop Halfmann stated that Krepper "asks for the payment of his pension. . . . A formal request made by Mrs. Mayer is to be expected soon." The bishop was unsure if the "judgment by the American court" would have "any consequences for his position as a minister of the

Lutheran Church." Mayer had stated to Bishop Halfmann that the court's decision was based on a "war-psychosis." The bishop knew the basics of Krepper's case, that he had been accused of "setting up a code for communication" with Germany. "Mrs. Mayer," he noted, "and some American pastors are attempting, through the mediation of *Kirchenprasesidenten* Dr. Fry, to bring the matter to President Truman to jump over the impenetrable wall of the American Gestapo. . . . So Mrs. Mayer openly calls the FBI, Federal Board (sic) of Investigation. . . ." Mrs. Mayer stated for a fact that "probably even before his departure from Germany" in 1935 the FBI was already shadowing Krepper. Bishop Halfmann doubted that this was the case, yet on its own the German church could "do nothing to help ensure Krepper's rehabilitation." Nonetheless, Halfmann wrote to Pastor Kropp to try and secure a "certificate" that stated that "if pastor Krepper was able to get out of his war-related conviction there would be no consequences for his ecclesiastical position." "If we would get such a certificate, then I think we would have a free hand in matters." Eventually, Mrs. Mayer was successful. Krepper was given official status as "retired" on the German church clergy roster. Krepper was then eligible to receive his pension from the German church.

THE FETZ RÉSUMÉ

Erick Fetz, a chemist from Orange, New Jersey, made the most vocal petition to the ULCA on Krepper's behalf. He claimed to have "intimate ties of friendship and creed" with Pastor Krepper, and he wrote a rambling 18-page document that he called a "résumé of the Case Krepper." Many of Erick Fetz's reflections in his summary of Krepper's story clearly contradict the facts as they are displayed in Krepper's German church personnel record, the parish records from St. John's Church, Newark, and his FBI file.

Fetz claimed that "Pastor Krepper was sent to prison in a wartime trial in 1944, which was a direct result of his pastoral work in Germany from 1935–1941."[6] Contrary to what Krepper himself had said of his return to Germany (that he went because he received a call to a congregation there), Fetz claimed that Krepper went back to Germany in 1935 "on a hurried call . . . to visit his dying mother."[7] As Erick Fetz became the spokesperson for Krepper's "defense," his words may express what Carl Krepper himself narrated of his personal story.

Fetz left out some pertinent information about Krepper's life, and he altered other details to suit his creative rewriting of Krepper's biography. Details that were incorrect in Fetz's résumé included the name of his first parish (St. John's Church in Williamstown, New Jersey); Krepper's ordination date (Fetz asserted that Krepper was ordained on January 10, 1910, instead of January 5, 1910, which Krepper stated); that Krepper submitted his resignation to his bishop in Germany, Bishop Paulsen, when he came to the United States in 1941 (which completely contradicts his German personnel record, which states that he remained a salaried pastor of the congregation until after the Second World War); that Krepper came back to the United States in 1941 because of the "attention of the Nazis," and because "he remained loyal to his principles and to the country which had adopted him, the United States" (contrary to the claims made by Krepper that he came back to the United States to make sure he did not lose his American passport, and to what came out in the FBI investigation, that he came on a mission from Walter Kappe);[8] that the Rev. Dr. Samuel Trexler, the president of the United Lutheran Synod of New York, promised "to look for such a vacancy" (contrary to what Trexler told the FBI agent who interviewed him during Krepper's investigation); that Trexler had him "stricken off the membership list . . . from the New York Synod" (he was actually transferred to the care of the German church, which was required and expected in such a situation); that Krepper had "brushes with Nazism" that "led him to . . . Berlin, in order to protest against the underhand maneuver of deliberately arranging the Hitler Youth Meetings at the same hours the Lutheran Church was giving her religious instructions" (this claim that Krepper had "brushes with Nazism" totally contradicts Krepper's own words, both in the parish record book of St. John's Church in Newark, and his German personnel record, where he boasted of flying the swastika in church and used the "Order Service" men to carry them into the church building; that the Nazi government did just that, arrange for Hitler Youth meetings during the hours of Confirmation classes was quite common); that Bishop Paulsen called him into his office and placed before him a document that declared his loyalty to the Führer, to which Krepper "violently [shook] his head"—that such loyalty oaths were common and required is the case, but in no document except the Fetz résumé is there any indication of Krepper not supporting the Führer through and through.

Fetz actually claimed that Krepper suffered through "personal surveillance by the Gestapo . . . and many personal humiliations because of his profession and American citizenship." Fetz also touched on the split between the clergy of the "German Christians" and the mainstream of

Lutheran clergy in Germany, who did not fully support the subjugation of church interests to the ideology of the Nazi Party. Fetz even made the audacious and fallacious claim that Krepper was never accepted onto the German church clergy roster. As his German church personnel records attest and his call documents in Germany make clear, he was indeed placed on the German church clergy roster. He even had received permission from the Reich minister of church affairs to be exempted from the requirement of citizenship in order to be permanently employed by the church. Contrary to what Fetz stated as fact, Krepper would eventually draw a pension from the German church. Fetz outrageously painted a picture of Pastor Krepper in Germany that portrayed him as "a Lutheran minister among the swaggering Nazi pagans."

In his résumé, Fetz also went through the FBI investigation and the federal charges against Krepper. He "contrasted" Krepper as a "loyal," "law abiding," and "unpolitical" [sic] American clergyman who "is serving a 10-year prison sentence as an innocent man!" Bertha Krepper, for her part, was portrayed as a victim of Walter Kappe, who was a "Nazi agent" who "gained Mrs. Krepper's confidence by posing as a friend." Fetz went on to explain how the FBI conducted a blundering investigation based not on facts, but on an almost personal dislike for Krepper (using Fetz's description of events). The prosecution, Fetz asserted, "strong-armed" the whole process, denying Krepper a fair trial. Fetz stated that Judge Meaney made a "calamitous mistake" in Krepper's trial, and therefore Fetz hoped to enlist the ULCA to correct the "scandalous frame-up of innocent Lutheran Pastor Krepper."

The Fetz manifesto offers a unique perspective on why Krepper accepted the call in Oldenburg in 1935. Without a doubt, this summed up what Krepper told others about his experiences as a pastor in Germany and in America:

> Pastor Krepper . . . subordinated his personal feelings and interests to the feelings and interests of the church—and in this case of ALL churches: Pastor Krepper perceived a unique opportunity of upholding the banner of the church in the rising tide of Nazism in view of the protection granted by his American citizenship.[9]

His congregation in Germany knew better. They fully understood that he came to the United States on a mission from the Nazi government, as "conscript of the *Wehrmacht*." That is why they were compelled to continue paying his salary of 6,000 Reichsmarks until November 26, 1945.

"TO TELL THE TRUTH IN LOVE"

In response to the Fetz résumé and the clergy who supported the PKDC, ULCA president Franklin Clark Fry reflected on the claims that Krepper and Erick Fetz asserted. He wanted to satisfy the "minds" and "consciences" of the leadership of the ULCA before he got involved in any plea for executive clemency on behalf of Krepper.[10] He wrote to the Reverend John Teutsch, who supported Krepper's clemency appeal, "To tell the truth in love, I have not been impressed with the judicial quality of the mind which prepared most of the documents in behalf of Pastor Krepper." He was referring specifically to claims made in the Fetz résumé, but behind it was a concern of the larger picture of what such support of Krepper would mean to the larger church. Fry had no patience with Fetz or his diatribe. In an April 10, 1950, letter to Erick Fetz, President Fry stated that the ULCA "will be unable to assume initiative in this case." His arguments were, first, that the church did not retain attorneys for such work, and second, that Krepper was no longer a member of a constituent synod of the ULCA.

Despite this setback, the PKDC continued to lobby on Krepper's behalf. Carl Krepper ended up living on Bathgate Avenue in the Bronx, not far from the Bronx Zoo. From there he fought for a full pardon. The PKDC secured the services of an attorney from Hoboken, Edward Stover, to represent Krepper's appeal for executive clemency. Stover exchanged a series of letters with Dr. Franklin Fry and the Reverend Robert E. Van Deusen, the secretary of the National Lutheran Council in Washington, D.C. On January 15, 1953, Van Deusen communicated to Stover that President Harry Truman had denied Krepper's petition for a pardon:

> President Truman has given specific instructions to his staff that there are to be no appointments of any kind between now and the end of his term in office. He is completely engrossed in the last-minute activities which will let him leave the White House with a clean desk next Tuesday.[11]

On January 22, Stover sent a formal request for a meeting to President Dwight D. Eisenhower. Van Deusen responded by reporting to Stover a conversation he had had with one of Eisenhower's administrative assistants regarding Krepper's request for a pardon. He was informed that "such an interview would not be possible and would have no particular value at this time."[12]

Attempting to be fair and just in regard to the Krepper case, on December 22, 1952, Dr. Fry forwarded Krepper's request to the U.S. pardon attorney. The attorney, Daniel M. Lyons, responded on July 6, 1953, denying the request. Krepper's term for parole would expire on March 4, 1957. Any requests to pardon Pastor Krepper would have to wait.

Instead of returning to Germany to join his wife, Carl Krepper remained in the United States. Even though he had claimed to "Otto Kasten" that his heart was in Germany, he ended up retiring to Sandisfield, Massachusetts. Krepper's wife Bertha traveled back to the United States one more time. She traveled on a German passport, and arrived in New York on October 18, 1956. She did not remain. Her son Eugene had died on July 7, 1947, and she was unable to attend his funeral as she had been co-indicted with her husband in 1945. When she returned to Germany, she left behind the husband who had left her as a conscript of the *Wehrmacht* and risked his life and well-being on a mission for the Third Reich. She had not seen her husband in 15 years. She retired to Wedel, a small city near Hamburg located on the Elbe River in Schleswig-Holstein, Germany, and died there on April 25, 1959.

Carl Krepper, who had transformed himself from a pastor in Newark into "the man with the satchel," died of bronchial pneumonia at the Pine Nursing Home in Great Barrington, Massachusetts on June 21, 1972, at the age of 88. A funeral service was held at the Hickey-Roy Funeral Home in Great Barrington and was conducted by the Rev. Walter K. Miller, previously pastor of the First Congregational Church (United Church of Christ) of Sheffield, Massachusetts.[13] His death certificate listed him a widower and his occupation was listed as "Minister." Krepper had no living relatives, and no one claimed his cremated remains. His ashes were eventually interred in an unmarked grave with other cremated remains at the Pittsfield Cemetery in Pittsfield, Massachusetts.

If Carl Krepper had been at the home of his stepson in Rahway, New Jersey, on June 21, 1942, the war in the United States could have become a very deadly thing. Adolf Hitler and Walter Kappe wanted to bring the war into the heart of America. Carl Krepper was to be the man to help make that happen. The Pastorius saboteurs might have succeeded in at least a portion of their deadly plan if they had met with him in Rahway. He was not home, and the saboteurs did not succeed. They were executed in the electric chair, and Carl Krepper went on to federal prison. He had come to the United States in 1909 to serve German-American

Lutheran Christians, but he returned in 1941 to help bring the Second World War to the very democratic system that had supported and nurtured him for two and half decades. His life concluded in obscurity, his legacy one of betrayal and subterfuge. The last word on the legacy of Carl Krepper should come from the man who wished to "speak the truth in love" regarding the Lutheran pastor turned Nazi spy. Reflecting on the case of Krepper's appeal for executive clemency, Dr. Franklin Clark Fry[14] noted: "Yes, Krepper was strongly pro-Nazi in sentiment. God and the Reich were closely identified in his mind."[15]

NOTES

CHAPTER ONE

1. E. Clifford Nelson (ed.), *The Lutherans in North America* (Philadelphia: Fortress Press, 1980), 37.

2. Harry J. Kreider, *The Beginnings of Lutheranism in New York* (Gettysburg, PA: Times and New Publishing Company, 1949), 7–12. The Lutheran Church in New Netherland dates to 1649, as Lutherans in Albany and Manhattan organized what in 1669 eventually became two separate congregations (First Lutheran Church in Albany, and St. Matthew's Lutheran Church in Manhattan).

3. *Protocol of the Lutheran Church in New York City, 1702–1750*, trans. Simon Hart and Harry J. Kreider (New York: United Lutheran Synod of New York and New England, 1958), xiii.

4. On Justus Falckner, see Kim-Eric Williams, *The Journey of Justus Falckner, 1672–1723* (Delhi, NY: American Lutheran Publicity Bureau, 2003), and *Fundamental Instruction: Justus Falckner's Catechism*, trans. and ed. Martin Kessler (Delhi, NY: American Lutheran Publicity Bureau, 2003).

5. Marianne S. Wokeck, "Henry Melchior Muhlenberg's Views of the Immigrant Church: 'The Desert Is Vast and the Sheep Are Dispersed,'" in *Henry Melchior Muhlenberg—The Roots of 250 Years of Organized Lutheranism in North America*, ed. John W. Kleiner (Lewiston, NY: The Edwin Mellen Press, 1998), 86–92.

6. On Muhlenberg's preparation and arrival in America see Paul A. Wallace, *The Muhlenbergs of Pennsylvania* (Philadelphia: The University of Pennsylvania Press, 1950), 1–24. Also see Karl-Otto Strohmidel,

"Henry Melchior Muhlenberg's European Heritage," *Lutheran Quarterly* VI, no. 1: 5–34.

7. The Ministerium was established on August 15 (August 26 new style), 1748. On the founding of the Ministerium, see volume 1 of *The Journals of Henry Melchior Muhlenberg*, ed. Theodore G. Tappert and John W. Doberstein (Philadelphia: The Muhlenberg Press, 1942), 202. Also note the "Jubilee Memorial," *Documentary History of the Evangelical Lutheran Ministerium of Pennsylvania and Adjacent States—Proceedings of the Annual Conventions from 1748–1821* (Philadelphia: Board of Publication of the General Council of the Evangelical Lutheran Church in North America, 1898), 3–23.

8. Listed under "Special Interest Conferences/Ethnic Associations" in the *2013 Yearbook* of the Evangelical Lutheran Church in America (Minneapolis: Augsburg Fortress, 2013), 635. Also see the German Evangelical Lutheran Conference in North America Web site, www.delkina.org.

9. Rev. J. N. Lenker, *Lutherans in All Lands—The Wonderful Works of God*, vols. 1 and 2 (Milwaukee, WI: Lutherans in All Lands Company, 1893), 180. These statistics come from the section titled "Laborers Sent to the Transmarine Emigrants by the Lutheran Institutions and Societies of Germany" (taken from a table "published by the Immigrant Society in Stall's Lutheran Year Book of 1886").

10. *The Lutherans in North America*, ed. E. Clifford Nelson (Philadelphia: Fortress Press, 1975), 284–86.

11. J. N. Lenker, *Lutherans in All Lands* (Milwaukee, WI: Lutherans in All Lands Company, 1893), 180.

12. J. N. Lenker, *Lutherans in All Lands* (Milwaukee, WI: Lutherans in All Lands Company, 1893), 180. Lenker notes that the seminary in Mecklenberg, which was founded in 1853, sent out 28 pastors, and that "most men [were sent] to Catholic countries."

13. "Describes Plot by German Spies to Incite Negroes," *The New York Times*, December 15, 1918. This article discusses the case against Kropp Seminary graduates in the United States who were accused of being involved in a plot to keep America out of the war and to incite racial conflict in the Southern states to help keep the United States' attention away from Germany. "Loyal" Lutheran clergymen "check[ed] pulpit propaganda sown by some of the pastors."

14. From Krepper's July 16, 1941, letter to the Information Department of the Foreign Office in Berlin (in his personnel record from the *Landeskirchliches* Archives of the Evangelical Lutheran Church in North Germany).

15. These dates were recorded in a March 25, 1940, communication to the Reich minister of church affairs, Müller (*Ev/-Luth. Landeskirchenamt* B 791) (Dez. II) C944, contained in Krepper's personnel record (Bestand Nr. 12.03, Nr. 676) in the *Landeskirchliches* Archives of the Evangelical Lutheran Church in North Germany. Blankenese was an independent town until it merged with

Altona in 1927, and then Altona and Blankenese were brought into Hamburg through the Greater Hamburg Act in 1938.

16. Friedrich Hammer, *Verzeichnis der Pastorinnen und Pastoren der Schleswig-Holsteinischen Landeskirche 1864–1976* (Neumünster, DE: Karl Wachholtz Verlag, for the Schlswig-Holstein Church History Society, 1976), 282. There is a paucity of material on Paulsen's personal life that is evident in Hammer's biographical data on clergy who served in Schleswig-Holstein.

17. This history is briefly told in a February 4, 1954, personal letter of Pastor R. Hoffman (rector of the Bethanien Deaconess center in Kropp, the successor body to the Kropp seminary) to Dr. Franklin Clark Fry, the president of the United Lutheran Church in America (contained in the Archives of the Evangelical Lutheran Church in America, Elk Grove Village, IL; record group ULCA 4/2, Box 22, United Lutheran Church in America, Office of the President, Franklin Clark Fry Papers, 1945–1962).

18. See the discussion from the standpoint of one prominent American Lutheran leader who was involved in the discussion with Kropp Seminary in *Life of Adolph Spaeth, D.D., LL.D.*, ed. Harriett R. Spaeth (Philadelphia: General Council Publication House, 1916), 193–94:

> In the last few years we had experienced that, in spite of the fine training received there, many of the young pastors from Kropp found it difficult to accommodate themselves to conditions here; and that there was danger of estrangement and dissension between them and other pastors of our American Church, especially those trained in the Philadelphia Seminary. It was the opinion of many intelligent men, pastors and laymen, besides the professors in the Seminary, that one finishing year with us would make them better acquainted with our land, and would conduce to mutual understanding with pastors born and bred in America. It was my hope especially, that such a regular influx of German blood and German education in our Seminary would act as leaven, and as a stimulus to our American students.

19. For the details of the "Kropp War" see *Life of Adolph Spaeth, D.D., LL.D.*, ed. Harriett R. Spaeth (Philadelphia: General Council Publication House, 1916), 198–204.

20. Personal letter from seminarian Erick Lindner written on February 20, 1929, for publication in *Der Lutherische Herald*, which was published by the Lutheran Publication House in Philadelphia, Pennsylvania. This letter detailed the seminarian's financial obligations, for he sought assistance from the American church. He did not receive any assistance in the funding of his theological education from the German church because, in his own words, "I am not entering into the German church, but into the United Lutheran Church in America" (in the Kropp archives housed at the Lutheran Archives Center at Philadelphia).

21. In the file titled *"Namensverzeichnis sämtlicher Zöglinge des Evang.-Luth. Predigerseminars* in Kropp von 1882 bis 1931," 50, maintained in the Lutheran Archives Center at Philadelphia.

22. From the "Report of the Board of Education" in *Minutes of the Eighth Biennial Convention of the United Lutheran Church in America, Philadelphia, Pennsylvania, October 12–19, 1932* (Philadelphia: The United Lutheran Publication House, 1932), 104.

23. *The Lutherans in North America*, ed. E. Clifford Nelson (Philadelphia: Fortress Press, 1975), 285.

24. Theodore G. Tappert, *Lutheran Theological Seminary at Philadelphia 1864–1964* (Philadelphia: Lutheran Theological Seminary, 1964), 65.

25. See Emerson Hough, *The Web* (Chicago: The Reilly and Lee Co., 1919), 82–106, and 107–19; also note *Brewing and Liquor Interests and German Propaganda; Hearings before a Sub-Committee on the Judiciary of the United States Senate; Sixty-First Congress, Second and Third Sessions* (Washington, DC: Government Printing Office, 1919), 1910–1934.

26. "MEMORANDUM, RE: Carl Krepper, Alias Father Krepper," June 25, 1942, Copy-3/24/44-hs, 1; 98-15929.

27. When he was called to serve the Friedens Church as pastor in 1911, Krepper actually replaced a pastor who had tried unsuccessfully to move the congregation from German to English services. There was a split in the congregation in 1911 over this attempt by Krepper's predecessor to move the language of worship to English. Interestingly, when Krepper left the parish to take a two-point German parish in New Jersey (Zion in Carteret and Zion in Rahway), the Friedens Church recalled Krepper's predecessor and began the move to use English in its liturgy. This story is spelled out in the congregation's fortieth, fiftieth, sixty-fifth, and seventy-fifth anniversary booklets (in the archives of the Friedens Church located at the Lutheran Archives Center at Philadelphia).

28. Letter of "Pastor Krepper, Oldenburg," written May 4, 1937, to the *Evang. Luth. Landeskirchenamt in Kiel*. Found on page four of a five-page letter detailing his pastoral work in America (on page 48 of his German Church personnel record).

29. See Walter Struve, "Georg von Bosse," in *Germany and the Americas: Culture, Politics, and History*, vol. 1, ed. Thomas Adam (Santa Barbara, CA: ABC-CLIO, 2005): "Essential . . . was maintenance of German language, culture, and religious practices . . ." 156.

30. Ibid.

31. Ibid.

32. From the report entitled *"An den Herrn Reichsminster für die kirchlichen Angelegenheiten,* filed on March 11, 1940, 1, in the personnel file on Carl Krepper in the *Landeskirchliches Archiv* of the Evangelical Lutheran Church in Northern Germany in Kiel.

CHAPTER TWO

1. The lawyer retained by Krepper's friends to secure a pardon for the convicted Nazi agent was Edward Stover, "Counselor at Law and Master of Superior Court," who had his office in Hoboken, New Jersey. Pastor Fritz Evers of Baltimore, Maryland, appears with Pastor Heinrich Kropp of Brooklyn (along with Krepper's one-time girlfriend and landlady in Newark, Mrs. Marianne Mayer) and the Rev. Franklin Fry, the president of the United Lutheran Church in America, and Carl Krepper, who was living after his release from prison on Bathgate Avenue in the Bronx, as addressees in correspondence from Stover concerning attempts to secure a federal pardon in correspondence dated July 8 and 14, 1953. Mr. Stover was apparently unaware that Fritz Evers had died the previous year. This record is contained in the archives of the Evangelical Lutheran Church in America, ULCA 4/2, United Lutheran Church in America, Office of the President Franklin Clark Fry Papers, 1945–1962, Box 48 of 87; Folder K, 1953–54.

2. Carl and Bertha Krepper left for Germany in October 1935. The *Yearbook of the United Lutheran Church in America* (Philadelphia: United Lutheran Publication House, 1938) listed Krepper as removed from the clerical roster of United Lutheran Church in America due to his transfer to the German church (92).

3. See the discussion in Robert F. Scholz, *Press toward the Mark: History of the United Lutheran Synod of New York and New England 1830–1930* (Metuchen, NJ: The Scarecrow Press and the American Theological Library Association, 1995), 162–64.

4. There is a discrepancy between several sources concerning the date of Krepper's ordination. In correspondence contained in his German ecclesiastical personnel record, Krepper recorded that he was ordained on January 5, 1910 (he made this statement in his July 16, 1941, letter to the Information Ministry of the German Foreign Office in which he presented his case for his trip back to the United States in December 1941, as well as in his April 27, 1937, curriculum vitae, contained in his German personnel record). In their September 20, 1948, summary of the case against Krepper (I.C. # 98-15929), the Federal Bureau of Investigation reported that Krepper was ordained on January 6, 1910 (1). In a March 26, 1950, summary of the "Case Krepper," that was put forth by the "Pastor Krepper Defense Committee," the chairman of this committee, an E. Fetz, stated that Krepper was ordained on January 10, 1910 (this document is contained in the Archives of the Evangelical Lutheran Church, Elk Grove Village, Illinois; found in ULCA 4/2, Box 22, United Lutheran Church in America, Office of the President, Franklin Clark Fry Papers 1945–1962). This rambling document of Krepper's case was first sent to the Rev. Heinrich Kropp, the pastor of the German Evangelical Lutheran Zion Church, Brooklyn, New York, and chairman of the Committee on

German Interests of the United Lutheran Church in America. The manifesto was then sent by Mr. Fetz to the Rev. Dr. Franklin Clark Fry on April 5, 1950. The purpose of this document was to secure support of the Lutherans in the United States in obtaining an American church pension for Carl Krepper. This effort was rejected out of hand by the United Lutheran Church in America.

5. *New York Ministerium Legacy* (New York: Lutheran Church in America, 1986), NJS 118.

6. The controversy was treated in the 20th anniversary booklet, written in German in 1917, during Pastor Krepper's pastorate. In 1917, the controversy was treated as a sad episode in the church's otherwise glorious history of German-language ministry. While the congregation's 40th anniversary booklet (1937) steered clear of telling this story, every other congregational history in the church's anniversary books detailed the controversy over the use of English, and sided with Pastor Schmidt's attempts to introduce English into the worship life of the parish. In a post–World War II environment, the church's 50th anniversary booklet (1947) proclaimed: "In August 1911, following a controversy regarding the use of the English language in the services, Pastor Schmidt accepted a call to Harrisburg, and Rev. Karl Krepper [sic] of Williamstown, N. J., was elected Pastor." Noting that a fire in 1904 had almost destroyed the congregation, the 65th anniversary booklet (1962) stated,

> What fire could not do to the young congregation, human stubbornness almost succeeded to accomplish. In 1911, a controversy—only too well known among Lutheran Congregations with German background—arose regarding the use of the German language. Pastor Schmidt with keen foresight and with great courage (in those days!) asked for permission to conduct bilingual services. He was refused. He left and many members did the same. A young Pastor who was willing to continue services in German only was called: The Rev. Karl Krepper [sic] of Williamstown, N.J.

In 1972, the year that Carl Krepper died, Friedens Church celebrated its 75th anniversary. The anniversary booklet for that year stated, "Looking to the future he (Pastor Schmidt) urged the use of English along with the German in conducting services. Rebuffed in his request, controversy entered the life of our congregation. Pastor Schmidt left for another pastorate and Pastor Karl Krepper was called. Pastor Krepper served 13 years ministering in the German language." The story was repeated in the congregation's 100th anniversary booklet in 1997. The parish has since closed, and its records are preserved at the Lutheran Archives Center at Philadelphia.

7. From the 1912 booklet *Kurze Gemeindegeschichte und Ordnung für die Fest-Gottesdienste bei der 15jarigen Jubelfeier* (The Brief Congregational History and Order for the Festival Divine Service upon the 15th Year Jubilee Celebration). The 15th anniversary celebrations were held on May 5 and 6, 1912.

8.   Krepper's installation was advertised in a special announcement to the congregation dated November 26, 1911.

9.   From the congregation's "Golden Anniversary" booklet (1947).

10.   Krepper served St. John's Lutheran Church in Bridgeton, New Jersey, from February 1 to September 1, 1923 (as in a letter to Reich Minister Kerrl; *Ev/-Luth. Landeskirchenamt* B 791 [Dez. II] C944, p. 134, contained in Krepper's personnel record [Bestand Nr. 12.03, Nr. 676] in the *Landeskirchliches* Archives of the Evangelical Lutheran Church in North Germany). This German congregation helped organize another Lutheran Church in Bridgeton, Christ Lutheran Church, in 1892. In 1931, after Krepper's pastorate, St. John's Church joined the Lutheran Church-Missouri Synod.

11.   On the history of the Ministerium of New York, see Harry J. Kreider, *History of the United Lutheran Synod of New York and New England, Vol. 1* (Philadelphia: The Muhlenberg Press, 1954), and Robert F. Scholtz, *Press toward the Mark: History of the United Lutheran Synod of New York and New England 1830–1930* (Metuchen, NJ: The American Theological Library Association and the Scarecrow Press, 1995).

12.   "Bicentennial Plan Underway Here," *Carteret Press*, February 26, 1932. This front-page story stated that "Rev. Carl Krepper pledged the support of the Lutheran Church" (http://archive.woodbridgelibrary.org/Archive/CarteretPress/1932/1932-02-26/pg_0001.pdf). See also "Arthur L. Perry Heads Committee on Bi-Centennial," *Rahway Record*, February 2, 1932. In this front-page story, Rev. Carl Krepper is listed as one of the speakers (http://50.242.30.250:8080/TheRahwayRecord/1932/1932-02-02/pg_0001.pdf).

13.   *New York Ministerium Legacy*, NJS, 14.

14.   "George John Dasch, with aliases; et al.," 7-14-42, 7, from Kenneth P. Pettijohn, 65-2697; HQ 98-15929.

15.   "George John Dasch, with aliases, et al., Sabotage, Espionage G," Newark, 8-1-42, 21, from Kenneth P. Pettijohn, 65-2697; HQ 98-15929.

16.   *Carteret Press*, "New Building and Loan Elects Staff and Officers." In this front-page article, it was reported that Rev. Carl Krepper was elected treasurer of the association. See http://archive.woodbridgelibrary.org/Archive/CarteretPress/1927/1927-11-04/pg_0010.pdf.

17.   *Carteret Press*, "Bids Are Opened at School Meeting," June 10, 1932. It was noted in this front-page article that Krepper had applied to serve as a schoolteacher. See http://archive.woodbridgelibrary.org/Archive/CarteretPress/1932/1932-06-10/pg_0001.pdf.

18.   Krepper had left Germany aboard the SS Reliance sailing from Hamburg on September 11, 1928. The ship arrived in New York on September 20. The details of his welcome are found in the *Carteret Press*, October 5, 1928, "B. & L. Directors Give Welcome to Minister," 1. See http://archive.woodbridgelibrary.org/Archive/CarteretPress/1928/1928-10-05/pg_0001.pdf.

19.   *The Rahway Record*, "Lutherans Greet Returning Pastor—Surprise Rev. Carl Krepper, Home from Germany," October 2, 1928, 1.

20. According to Krepper's Rutgers University "Alumni Records Data Form," he graduated in 1931 with an AB in arts and sciences. He is listed in his university record as being born on May 11, 1884, in Altona, Germany. The record of his financial contributions to the alumni fund is very telling. Within his alumni record, his address on June 25, 1931, was listed as 710 Roosevelt Avenue, Carteret, New Jersey, when he was serving Zion Lutheran Churches in Carteret and Rahway, and it was stated that he contributed $10.00 to the alumni fund. In 1932, Krepper contributed $8 to the alumni fund. On May 14, 1935 (after he had received his master's degree from the seminary), he was listed as living at 140 Court Street, Newark. On January 30, 1936, Krepper's address was listed at 767 Roosevelt Avenue, Carteret, care of "Frey." That Krepper had put his forwarding address as that of his stepson Eugene Frey is significant. By 1942, Eugene had moved to Rahway, and the Pastorius saboteurs would be given that address as Krepper's contact, written in invisible ink on handkerchiefs that were given to them in Germany by Lt. Kappe, the head of the sabotage plot. When the alumni fund folks at Rutgers tried to catch up with Krepper again on April 17, 1952, Krepper's address was listed as "unknown." The reason Krepper could not be contacted by the alumni fund in 1952 was that his stepson Eugene Frey had died in 1947, and Krepper had only been released from Lewisburg Federal Penitentiary in Pennsylvania on February 3, 1951 (he was paroled), and was living in the Bronx. Krepper had obviously not kept current with his alumni record at Rutgers.

21. *Newark Evening News*, "Suspicious of Krepper: Neighbors Tell of 'Old Man with Satchel,'" December 21, 1944. As found in the clippings files of the *Newark Evening News* in the Newark Public Library.

CHAPTER THREE

1. On these developments, see the discussion in Robert F. Scholz, *Press toward the Mark: History of the United Lutheran Synod of New York and New England 1830–1930* (Metuchen, NJ: The Scarecrow Press and the American Theological Library Association, 1995), 89–90, as well as Harry J. Kreider, *History of the United Lutheran Synod of New York and New England*, volume I (1786–1860) (Philadelphia: Muhlenberg Press, 1954), 32–37, on the earlier German-language controversy within the New York Ministerium in the later eighteenth to earlier nineteenth centuries.

2. See page 3 of "RHH:FK," NY 65-11065, HQ 98-15929. Through a confidential source, FBI special agent Robert H. Hodgin had ascertained that Krepper's stepdaughter-in-law, Hilda Frey, had said that Krepper "had obtained a Lutheran Church in New York City." Dr. Ralph Long told Special Agent Hogdin that there had been no new appointments in recent months of which he was aware. Long then checked with the Rev. Dr. Samuel Trexler, the president of the United Lutheran Synod of New York, who confirmed that there

were no new parish calls issued during the time in question. Agent Hodgin then personally interviewed Trexler about Krepper. Trexler said that Carl Krepper "had approached him and attempted to obtain a position in a New York Lutheran Church." According to Agent Hodgin, "Trexler stated that he would not consider appointing Krepper under any circumstances because he believed that Krepper was pro-German in sentiment and that the Church would not be benefited by the services of such a man." Trexler also told the agent that he would not bring the inquiry to Krepper's attention, and that Krepper might be reached through a close personal friend the Rev. Frederick Noledeke, of Glen Ridge, NJ. On Samuel Trexler, see Edmund Devol, *Sword of the Spirit: A Biography of Samuel Trexler* (New York: Dodd, Mead and Company, 1954), as well as his entry in John Kaufmann's *Biographical Record of the Lutheran Theological Seminary at Philadelphia 1864–1962* (Philadelphia: Lutheran Theological Seminary at Philadelphia, 1962), 64.

3.   See Philip Jenkins, "Spy Mad: Investigating Subversion in Pennsylvania 1917–1919," *Pennsylvania History*, 63, no. 2 (1996): 204–231 (available at http://www.personal.psu.edu/faculty/j/p/jpj1/Spy%20Mad%20.htm).

4.   Named after the German immigrant and Union major general who served in the army both in his native Germany and during the American Civil War. Sigel was successful in recruiting German immigrants during the Civil War. He died in New York City in 1902.

5.   Found in the archives of First German Evangelical Lutheran Church in Newark, New Jersey, it is part of the archives of the now-closed Redeemer Lutheran Church, Irvington, New Jersey.

6.   On the anti-Nazi boycott in the United States, see the excellent treatment by Warren Grover, *Nazis in Newark* (New Brunswick, NJ: Transaction Publishers, 2003; fifth printing, 2009), 111–37.

7.   Warren Grover, *Nazis in Newark* (New Brunswick, NJ: Transaction Publishers, 2003; fifth printing, 2009), 188. Grover cites the statistic from a leader of the boycott movement that overall, U.S. trade with Germany decreased from 5.6 percent to 3.2 percent of total foreign trade during this period.

8.   *The Jewish Daily Bulletin* (New York), "Foresees Return of Rights to Jews," XI, no. 2899, Tuesday, July 17, 1934, 7 (available at http://pdfs.jta.org/1934/1934-07-17_2899.pdf). The article quoted Charles Courtney, a "master locksmith who salvages millions of dollars' worth of gold from sunken ships' treasure chests." According to the article, "Just back from Europe and a special trip to Germany to investigate Nazi conditions, Courtney . . . declared 'that if the Jews lift the boycott they can get somewhere, German leaders told me that, and they said if it was not lifted there will be indelible hatred. What boycott there is now is extremely harmful to the Jews." Whatever the value of Mr. Courtney's assessment, or his expertise in making such a judgment, the fact is that Nazis in Germany tried to force American Jews to stop their boycott, even to the point of

making the preposterous claim that if Jews in America gave up the boycott things would get better for the Jewish population of Germany.

9. Information on the background of the Rev. Heinz Kugler comes from his son, the Rev. Gary Kugler, pastor of St. John's Lutheran Church, Union City, New Jersey (personal conversation). As they were usually published with the previous year's statistics, the *Yearbook of the United Lutheran Church in America* (Philadelphia: United Lutheran Publication House) for 1936 still listed Carl Krepper as pastor of St. John's, Newark (Krepper had not left his pastorate there until the end of October 1935). In the 1937 *Yearbook*, St. John's was listed as vacant (101), and Krepper was listed as living in Oldenburg, Holstein, Germany, and as still rostered in New York (74). In the 1938 *Yearbook*, Krepper was listed among the names who "have been removed from the clerical roster" (92), while the Rev. Heinz Kugler was listed as the pastor of the congregation (103). Even though it occasionally occurred (as in the case of the Rev. Reinhold Schmidt, Krepper's predecessor and successor at Friedens Church in Philadelphia who served both immediately before and immediately after Krepper's ministry there), it was unusual for clergy to return to congregations they had previously served. Even if St. John's had remained vacant during the years Krepper was in Germany, Krepper would not likely have been considered for the parish, especially given his penchant for taking extended leaves of absence to the Fatherland.

10. Cited in Warren Grover, *Nazis in Newark* (New Brunswick, NJ: Transaction Publishers, 2003; fifth printing, 2009), 74; this was quoted from the U. S. Congressional Hearings, Investigation of Nazi Propaganda Activities and Investigation of Certain Other Propaganda Activities Subcommittee of the Special Committee on Un-American Activities (Hearing No. 73).

11. On Spanknöbel, see Donald M. McKale, *The Swastika Outside Germany* (Kent, OH: The Kent State University Press, 1977), 34–35, 69–72.

12. Donald M. McKale, *The Swastika outside Germany* (Kent, OH: The Kent State University Press, 1977), 13.

13. FBI "Memorandum for the Director," John Edgar Hoover, dated September 5, 1942, 3–4, in FBI file HQ 98-15929.

14. "Bund Leader and Others Given Jail Terms," *Dunkirk (NY) Evening Observer*, January 31, 1941, 3. This story was carried in newspapers across the country.

15. This may have been a Rev. O. Mordhorst, a graduate of the Lutheran Theological Seminary at Philadelphia who was ordained by the Ministerium of Pennsylvania in 1899 to serve in Western Canada. The Rev. O. Mordhorst who wrote from Parchau, Germany, to the Bund leadership in New Jersey certainly knew who to contact in America to verify Krepper's pro-Nazi leanings.

16. "George John Dasch, with Aliases, et al., Sabotage, Espionage G," Newark, 8-1-42, 17, from Kenneth P. Pettijohn, 65-2697; HQ 98-15929.

17. The school closed its doors three days after Germany declared war on the United States. Just continued to support this German-language school

after it finally reopened in 1951. Now located in Union County, the *Deutscher Sprachschule* continues to be a thriving educational institution that offers a variety of high-quality courses for students of the German language.

18. Walter Stein, "Revocation of Citizenship—Denaturalization," *Marquette Law Review* 28, no. 2 (Summer 1944): 69, available at http://scholarship.law.marquette.edu/cgi/viewcontent.cgi?article=3512&context=mulr). On the "Denaturalization Program" during World War II, see Patrick Weil, *The Sovereign Citizen: Denaturalization and the Origins of the American Republic* (Philadelphia: University of Pennsylvania Press, 2013), 92–110.

19. Walter Stein, "Revocation of Citizenship—Denaturalization."

20. Letter of "Pastor Krepper, Oldenburg," written May 4, 1937, to the *Evang. Luth. Landeskirchenamt in Kiel.* Found on page four of a five-page letter detailing his pastoral work in the United States and his support of German culture before and after World War I, as well as his enthusiasm for Nazism while serving in the United States (on page 48 of his German church personnel record).

21. Krepper claimed that "at that time [1934] both American President Mr. Franklin Roosevelt and Reich Bishop Müller had expressed their personal desires as to its success." Letter of "Pastor Krepper, Oldenburg," written May 4, 1937, to the *Evang. Luth. Landeskirchenamt in Kiel.*

22. On Kappe's role in the German-American Bund, see Marvin D. Miller, *Wunderlich's Salute* (Smithtown, NY: Malamud-Rose Publishers, 1983), 17–20.

23. On Fritz Kuhn and the Bund, see the detailed study by Arnie Bernstein, *Swastika Nation: Fritz Kuhn and the Rise and Fall of the German-American Bund* (New York: St. Martin's Press, 2013).

CHAPTER FOUR

1. On the title page of his thesis, Krepper misspelled Hoffman's name as "Hofman." The Rev. Dr. Milton J. Hoffman was born in Overisel, Michigan, on January 31, 1886.

2. "Protestant Churches and Slavery. A Study Prepared for the Faculty of the New Brunswick Theological Seminary. In Completion of the Work for the Degree of Master of Theology. Department of Church History. Doctor Milton J. Hofman [sic]; May 7, 1934, E. L. Carl Krepper, 140 Court Street, Newark, NJ," 50.

3. Ibid., 40.

4. Note, for example, the reflections of a German-American pastor in 1940, the Rev. Otto Heick, "Hitler ist Diktator, der Staat is er" [Hitler is dictator, he is the state], found in a November 3, 1940, letter from the Rev. Dr. Otto Heick to the Rev. Dr. Tappert. Heick had served as a professor at the Martin Luther Seminary in Lincoln, Nebraska, before becoming pastor of Christ Lutheran Church in Ellis, Kansas, in 1936. Heick had taken a leave of absence from his parish in 1939 to travel back to Germany. On his return trip to the United States he traveled aboard

the SS Gripsholm, which sailed September 22 from Gothenburg, Sweden, to New York, arriving on October 2. Traveling on board this ship was the prominent Lutheran theologian and professor at the Lutheran Theological Seminary at Philadelphia, the Rev. Dr. Theodore Tappert, who translated the *Book of Concord* and the *Journals of Henry Melchior Muhlenberg*, as well as Martin Luther's *Table Talk*, for American Lutherans. Starting in 1944, Pastor Heick and his congregation invited German prisoners of war at nearby Walker Army Air Base to attend its weekly German services (from the Christ Lutheran Church 75th anniversary booklet, http://ellisclc.org/userFiles/3341/75_years_of_history.pdf).

5.   *Newark Evening News*, "Krepper Trial Defense Rests: Denies He Was Forced to Join Nazi Party to Hold Pastorate," February 21, 1945. "Asked 'why Pastor Niehmoeller was arrested in Germany,' Krepper replied: 'Because he said the German people were bestowing upon Hitler the honors that only belong to God.'"

6.   See the February 25, 1953, letter from United Lutheran Church in America president Franklin Clark Fry to the Rev. Robert E. Van Deusen of the National Lutheran Council in Washington, DC, as Krepper tried, unsuccessfully, for a federal pardon (ULCA 4/2 United Lutheran Church in America, Office of the President Franklin Clark Fry Papers, 1945–1962, Box 48 of 87, Folder K, 1953–1954).

7.   As found on the United States Department of Justice, Foreign Agents Registration Act Web site, http://www.fara.gov/. The full text of the act is available online at http://www.gpo.gov/fdsys/pkg/USCODE-2009-title22/pdf/USCODE-2009-title22-chap11-subchapII.pdf.

8.   On the troubles over Nazi efforts within Newark in 1935, see Warren Grover, *Nazis in Newark* (New Brunswick, NJ: Transaction Publishers, 2003; 2009 edition), 98–105.

9.   "Order Strikes Blow at Nazis; Decline Is Seen," *The Jewish Daily Bulletin* (New York), XI, no. 2899, Tuesday, July 17, 1934, http://pdfs.jta.org/1934/1934-07-17_2899.pdf.

10.   Donald M. McKale, *The Swastika outside Germany* (Kent, OH: Kent State University Press, 1977), 89–91.

11.   "*Pastor C. Krepper, Lebenslauf*," *Personalakten*, 12.03, Nr. 676 in the *LandesKirchliches Archiv*, Kiel, personnel record, 51.

12.   "*Memorandum*," 2, *Ev.-Luth. Landeskirchenamt, Kiel, January 22, 1937*," *Personalakten, 12.03, Nr. 676* in the *LandesKirchliches Archiv, Kiel*, personnel record, 33.

13.   Archival summary in personal letter to the author from Benjamin Hein of the *Landeskirchliches Archiv, Kiel, Evangelisch-Lutherische Kirche in Norddeutschland*, June 4, 2012.

14.   *Yearbook of the United Lutheran Church in America* (Philadelphia: United Lutheran Publication House, 1938), 92.

15.   See Pastor Loos's letter on the question of Krepper's permanent employment at St. John's, Oldenburg, in Krepper's *Personalakten*, 12.03, Nr. 676 in the *LandesKirchliches Archiv*, Kiel: *Kirchenpropstei*, Oldenburg i. Holst, January 20, 1937; Tgb.-Nr. 105; personnel record, 36–37; on Pastor Loos also

see Friedrich Hammer, *Verzeichnis der Pastorinnen und Pastoren der Schleswig-Holsteinischen Landeskirche 1864–1974* (Kiel, DE: Verein für Schleswig-Holsteinische Kirchengeschichte, 1976), 229.

16. "George John Dasch, was. ET AL, Sabotage," 7/16/42, report by E. B. Bruninga, Washington, DC, 65-3479; 98-15929.

17. This may be one of the few "facts" of Krepper's life that is accurate in Erick Fetz's rambling and fictional "résumé of the Case Krepper," in his March 26, 1950, letter to the Rev. Heinrich A. Kropp; Letter from Erick Fetz to Rev. H. A. Kropp, German Ev. Luth. Zion Church, Brooklyn, NY, March 26, 1950, found in ULCA 4/2, United Lutheran Church in America, Office of the President Franklin C. Fry Papers, 1945–1962, 3, Box 22.

18. "*Der Propst. Tgb. 741, Schönwalde, den 25.6.1937*"; *An das Landeskirchenamt in Kiel; Betr. Oldenburg, P. Krepper; Personalakten*, 12.03, Nr. 676 in the *LandesKirchliches Archiv*, Kiel, personnel record, 106.

19. "George John Dasch, with aliases, et al.," NY File No. 65-11065, 7/15/42, New York, 1; HQ 98-15929.

20. Friedrich Hammer, *Verzeichnis der Pastorinnen und Pastoren der Schleswig-Holsteinischen Landeskirche 1864–1974* (Kiel, DE: Verein für Schleswig-Holsteinische Kirchengeschichte, 1976), 208, lists the effective date of Krepper's call in the Third Church as June 30, 1940. Amazingly, a copy of Krepper's letter of call to this congregation exists in Krepper's FBI file, HQ 98-15929, in a November 16, 1942, letter from FBI director J. Edgar Hoover to the special agent in charge, New York. Hoover attached translations of four letters received by Carl Krepper. Krepper had apparently asked his wife Bertha to send along a copy of his letter of call to the Third Church in Rendsburg-Neuwerk (Büdelsdorf), which states that he was appointed as pastor of the church as of June 1, 1942, which was certified by church authorities in Kiel on June 4, 1942. As this text in the FBI files is a copy of the ecclesiastical document and not the original document, it would seem that the official listing of the date of the start of Krepper's call in Hammer (June 30) should be accepted as the more accurate date.

21. Warren Grover, *Nazis in Newark* (New Brunswick, NJ: Transaction Press, 2003; 2009 edition), 179.

22. *Newark Evening News*, "Eavesdropped upon Krepper: FBI Man says Ex-Pastor Preferred Nazi Army Post to Being Here," February 17, 1945.

CHAPTER FIVE

1. *Newark Evening News*, "Krepper Self-Addressed Two Letters from Spain," February 15, 1945 (from the clippings file at the Newark Public Library).

2. *Newark Evening News*, "Krepper Self-Addressed Two Letters from Spain," February 15, 1945 (from the clippings file at the Newark Public Library).

3. "*Der Kirchenvorstand der Neuwerker Kirchengemeinde; An die Vorl. Kirchenleitung z.H. Herrn Präses Halfmann,*" *Personalakten*, 12.03, Nr. 676 in the *LandesKirchliches Archiv, Kiel*, personnel record, 159–60.

4. "Pre-War Propaganda Admitted by Krepper," *New York Times*, February 21, 1945: "Newark, N.J., February 20 – Carl E. Krepper, former Lutheran minister accused of conspiracy to violate the sabotage and censorship laws, admitted today in Federal court, here that he had agreed with Lieut. Walter Kappe of the German Propaganda Ministry in Berlin in 1941 to do propaganda work in this country that 'would keep United States out of the war.'"

5. Dennis P. McIlnay, *The Horseshoe Curve: Sabotage and Subversion in the Railroad City* (Hollidaysburg, PA: Seven Oaks Press, 2007), 43; see also David Alan Johnson, *Betrayal: The True Story of J. Edgar Hoover and the Nazi Saboteurs Captured during WWII* (New York: Hippocrene Books, Inc., 2007), 11.

6. Alex Abella and Scott Gordon, *Shadow Enemies: Hitler's Secret Terrorist Plot against the United States* (Guilford, CT: The Lyons Press, 2002), 29; and Johnson, *Betrayal*, 10–16.

7. Johnson, *Betrayal*, 11.

8. "*An das Auswaertige Amt, Informationsabteilung, Berlin*"; *Personalakten*, 12.03, Nr. 676 in the *LandesKirchliches Archiv*, Kiel, personnel record, 140.

9. The FBI discovered that Krepper traveled to the United States aboard the Excalibur in cabin A-26.

10. "*Der Kirchenvorstand der Neuwerker Kirchengemeinde; An die Vorl. Kirchenleitung z.H. Herrn Präses Halfmann*," *Personalakten*, 12.03, Nr. 676 in the *LandesKirchliches Archiv*, Kiel, personnel record, 159–60.

11. On Halfmann, see Friedrich Hammer, *Verzeichnis der Pastorinnen und Pastoren der Schleswig-Holsteinischen Landeskirche 1864–1974* (Kiel, DE: Verein für Schleswig-Holsteinische Kirchengeschichte, 1976), 126.

12. See the FBI summary of I.C. # 98-15929, "Carl Emil Ludwig Krepper, with aliases E.L.C. Krepper, Charles Krepper—Censorship Matters, Trading with the Enemy, Conspiracy to Commit Sabotage and to Violate Censorship Laws," September 20, 1948, 1. "Kappe told them (the Pastorius saboteurs) Krepper was reliable, would furnish them a hide-out in the United States, and would give them other assistance."

13. See "Former Pastor Seized in Newark on Charges of Being Spy Aide," *New York Times*, December 21, 1944.

14. FBI summary of I.C. # 98-15929, 2.

15. March 6, 1942, letter from J. Edgar Hoover to "Special Agent in Charge, Newark, NJ," contained in HQ 98-15929.

CHAPTER SIX

1. See Michael Ganon, *Operation Drumbeat* (New York: HarperCollins, 1991).

2. Pierce O'Donnell, *In Time of War: Hitler's Terrorist Attack on America* (New York: The Free Press, 2005), 9.

3.   On the Quentz Lake facility and the saboteur's training, see Michael Dobbs, *Saboteurs: The Nazi Raid on America* (New York: Vintage Books, 2005), 15–16; also see Alex Abella and Scott Gordon, *Shadow Enemies: Hitler's Secret Terrorist Plot against the United States* (Guilford, CT: The Lyons Press, 2002), 20, as well as Dennis P. McIlnay, *The Horseshoe Curve: Sabotage and Subversion in the Railroad City* (Hollidaysburg, PA: Seven Oaks Press, 2007), 65–70, and Pierce O'Donnell, *In Time of War*, 4–5.

4.   For profiles of the saboteurs see Pierce O'Donnell, *In Time of War*, 21–34, 79; also see the detailed treatment on the Pastorius men in Alex Abella and Scott Gordon, *Shadow Enemies*, 5–44, and Dennis P. McIlnay, *The Horseshoe Curve*, 52–64.

5.   Dobbs, *Saboteurs*, 227–28.

6.   Abella and Gordon, *Shadow Enemies*, 93.

7.   "Memorandum for the Director, RE: George John Dasch, with aliases, et al., Sabotage," September 5, 1942, from D. Milton Ladd, HQ 98-15929.

8.   Dobbs, *Saboteurs*, 91–102, also see David Alan Johnson, *Betrayal: The True Story of J. Edgar Hoover and the Nazi Saboteurs Captured during WWII* (New York: Hippocrene Books, 2007), 67–99.

9.   Abella and Gordon, *Shadow Enemies*, 105.

10.   "Memorandum for Mr. Tamm, RE: George Dasch, et al., Sabotage," Federal Bureau of Investigation, D. M. Ladd, June 22, 1942, 1, copy 12/28/42, HQ 98-15929.

11.   Louis Fisher, "Military Tribunals: The Quirin Precedent," *CRS Report for Congress* (March 26, 2002), 6.

CHAPTER SEVEN

1.   On D. Milton Ladd, see the entry on his life in *The FBI: A Comprehensive Reference Guide*, Athan G. Theoharis, ed., with Tony G. Poveda, Susan Rosenfeld, and Richard Gid Powers (Phoenix, AZ: Oryx Press, 1999), 338. Assistant Director, Domestic Intelligence Division D. M. Ladd wrote a great deal of the summary correspondence in Carl Krepper's FBI file.

2.   On Edward A. Tamm, see the entry on his life in *The FBI: A Comprehensive Reference Guide*, 356.

3.   "Memorandum for Mr. Tamm, RE: George Dasch, et al., Sabotage," Federal Bureau of Investigation, D. M. Ladd, June 22, 1942, 1–2, copy 12/28/42, HQ 98-15929.

4.   On Earl Connelley, see the entry on his life in *The FBI: A Comprehensive Reference Guide*, 320–21.

5.   Michael Dobbs, *Saboteurs: The Nazi Raid on America* (New York: Vintage Books, 2005), 267.

6.   Michael Dobbs, *Saboteurs: The Nazi Raid on America*, 50, 170, relying on one of the handkerchiefs as well as the initial FBI reports from the early days

of the Pastorius investigation, calls him "Father Emil Krepper" and identifies him as "a pro-Nazi Lutheran priest in New Jersey" (50); Dennis P. McIlnay, *The Horseshoe Curve: Sabotage and Subversion in the Railroad City* (Hollidaysburg, PA: Seven Oaks Press, 2007), calls him "Pastor Emil Krepper," 85 and 145; Alex Abella and Scott Gordon, *Shadow Enemies: Hitler's Secret Terrorist Plot against the United States* (Guilford, CT: The Lyons Press, 2002), 93 and 105, call him "Pastor Krepper," as does David Alan Johnson in *Betrayal: The True Story of J. Edgar Hoover and the Nazi Saboteurs Captured during WWII* (New York: Hippocrene Books, 2007), 127 and 216 (literally quoting one of the handkerchiefs, Johnson also calls him "Pas Krepper," 135 and 167). The only account that connects the full story of Carl Krepper with Operation Pastorius is J. Francis Watson and William E. Watson, "Carl Krepper, American Pastor and Nazi Saboteur," *Lutheran Quarterly*, XXIII (2009): 388–405; also see "Revisiting Carl Krepper, American Pastor and Nazi Saboteur," *Lutheran Quarterly*, XXIV (2010): 474–75.

7.   "FBI Newark, June 24, 1942, 8:15 PM, EMF, Director, SAC New York," 1–2, copy, HQ 98-15929.

8.   From an earlier June 22, 1942, "Memorandum for Mr. E. A. Tamm, RE: George Dasch, et al., Sabotage," Federal Bureau of Investigation, D. M. Ladd, copy 12/28/42, HQ 98-15929.

9.   "Personal and Confidential, Memorandum for the Attorney General," 6-24-42, J. Edgar Hoover, HQ 98-15929.

10.   "United States Department of Justice, Washington, D.C., June 25, 1942, Memorandum for Mr. Ladd, RE: George John Dasch, et al., Sabotage," 1–2, copy 3/24/44, HQ 98-15929.

11.   "Memorandum, June 25, 1942, RE: Carl Krepper, alias Father Krepper," 1–2, copy 3/24/44, HQ 98-15929.

12.   "FBI Newark, 6-26-42, 11-40 PM, EWT, Director and SAC New York City," teletype, HQ 98-15929.

13.   "Memorandum for Mr. Ladd," Washington, D.C., June 30, 1942, from R. P. Kramer, HQ 98-15929.

14.   "Memorandum for Mr. Tracy, RE: George John Dasch; Sabotage G," Q269, from Special Agent Edmund P. Coffey, includes translation of letter from Bertha Krepper to Carl Krepper, 2, HQ 98-15929. The letter, written in German, was sent via Spain to "Sr. Don Carl Krepper, C/O Gene Frey, R.F.D. #2, Box 40F, Rahway, N. J. Estados Unidos."

15.   "Memorandum For the Director," New York, New York, October 15, 1942, RE: George John Dasch with aliases, Reverend Karl [sic] E. Krepper et al., Espionage. Sabotage," 65-11352, HQ 98-15929.

16.   "Memorandum for the Attorney General" 7-22-42, 2, from J. Edgar Hoover, CC: Mr. Tamm, Mr. Ladd, Mr. Traynor; HQ 98-15929.

17.   On Foxworth, see the entry on his life in *The FBI: A Comprehensive Reference Guide*, 326–27. After serving as a special agent in Newark, New Jersey, Foxworth was promoted to special agent in charge of the New York field

office. He then became, successively, assistant director of the administrative division and assistant director of the domestic intelligence division. During World War II, J. Edgar Hoover named him assistant director of the New York field office as well as the head of the National Defense Office in New York City. He died in a plane crash while on a secret mission in Dutch Guiana on January 15, 1943.

18. "FBI NYC to Director and SAC Newark, 7-1-42, 11-59 PM," HQ 98-15929.

19. "Memorandum for Mr. Tamm, Mr. Ladd," July 2, 1942, from J. Edgar Hoover, HQ 98-15929.

20. "Memorandum for the Attorney General, RE: George John Dasch, et al., Sabotage," 7-22-42, cc: Mr. Tamm, Mr. Ladd, Mr. Traynor; 1–3; HQ 98-15929.

21. "George John Dasch, with aliases; et al., sabotage, espionage," 7-14-42, Newark, New Jersey, report by Kenneth P. Pettijohn, 13–15; 65-2697; HQ 98-15929.

22. "Memorandum for the Director, RE: George John Dasch, with aliases, et al., Sabotage," September 5, 1942, from D. M. Ladd, 3; HQ 98-15929.

CHAPTER EIGHT

1. The handwritten letter and envelope are both attached to an August 4, 1942, letter from J. Edgar Hoover to "Special Agent in Charge, Newark, New Jersey, Re: Mr. Krepper, Anna Kretzhaum," HQ 98-15929.

The anonymous letter and Hoover's cover letter were cc'd to the New York field office as well.

2. "Memorandum for E. A. Tamm, RE: George Dasch, et al., Sabotage," June 26, 1942, from D. M. Ladd, HQ 98-15929.

3. In a March 9, 1942, letter to her husband, son Eugene, and daughter-in-law Hilda, Bertha Krepper sent greetings to Mrs. Sophie Jenewein: "Please give my greetings to Mrs. Jenewein"; this letter, written in German, was sent by the postal inspector in Washington, D.C., to the FBI and examined at the bureau's laboratory for secret messages and codes. After it was decided that the letter contained no codes or secret messages, D. M. Ladd determined to send them on to Krepper after September 26, 1942. The two-page letter is found attached to "Memorandum to Mr. Traynor," October 3, 1942, from W. C. Hinze, Jr., HQ 98-15929.

4. "Memorandum for Mr. Ladd, RE: George Dasch et al., Sabotage," June 25, 1942, from R. P. Kramer, HQ 98-15929.

5. "FBI Newark, 6-26-42, 11-40 PM, EWT, Director and SAC New York City," teletype, HQ 98-15929.

6. "Memorandum for the Attorney General, Personal and Confidential," 6-27-42, HQ 98-15929.

7. "Re: Alvis Louis Jenewein," June 27, 1942, Copy-3/24/44-hs, HQ 98-15929.

8. Jenewein later operated a Volkswagen sales and service shop in Princeton, New Jersey. He died while visiting Germany in 1966.

9. "Alvin Schoenbach, alias Alwin Schonbach, alias Alvin Shoenbach, alias Alvin Schoenboch, Internal Security G," New York City, 2/24/42, report by R. W. Meadows.

10. "Carl Emil Ludwig Krepper, was et al., sabotage," FBI, New York, 11-5-42, 9-25 PM, from Special Agent Foxworth to Director, WHS, HQ 98-15929.

11. "Memorandum for the Attorney General, Personal and Confidential," 6-30-42, from J. Edgar Hoover, HQ 98-15929.

12. "Carl Emil Ludwig Krepper, was et al., sabotage," FBI, New York, from Special Agent Foxworth to Director, 11-5-42, 9-25 PM, WHS, HQ 98-15929.

13. "Unknown subjects, Landing of Sabotage Equipment at Amagansett, Long Island, June Thirteenth, Nineteen Forty-Two," 7-1-42, 11-06 PM, from Special Agent Conroy, FBI Newark to Director and SAC New York, HQ 98-15929.

14. "RHH:FK," 3, NY 65-11065, HQ 98-15929.

15. "George John Dasch, with aliases, et al., Sabotage," 11, 7-14-42, Newark, from Kenneth P. Pettijohn; 65-2697; HQ 98-15929.

16. "RHH:FK," 1, NY 65-11065, HQ 98-15929.

17. Kerry Segrave, *Vending Machines: An American Social History* (Jefferson, NC: McFarland and Company, Inc., 2002), 117.

18. Ibid., 117.

19. Ernst Krepper's *Family Life* magazine has nothing to do with the modern *Family Life*, published for the Old Order Amish by Pathway Publishers in Ontario, Canada. There is no indication of the intended audience of Krepper's publication, and no record that it was ever published.

20. "CLG:VCD—1," NY 65-11065, HQ 98-15929.

21. "Memorandum for the Director, RE: George John Dasch, with aliases, et al., Sabotage," September 5, 1942, from D. Milton Ladd, 1; HQ 98-15929.

22. "CLG:SvB," 1, NY 65-11065, HQ 98-15929.

23. "Die Personalakte Krepper," Kiel, September 25, 1951, Bischof D. Halfmann; *Personalakten*, 12.03, Nr. 676 in the *LandesKirchliches Archiv*, Kiel, personnel record, from Bishop Wilhelm Halfmann, 203. Writing of this for Krepper's personnel record, Bishop Halfmann noted:

Mrs. Mayer knew a lot about the whole Krepper affair and she seems among his friends to be the one who has the courage to stand up for him. . . . The situation is the following: Krepper is released on parole, which may correspond to something like our release under police supervision. He is penniless and is sustained by friends. He asks for the payment of his pension. A formal request made by Mrs. Mayer is to be expected soon.... Mrs. Mayer and some American pastors are making the attempt, through the mediation of Church President Dr. Fry, to bring the matter to President Truman to jump over the impenetrable wall of the American Gestapo. So Ms. Mayer openly calls the FBI, Federal Board [sic] of Investigation that had shadowed Krepper, probably even before his departure from Germany . . . and then brought him down.

Mayer's characterization of the FBI as the "American Gestapo" did not agree with Halfmann's, but he tried to be realistic about the prospects of going through Franklin Clark Fry to get to President Truman: "The prospects for that are doubtful. We can also do nothing to help ensure Krepper's rehabilitation."

24. "Memorandum for E. A. Tamm," October 16, 1942, New York, from D. M. Ladd; HQ 98-15929.

25. "Memorandum for the Director, RE: George John Dasch, with aliases, et al., Sabotage," September 5, 1942, from D. M. Ladd, 3; HQ 98-15929.

26. "Memorandum for the Director, RE: George John Dasch, with aliases, et al., Sabotage," September 5, 1942, from D. M. Ladd, 3; HQ 98-15929.

CHAPTER NINE

1. "Memorandum for the Director, George John Dasch with aliases. Reverend Karl [sic] E. Krepper et al. Espionage. Sabotage," New York, October 15, 1942, from Earl J. Connelley; 65-11352; HQ 98-15929.

2. On his draft registration card, Krepper listed his stepson's address, 5 Mountainview Road, Clark Township, Rahway, Union County, New Jersey. Krepper was then 58 years old, and he listed himself as self-employed and his stepson's address as his business address. The place and date of his birth were listed, as was his height (5'7"), his weight (165 pounds), his hair (brown), eye color (gray), race (white), and complexion (ruddy); it was also noted that Krepper had an angular scar on the fourth finger of his left hand. Krepper registered at Local Board No. 5, Cranford, Union County.

3. "John George Dasch, et al., with aliases. Sabotage Espionage G," New York, 7/15/42, from C. L. Green, 65-11065; HQ 98-15929.

4. On the Rumrich case, see *The FBI: A Comprehensive Reference Guide*, Athan G. Theoharis, ed., with Tony G. Poveda, Susan Rosenfeld, and Richard Gid Powers (Phoenix, AZ: Oryx Press, 1999), 58–59.

5. "CLG:AMT," 1, 65-11065; HQ 98-15929.

6. "CLG:AMT," 1, 65-11065; HQ 98-15929.

7. Alex Abella and Scott Gordon, *Shadow Enemies: Hitler's Secret Terrorist Plot against the United States* (Guilford, CT: The Lyons Press, 2002), 222–28.

8. Michael Dobbs, *Saboteurs: The Nazi Raid on America* (New York: Vintage Books, 2005), 232.

9. "DLT:EH," August 7, 1942; copy 3/24/44-hs; HQ 98-15929. There is a handwritten annotation on the side of this copy with the name "Carl Krepper" scrawled upon it.

10. For Krepper's activities during the execution of the Pastorius sabo-teurs, see "Reverend Carl Emil Ludwig Krepper, Espionage G," 8/19/42, New York, from C. E. Airhart, 65-11352, 10-11; HQ 98-15929.

11. "Memorandum for Mr. Ladd, RE: George John Dasch, with aliases, et al., Sabotage," August 12, 1942, from W. C. Hinze, Jr.; HQ 98-15929.

12. "WCH:DO, Re: George John Dasch, with aliases et al.; Sabotage," August 20, 1942, from J. Edgar Hoover; HQ 98-15929.

13. "George John Dasch, with aliases et al.," August 20, 1942, from D. M. Ladd to E. A. Tamm, August 20, 1942; HQ 98-15929.

14. "FBI NYC Director," 8-23-42, 9 PM, from Assistant Director P. E. Foxworth; HQ 98-15929.

15. "FBI Newark, Director and SAC NYC, Carl Emil Ludwig Krepper, Espionage," 8-26-42, 10-14 PM, from Agent Conroy; HQ 98-15929.

16. "George John Dasch, with Aliases, et al., Sabotage, Espionage G," Newark, 8-1-42, from Kenneth P. Pettijohn, 65-2697; HQ 98-15929.

17. Letter from Bertha Krepper from Büdelsdorf-Rendsburg, March 9, 1942, attached to "Memorandum for Mr. Traynor," October 3, 1942, Washington, DC, 2, from W. C. Hinze; HQ 98-15929. This letter, together with another, was screened by the chief postal censor in Washington, and then they went to the FBI laboratory for secret messages and codes. None were discov-ered, and the letter was eventually sent on to Krepper.

18. "Memorandum for Mr. Ladd, RE: George John Dasch, with aliases, et al., Sabotage," August 28, 1942, from Duane L. Traynor; HQ 98-15929.

19. "Re: Emil Ludwig Carl Krepper; Alvin Schoenbach; Eugene Frey; Sabotage," August 29, 1942, Confidential; Director, Federal Bureau of Investigation, Washington, DC, from P. E. Foxworth; HQ 98-15929.

20. "Special Agent in Charge, New York, New York; RE: George John Dasch with aliases, Sabotage," September 12, 1942, from J. Edgar Hoover, Director; HQ 98-15929.

21. "Memorandum for E. A. Tamm," October 16, 1942, 2, from D. M. Ladd, 98-10288; HQ 98-15929.

22. The transcript of the October 7, 1942, telephone conversation is included as an attachment to "Memorandum for E. A. Tamm," October 16, 1942, 2, from D. M. Ladd, 98-10288; HQ 98-15929.

23. "Memorandum for E. A. Tamm," October 16, 1942, 2, from D. M. Ladd, 98-10288; HQ 98-15929.

24. "Memorandum for the Director, RE: George John Dasch with aliases, Rev. Karl [sic] E. Krepper et al., Espionage, Sabotage," October 15, 1942, New York, 3, from Earl J. Connelley, 65-11352; HQ 98-15929.

25. "Special Delivery, Strictly Confidential, RE: Carl Emil Ludwig Krepper, with alias, et al., Sabotage," New York, to Director, Federal Bureau of Investigation, Washington, DC, October 9, 1942, 2, from Assistant Director P. E. Foxworth; 65-11352; HQ 98-15929.

26. "Memorandum for E. A. Tamm," October 16, 1942, 1, from D. M. Ladd, 98-10288; HQ 98-15929.

27. "Memorandum for the Director, RE: George John Dasch with aliases, Rev. Karl [sic] E. Krepper et al., Espionage, Sabotage," October 15, 1942, New York, 3, from Earl J. Connelley, 65-11352; HQ 98-15929.

28. Ibid.

29. "Memorandum for the Director, RE: George John Dasch with aliases, Rev. Karl [sic] E. Krepper et al., Espionage, Sabotage," October 15, 1942, New York, 4, from Earl J. Connelley, 65-11352; HQ 98-15929.

30. RE: Carl Emil Ludwig Krepper with alias, et al.; Sabotage, Strictly Confidential," Director, Federal Bureau of Investigation, Washington, DC, October 10, 1942, from P. E. Foxworth, 65-11352; HQ 98-15929.

31. "Reverend Carl Emil Ludwig Krepper, with alias: E. L. C. Krepper; Alvin Schoenbach, with alias Alvin James Schoenbach . . ., Sabotage," New York, 11/27/42, from Charles L. Green, 5, NY 65-11352; HQ 98-15929.

32. Abella and Gordon, *Shadow Enemies*, 42–43.

33. "Reverend Carl Emil Ludwig Krepper, with alias: E. L. C. Krepper; Alvin Schoenbach, with alias Alvin James Schoenbach . . ., Sabotage," New York, 11/27/42, from Charles L. Green, 11, NY 65-11352; HQ 98-15929.

34. "Memorandum for Mr. Ladd, RE: Carl Emil Ludwig Krepper, with alias, et al., Sabotage," October 17, 1942, from Duane L. Taynor; HQ 98-15929.

35. "Carl Emil Ludwig Krepper with aliases, et al., Sabotage," Office Memorandum, United States Government, March 26, 1946, to Mr. Nichols, from R. F. Cartwright; HQ 98-15929.

CHAPTER TEN

1. "Memorandum for Mr. Ladd, RE: George John Dasch, et al., Sabotage," October 19, 1942, from Duane L. Traynor; 98-15929.

2. "RE: Reverend Carl Emil Ludwig Krepper, Sabotage," November 19, 1942, Director, Federal Bureau of Investigation, Washington, DC, from Assistant Director P. E. Foxworth, 1, NY 65-11352; 98-15929.

3. Ibid.

4. "Personal and Confidential, RE: Reverend Carl Emil Ludwig Krepper, Sabotage," Chicago, Illinois, December 5, 1942, Director, Federal Bureau of Investigation, Washington, D.C., from Earl J. Connelley, 1; 98-15929.

5. Ibid.

6. "Reverend Carl Emil Ludwig Krepper," Assistant Director E. J. Connelley, New York, New York, December 16, 1942, from J. Edgar Hoover, Director; HQ 98-15929.

7. "Reverend Carl Emil Ludwig Krepper, with alias: E. L. C. Krepper; Alvin James Schoenbach, with alias Alvin James Shoenbach ... Sabotage," New York, 11/27/42, Charles L. Green, 2, 65-11352; HQ 98-15929.

8. Ibid.

9. Ibid.

10. Ibid.

11. Ibid.

12. Ibid.

13. "RE: Rev. Carl Emil Ludwig Krepper, Sabotage," February 5, 1942, Director, FBI, Newark, New Jersey, from Special Agent in Charge E. E. Conroy; 98-15929.

14. *Newark Evening News*, "Describes Krepper Trap: FBI Agent Tells Court of Fake Letter Written to Former Pastor Last March," February 16, 1945.

15. "Carl Emil Ludwig Krepper, was, et al., Sabotage," to FBI Director and SAC New York, 7-49 PM, from Conroy; 98-15929.

16. "Reverend Carl Emil Ludwig Krepper, with aliases, et al.; Sabotage," to SAC, New York City, March 24, 1943, from J. Edgar Hoover, Director, 98-15292; 98-15929.

17. "RE: Rev. Carl Emil Ludwig Krepper, with aliases; Sabotage," Personal and Confidential, Letter to the Director, February 19, 1943, Newark, New Jersey, from S. K. McKee, Special Agent in Charge, 1, 65-2749; 98-15929.

18. "Laboratory Report, Re: Rev. Carl E. L. Krepper, et al., Sabotage," November 4, 1942, Federal Bureau of Investigation, United States Department of Justice, 98-10288-2013; 98-15929.

19. "RE: Rev. Carl Emil Ludwig Krepper, with aliases; Sabotage," Personal and Confidential, Letter to the Director, February 19, 1943, Newark, New Jersey, from S. K. McKee, Special Agent in Charge, 2, 65-2749; 98-15929.

20. "Karl Emil Ludwig Krepper, et al., Sabotage," FBI Director, NYC, 12-5-42, 3-09 PM, from Foxworth; HQ 98-15929.

21. "Personal and Confidential, RE: Reverend Carl Emil Ludwig Krepper, Sabotage," Chicago, Illinois, December 5, 1942, Director, Federal Bureau of Investigation, Washington, DC, from Earl J. Connelley, 1; HQ 98-15929.

22. Ibid.

23. "Memorandum for Mr. Ladd, Re: George John Dasch, with aliases, et al., Sabotage," December 7, 1942, from Duane L. Traynor, 98-10288; HQ 98-15929.

24. "RE: Reverend Carl Emil Ludwig Krepper, with aliases, et al., Sabotage," New York, New York, March 1, 1943, to Director, FBI, from SAC E. E. Conroy, 1, 65-11352; HQ 98-15929.

25. Ibid.

26. *Time* magazine, "The Man with the Satchel," Monday, January 1, 1945, http://www.time.com/time/magazine/article/0,9171,791800,00.html. Also see *Newark Evening News*, "Suspicious of Krepper: Neighbors Tell of 'Old Man with Satchel,'" December 21, 1944.

CHAPTER ELEVEN

1. "Carl Emil Ludwig Krepper, with aliases E. L. C. Krepper, Charles Krepper—Censorship Matters, Trading with the Enemy, Conspiracy to Commit Sabotage, and to Violate Censorship Laws," September 20, 1948, 3; 98-15929.

2. *Newark Evening News*, "Eavesdropped upon Krepper: FBI Man Says Ex-Pastor Preferred Nazi Army Post to Being Here," February 17, 1945.

3. "Carl Emil Ludwig Krepper, with aliases E. L. C. Krepper, Charles Krepper."

4. Ibid.

5. *Newark Evening News*, "Eavesdropped upon Krepper."

6. *Newark Evening News*, "Krepper Trial Defense Rests: Denies He Was Forced to Join Nazi Party to Hold Pastorate," February 21, 1945.

7. *Newark Evening News*, "Eavesdropped Upon Krepper."

8. *Newark Evening News*, "Court Denies Krepper Plea: Dismissal Is Sought as Government Rests in Nazi Trial," February 20, 1945.

9. Ibid.

10. Ibid.

11. "Carl Emil Ludwig Krepper, with aliases E. L. C. Krepper, Charles Krepper."

12. *Newark Evening News*, "Court Denies Krepper Plea."

13. "Carl Emil Ludwig Krepper, with aliases E. L. C. Krepper, Charles Krepper."

14. *Time* magazine, "The Man with the Satchel," January 1, 1945.

15. *New York Times*, "Arrested in Newark," December 21, 1944.

16. Thomas Francis Meaney was born in Jersey City in 1888, and graduated from St. Peter's College, Jersey City, and Fordham University School of Law. He was nominated to be a federal judge for U.S. District Court for the District of New Jersey by President Franklin D. Roosevelt in 1942. He died in 1968.

17. *New York Times*, "Ex-Pastor Seized as Nazi Spy Aide: Conspiracy to Help 8 Saboteurs of June, 1942, Is Charged in Newark Indictments," 1, December 21, 1944.

18. A brief survey of newspapers that covered the arrest and trial of Krepper includes those from the following locales: Altoona, Pennsylvania (one of the targets of the saboteurs was the Horseshoe Curve near Altoona); Frederick, Maryland; Benton Harbor, Michigan; Miami, Oklahoma; Lowell, Massachusetts; Carteret, New Jersey; Salamanca, New York; Paris, Texas; Phoenix, Arizona; Hagerstown, Maryland; Racine, Wisconsin; Athens, Ohio; Camden, Arkansas; Burlington, North Carolina; Brownsville, Texas; El Paso, Texas; Gettysburg, Pennsylvania; Council Bluffs, Iowa; Long Beach, California; Del Rio, Texas; Albert Lea, Minnesota; Reno, Nevada; Kingston, New York; Ironwood, Michigan; Kokomo, Indiana; Las Cruces, New Mexico; and Lock Haven, Pennsylvania, as well as Newark, New Jersey, and New York, New York.

19. *New York Times*, "Ex-Pastor Seized as Nazi Spy Aide."

20. *Newark Evening News*, "Court Sets February 13 for Krepper Nazi Trial," January 30, 1945.

21. "Carl Emil Ludwig Krepper, with aliases E. L. C. Krepper, Charles Krepper."

22. *Newark Evening News*, "Krepper Jury Sits: Panel in Nazi Case Picked in 20 Minutes," February 13, 1945.

23. *Newark Evening News*, "Ink Links Krepper: Brought out on Handkerchief at Trial," February 14, 1945.

24. *New York Times*, "Secret Printing on Saboteur's Handkerchief Restored at Krepper's Spy Trial in Jersey," February 15, 1945.

25. *New York Times*, "Ex-Pastor Guilty in Sabotage Trial: Krepper Convicted by Jury in Newark as an Agent of the Nazi Government," February 22, 1945.

26. *Newark Evening News*, "Krepper Trial Defense Rests: Denies He Was Forced to Join Nazi Party to Hold Pastorate," February 21, 1945.

27. *Newark Evening News*, "Krepper Case Goes to Jury: No Witnesses Called in Support of Alleged Nazi Agent," March 14, 1945.

28. *Newark Evening News*, "Krepper Facing Second Sentence: 20 Years and $20,000 Fine Are Maximum on New Conviction as Nazi Agent," March 15, 1945.

29. "Carl Emil Ludwig Krepper, with aliases E. L. C. Krepper, Charles Krepper."

30. Kurt E. B. Molzahn, *Prisoner of War* (Philadelphia: Muhlenberg Press, 1962); also see "Nazi Swastika and Luther Rose," *Journal of the New England Lutheran Historical Society*, 12 (Spring 1996): 1–22.

31. *Newark Evening News*, "Krepper Ordered Released in Bail: But Counsel Says Convicted Nazi Agent Unable to Raise $25,000," November 12, 1946. Frederic M. Pearse argued that it was "ridiculous" to put such a high bail on Krepper, as it was "impossible" for him to secure that amount of money. Charles Stanzialse, Chief Assistant United States Attorney for New Jersey, successfully argued that Krepper would be a flight risk, and that he might "'jump' the country if he got out of prison." Thus it was that bail was set at 25,000 dollars.

32. *United States v. Krepper, 159 F.2d 958 (3rd Cir. 12/11/1946)*, 159 F.2d 958, http://www.versuslaw.com.

33. *Carl Emil Ludwig Krepper, Petitioner, v. the United States of America, U.S. Supreme Court Transcript of Record with Supporting Pleadings, in The Making of Modern Law: U.S. Supreme Court Records and Briefs, 1832–1978* (Farmington Hills, MI: Gale, U.S. Supreme Court Record, 2011), 1-26. The "Petition for Writ of Certiorari to the United States Circuit Court of Appeals for the Third Circuit and Brief in Support Thereof" was filed on January 10, 1947, by George R. Sommer.

34. *New York Times*, "Nazi Aide Case Review Denied," March 4, 1947.

35. *Newark Evening News*, "Drops 3 Charges against Krepper: U.S. Dismisses Indictments of Ex-Pastor Serving 12 Years as Nazi Agent," July 2, 1947.

36. Letter from Daniel Lyons, Department of Justice, Office of the Pardon Attorney, Washington, DC, July 6, 1953, to the Reverend Franklin C. Fry, President, the United Lutheran Church in America; found in ULCA 4/2, United Lutheran Church in America, Office of the President Franklin C. Fry Papers, 1945–1962, Box 48 of 87, Folder K, 1953–54.

CHAPTER TWELVE

1. This dating is found in a letter from Rev. John Teutsch to Franklin C. Fry, August 7, 1950; found in ULCA 4/2, United Lutheran Church in America, Office of the President Franklin C. Fry Papers, 1945–1962, Box 22. Writing to Dr. Fry on August 7, 1950, Pastor Teutsch stated, "About ten months ago a committee has been formed . . . to asked [sic] the respective Board of our great U.L.C. to protest in this matter."

2. Letter from Franklin C. Fry to Alfred Fetz, January 19, 1950; found in ULCA 4/2, United Lutheran Church in America, Office of the President Franklin C. Fry Papers, 1945–1962, Box 22.

3. Letter from Rev. John Teutsch to Franklin C. Fry, August 7, 1950; found in ULCA 4/2, United Lutheran Church in America, Office of the President Franklin C. Fry Papers, 1945–1962, Box 22.

4. Letter from C. Franklin Koch, General Secretary, to the Rev. Heinrich A. Kropp, July 31, 1950; found in ULCA 4/2, United Lutheran Church in America, Office of the President Franklin C. Fry Papers, 1945–1962, Box 22.

5. "*Zur Personalakte Krepper*, Kiel, 25 September 1951, the *LandesKirchliches Archiv*, Kiel," personnel record, 303–304.

6. Letter from Erick Fetz to Rev. H. A. Kropp, German Ev. Luth. Zion Church, Brooklyn, NY, March 26, 1950; found in ULCA 4/2, United Lutheran Church in America, Office of the President Franklin C. Fry Papers, 1945–1962, 1, Box 22.

7. Ibid., 2, Box 22.

8. Ibid., 3, Box 22.

9. Ibid., 2, Box 22.

10. Letter from Franklin C. Fry to the Rev. John Teutch, August 24, 1950; found in ULCA 4/2, United Lutheran Church in America, Office of the President Franklin C. Fry Papers, 1945–1962, Box 22.

11. Letter from Robert E. Van Deusen to Edward Stover, January 15, 1953; found in ULCA 4/2 United Lutheran Church in America, Office of the President Franklin Clark Fry Papers, 1945–1962, Box 48 of 87, folder K, 1953–54.

12. Letter from Robert E. Van Deusen to Edward Stover, February 19, 1953; found in ULCA 4/2 United Lutheran Church in America, Office of the President Franklin Clark Fry Papers, 1945–1962, Box 48 of 87, folder K, 1953–54.

13. Krepper's death record is found in the Social Security and the Massachusetts Death Indexes. The author also secured a certified copy of his death certificate from the Great Barrington Town Clerk, Marie Ryan, on February 3, 2012. Sources for Krepper's place of death, cremation, and funeral service are the Great Barrington Town Clerk's office, and the records of the former Hickey-Roy Funeral Home, now maintained by the Birches-Roy Funeral Home of Great Barrington. The parish historian of the First Congregational Church of Sheffield, Massachusetts, indicated to the author in a telephone interview that there are "big gaps" in the church records covering the years 1961–1973, and because the Rev. Walter K. Miller retired prior to Krepper's funeral, there are no congregational records for his funeral service.

14. On Franklin C. Fry, see *From Federation to Communion: The History of the Lutheran World Federation*, edited by Jens Holger Schjorring, Prasanna Kumari, Norman A Hjelm (Minneapolis: Fortress Press, 1997), 438–44, and E. Theodore Bachmann with Mercia Bachman and Paul Rorem, *The United Lutheran Church in America, 1918–1962* (Minneapolis: Augsburg Fortress, 1997). For a discussion on international reactions to Nazism among Lutheran world leaders, see E. Clifford Nelson, *The Rise of World Lutheranism: An American Perspective* (Philadelphia: Fortress Press, 1982), chapter 10.

15. Letter from Franklin C. Fry to the Rev. Robert E. Van Deusen, February 25, 1953; found in ULCA 4/2 United Lutheran Church in America, Office of the President Franklin Clark Fry Papers, 1945–1962, Box 48 of 87, folder K, 1953–54.

BIBLIOGRAPHY

Abella, Alex, and Scott Gordon, *Shadow Enemies: Hitler's Secret Terrorist Plot against the United States* (Guilford, CT: The Lyons Press, 2002).

Archives of First German St. John's Lutheran Church, Newark, New Jersey, contained in the Archives of Redeemer Lutheran Church, Irvington, New Jersey (The Lutheran Archives Center at Philadelphia).

Archives of Friedens Lutheran Church, Philadelphia, Pennsylvania (The Lutheran Archives Center at Philadelphia).

Bachmann, E. Theodore, with Mercia Bachman and Paul Rorem, *The United Lutheran Church in America, 1918–1962* (Minneapolis: Augsburg Fortress, 1997).

Barnett, Victoria, *For the Soul of the People: Protestant Protest under Hitler* (New York: Oxford University Press, 1992).

Barry, Quentin, *The Franco-Prussian War 1870–71, Vol. 1. The Campaign of Sedan. Helmuth Von Moltke and the Overthrow of the Second Empire* (Sulihull, UK: Helion and Company, 2009).

Bentley, James, *Martin Niemöller: 1892–1984* (New York: Macmillan Free Press, 1984).

Bernstein, Arnie, *Swastika Nation: Fritz Kuhn and the Rise and Fall of the German-American Bund* (New York: St. Martin's Press, 2013).

Bloomquist, Carl W. S., "Nazi Swastika and Luther Rose." *Journal of the New England Lutheran Historical Society*, 12 (Spring 1996): 1–22.

Brewing and Liquor Interests and German Propaganda; Hearings before a Sub-Committee on the Judiciary of the United States Senate; Sixty-First Congress, Second and Third Sessions (Washington, D.C.: Government Printing Office, 1919).

Canedy, Susan, *America's Nazis: A Democratic Dilemma* (Menlo Park, CA: Markgraf Publishing Group, 1990).

Carl Emil Ludwig Krepper, Petitioner, v. the United States of America, U.S. Supreme Court Transcript of Record with Supporting Pleadings, The Making of Modern Law: U.S. Supreme Court Records and Briefs, 1832–1978 (Farmington Hills, MI: Gale, U.S. Supreme Court Record, 2011).

"Carl Emil Ludwig Krepper, with aliases E. L. C. Krepper, Charles Krepper—Censorship Matters, Trading with the Enemy, Conspiracy to Commit Sabotage, and to Violate Censorship Laws," FBI file on Carl Krepper, 98-15929.

Carter, Guy Christopher, "Confession at Bethel, August 1933—Enduring Witness: The Formation, Revision and Significance of the First Full Theological Confession of the Evangelical Church Struggle in Nazi Germany" (dissertation submitted to the Faculty of the Graduate School, Marquette University, 1987).

Carteret Press, online database through the Woodbridge Public Library, Woodbridge, NJ.

Christ Lutheran Church 75th anniversary booklet, http://ellisclc.org/userFiles/3341/75_years_of_history.pdf.

Conway, John S., *The Nazi Persecution of the Churches, 1933–1945* (Vancouver, BC: Regent College Publishing, 1968).

Devol, Edmund, *Sword of the Spirit: A Biography of Samuel Trexler* (New York: Dodd, Mead and Company, 1954).

Dobbs, Michael, *Saboteurs: The Nazi Raid on America* (New York: Vintage Books, 2005).

Documentary History of the Evangelical Lutheran Ministerium of Pennsylvania and Adjacent States—Proceedings of the Annual Conventions from 1748–1821 (Philadelphia: Board of Publication of the General Council of the Evangelical Lutheran Church in North America, 1898).

Duffy, James P., *Target America: Hitler's Plan to Attack the United States* (Guilford, CT: The Lyons Press, 2004).

Emerson, Hough, *The Web* (Chicago: The Reilly and Lee Co., 1919).

Fisher, Louis, "Military Tribunals: The Quirin Precedent," *CRS Report for Congress* (March 26, 2002).

Foreign Agents Registration Act Web site, http://www.fara.gov/.

Fry, Franklin Clark, ULCA 4/2, United Lutheran Church in America, Office of the President Franklin Clark. Fry Papers, 1945–1962, 1, Box 22.

Fry, Franklin Clark, ULCA 4/2, United Lutheran Church in America, Office of the President Franklin Clark Fry Papers, 1945–1962, Box 48 of 87, folder K, 1953–54.

Fundamental Instruction: Justus Falckner's Catechism. Translated and edited by Martin Kessler (Delhi, NY: American Lutheran Publicity Bureau, 2003).

Gannon, Michael, *Operation Drumbeat* (New York: Harper Collins, 1991).

Gerlach, Wolfgang, *And the Witnesses Were Silent: The Confessing Church and the Jews* (Lincoln, NE: University of Nebraska Press, 2000).

Gordon, Scott, *Shadow Enemies: Hitler's Secret Terrorist Plot Against the United States* (Guilford, CT: The Lyons Press, 2002).

Grover, Warren, *Nazis in Newark* (New Brunswick, NJ: Transaction Publishers, 2003).

Hammer, Friedrich, *Verzeichnis der Pastorinnen und Pastoren der Schleswig-Holsteinischen Landeskirche 1864–1974* (Kiel, DE: Verein für Schleswig-Holsteinische Kirchengeschichte, 1976).

Hausmann, Franz-Rutger, *Ernst-Wilhelm Boehle: Gauleiter im Dienst von Partei und Staat* (Berlin: Duncker & Humblot, 2009).

Herrmann, Wilhelm F., *The Kropp Lutheran Seminary*, unpublished STM thesis, the Lutheran Theological Seminary at Philadelphia, 1938.

Jacobsen, Hans Adolph, and Arthur L. Smith, *The Nazi Party and the German Foreign Office* (New York: Routledge, 2007).

Jenkins, Philip, *Hoods and Shirts: The Extreme Right in Pennsylvania 1925–1950* (Chapel Hill, NC: University of North Carolina Press, 1997).

Jenkins, Philip, "Spy Mad: Investigating Subversion in Pennsylvania 1917–1919," *Pennsylvania History* 63, no. 2 (1996): 204–231, http://www.personal.psu.edu/faculty/j/p/jpj1/Spy%20Mad%20.htm.

The Jewish Daily Bulletin (New York), "Order Strikes Blow at Nazis; Decline Is Seen," XI, no. 2899, Tuesday, July 17, 1934, http://pdfs.jta.org/1934/1934-07-17_2899.pdf.

Johnson, David Alan, *Betrayal: The True Story of J. Edgar Hoover and the Nazi Saboteurs Captured during WWII* (New York: Hippocrene Books, 2007).

Kaufmann, John, *Biographical Record of the Lutheran Theological Seminary at Philadelphia 1864–1962* (Philadelphia: Lutheran Theological Seminary at Philadelphia, 1962).

Kleiner, John W., ed., *Henry Melchior Muhlenberg—The Roots of 250 Years of Organized Lutheranism in North America* (Lewiston, NY: The Edwin Mellen Press, 1998).

Koop, Volker, *Hitlers Fünfte Kolonne: Die Auslands-Organization der NSDAP* (Berlin: be.bra verlag, 2009).

Kreider, Harry J., *History of the United Lutheran Synod of New York and New England*, volume I (1786–1860) (Philadelphia: Muhlenberg Press, 1954).

Kreider, Harry J., *The Beginnings of Lutheranism in New York* (New York: 1949).

Krepper, Carl Emil Ludwig, "Protestant Churches and Slavery," MTh thesis, New Brunswick Theological Seminary, 1934.

Lenker, J. N., *Lutherans in All Lands* (Milwaukee, WI: Lutherans in All Lands Company, 1893).

Life of Adolph Spaeth, D.D., LL.D., ed. Harriett R. Spaeth (Philadelphia: General Council Publication House, 1916).

Lutheran World Almanac and Annual Encyclopedia (New York: National Lutheran Council, 1937).

McIlnay, Dennis P., *The Horseshoe Curve: Sabotage and Subversion in the Railroad City* (Hollidaysburg, PA: Seven Oaks Press, 2007).

McKale, Donald M. *The Swastika outside Germany* (Kent, OH: Kent State University Press, 1977).

Miller, Marvin D., *Wunderlich's Salute: The Interrelationship of the German-American Bund, Camp Siegfrieds and Their Relationship with American and Nazi Institutions* (Smithtown, NY: MalamudRose Publishers, 1983).

Minutes of the Proceedings of the Annual Convention of the Evangelical Lutheran Ministerium of Pennsylvania and Adjacent States (Philadelphia: General Council Publication House, 1913).

Minutes of the Tenth Annual Convention of the United Lutheran Synod of New York (New York: United Lutheran Synod of New York, 1938).

Minutes of the Thirty-Third Convention of the General Council of the Evangelical Lutheran Church in America (Philadelphia: General Council Publication Board, 1911).

Molzahn, Kurt E. B., *Prisoner of War* (Philadelphia: Muhlenberg Press, 1962).

Nelson, E. Clifford, *The Rise of World Lutheranism: An American Perspective* (Philadelphia: Fortress Press, 1982).

Newark Evening News, clippings morgue, Charles F. Cummings New Jersey Information Center at the Newark Public Library, Newark, New Jersey.

New York Times, online database.

Personalakte Krepper, Kiel, *LandesKirchliches Archiv*, Kiel, (Krepper's German personnel record).

Pine, Lisa, *Hitler's National Community: Society and Culture in Nazi Germany* (London: Hodder Arnold, 2007).

Protocol of the Lutheran Church in New York City, 1702–1750, translated by Simon Hart and Harry J. Kreider (New York: United Lutheran Synod of New York and New England, 1958).

Schjorring, Jens Holger, Prasanna Kumari, and Norman A. Hjelm, eds. *From Federation to Communion: The History of the Lutheran World Federation* (Minneapolis: Fortress Press, 1997).

Scholz, Robert F., *Press toward the Mark: History of the United Lutheran Synod of New York and New England 1830–1930* (Metuchen, NJ: The Scarecrow Press and the American Theological Library Association, 1995).

Segrave, Kerry, *Vending Machines: An American Social History* (Jefferson, NC: McFarland and Company, Inc., 2002).

Shirer, William, *The Rise and Fall of the Third Reich: A History of Nazi Germany* (New York; Simon and Schuster, 1959; reprint Greenwich, CT: Crest Books, 1962).

Stein, Walter, "Revocation of Citizenship—Denaturalization," *Marquette Law Review*, 28, no. 2 (Summer 1944): 69–70, http://scholarship.law.marquette.edu/cgi/viewcontent.cgi?article=3512&context=mulr.

Strohmidel, Karl-Otto, "Henry Melchior Muhlenberg's European Heritage," *Lutheran Quarterly*, VI, no. 1: 5–34.

Struve, Walter, "Georg von Bosse," in *Germany and the Americas: Culture, Politics, and History*, vol. 1, edited by Thomas Adam (Santa Barbara, CA: ABC-CLIO, 2005).

Svendsen, Nick, *The First Schleswig-Holstein War 1848–50* (Solihull, UK: Helion and Company, 2008, reprint 2009).

Tappert, Theodore G., *History of the Lutheran Theological Seminary at Philadelphia 1864–1964* (Philadelphia: Lutheran Theological Seminary, 1964).

Tappert, Theodore G., and John W. Doberstein, eds., *The Journals of Henry Melchior Muhlenberg*, vol. 1. (Philadelphia: The Muhlenberg Press, 1942).

Theoharis, Athan G., et al., eds., *The FBI: A Comprehensive Reference Guide* (Phoenix, AZ: Oryx Press, 1999).

Thomsett, Michael, C., *The German Opposition to Hitler: The Resistance, the Underground, and Assassination Plots, 1938–1945* (Jefferson, NC: McFarland and Company, 2007).

Time magazine, "The Man with the Satchel," Monday, January 1, 1945, http://www.time.com/time/magazine/article/0,9171,791800,00.html.

2013 Yearbook of the Evangelical Lutheran Church in America (Minneapolis: Augsburg Fortress, 2013).

United States v. Krepper, 159 F.2d 958 (3rd Cir. 12/11/1946), http://www.versuslaw.com.

Von Schlabrendorf, Farian, *The Secret War against Hitler*, translated by Hilda Simon (London: Hodder and Stoughton, 1966).

Wallace, Paul A., *The Muhlenbergs of Pennsylvania* (Philadelphia: The University of Pennsylvania Press, 1950).

Watson, J. Francis, "Revisiting Carl Krepper, American Pastor and Nazi Saboteur," *Lutheran Quarterly*, XXIV (2010): 474–75.

Watson, J. Francis, and William E. Watson, "Carl Krepper, American Pastor and Nazi Saboteur," *Lutheran Quarterly*, XXIII (2009): 388–405.

Williams, Kim-Eric, *The Journey of Justus Falckner, 1672–1723* (Delhi, NY: American Lutheran Publicity Bureau, 2003).

Yearbook of the United Lutheran Church in America (Philadelphia: United Lutheran Publication House, 1936).

Yearbook of the United Lutheran Church in America (Philadelphia: United Lutheran Publication House, 1937).

Yearbook of the United Lutheran Church in America (Philadelphia: United Lutheran Publication House, 1938).

INDEX

ABOUT THE AUTHOR

J. FRANCIS WATSON, PhD, is a Lutheran clergyman, historian, and ecclesiastical archivist in New Jersey. The author of numerous articles in journals, books, and magazines, he is coauthor of *The Ghosts of Duffy's Cut: The Irish Who Died Building America's Most Dangerous Stretch of Railroad*. He holds a doctorate in theological and religious studies (history) from Drew University.

4/1/23 DC